1/1/02

HIGH-SPIRITED ROSE IS ROSE

A COLLECTION OF ROSE IS ROSE COMICS BY PAT BRADY

Andrews McMeel Publishing

Kansas City

Rose is Rose® by Pat Brady is distributed internationally by United Feature Syndicate, Inc.

For information, write Andrews McMeel Publishing, an Andrews McMeel Universal company, 4520 Main Street, Kansas City, Missouri 64111.

02 03 04 05 06 BAH 10 9 8 7 6 5 4 3 2 1

ISBN: 0-7407-2367-7

Library of Congress Control Number: 2001096509

**Other _Rose is Rose_ books by Pat Brady
from Andrews McMeel Publishing**

She's a Momma, Not a Movie Star

License to Dream

Rose is Rose 15th Anniversary Collection

The Irresistible Rose is Rose

Rose is Rose Web site: www.comics.com
E-Mail Pat Brady: PBradyRose@aol.com

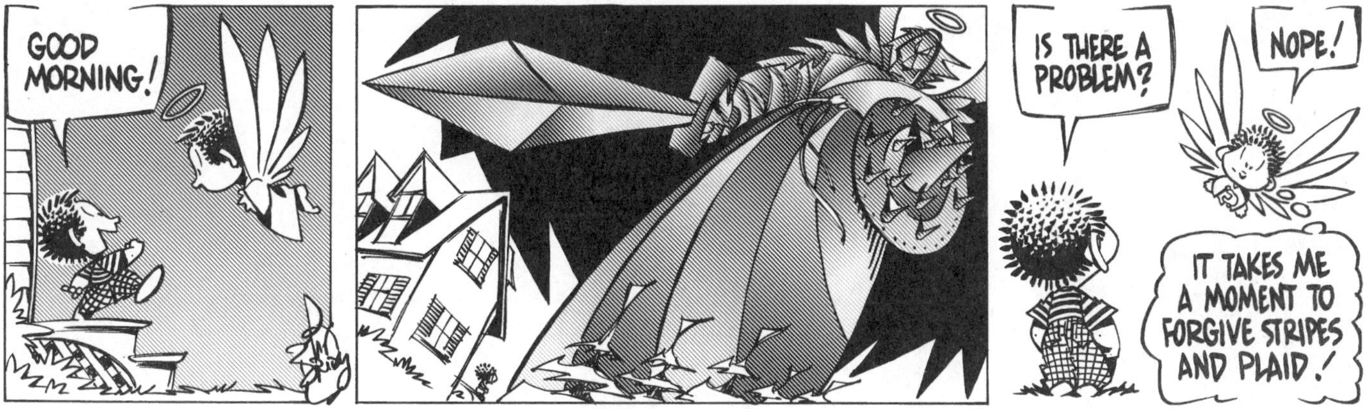
GOOD MORNING!
IS THERE A PROBLEM?
NOPE!
IT TAKES ME A MOMENT TO FORGIVE STRIPES AND PLAID!

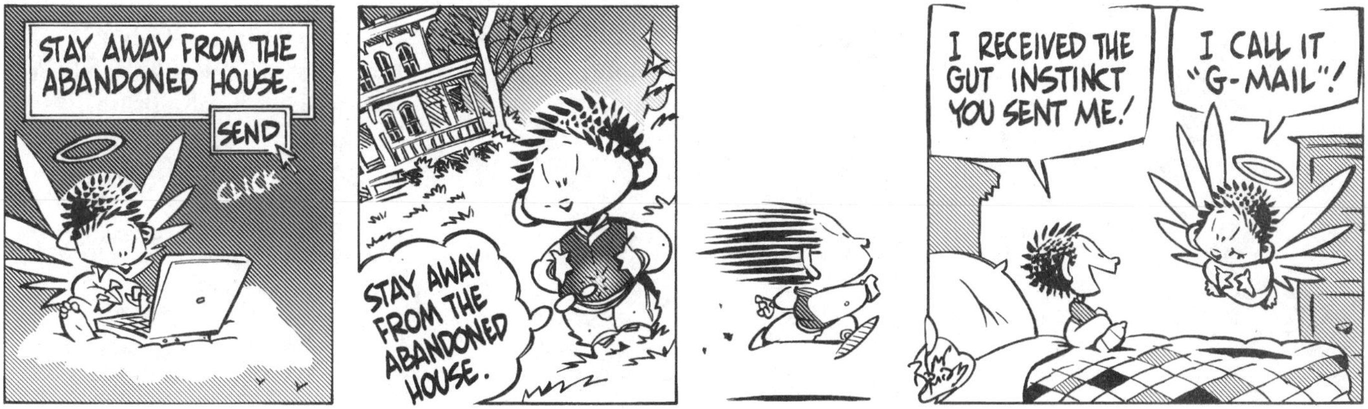
STAY AWAY FROM THE ABANDONED HOUSE.
SEND
CLICK
STAY AWAY FROM THE ABANDONED HOUSE.
I RECEIVED THE GUT INSTINCT YOU SENT ME!
I CALL IT "G-MAIL"!

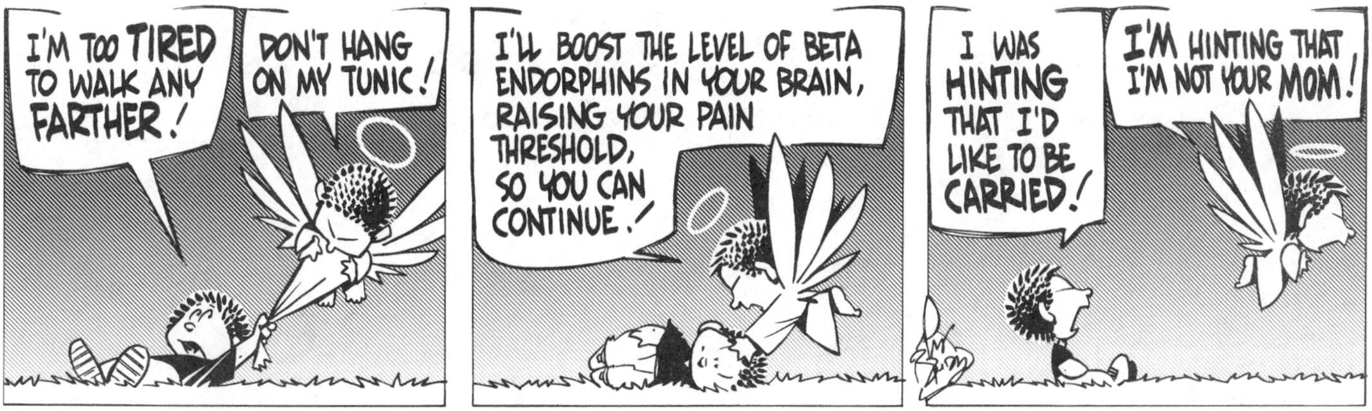
I'M TOO TIRED TO WALK ANY FARTHER!
DON'T HANG ON MY TUNIC!
I'LL BOOST THE LEVEL OF BETA ENDORPHINS IN YOUR BRAIN, RAISING YOUR PAIN THRESHOLD, SO YOU CAN CONTINUE!
I WAS HINTING THAT I'D LIKE TO BE CARRIED!
I'M HINTING THAT I'M NOT YOUR MOM!

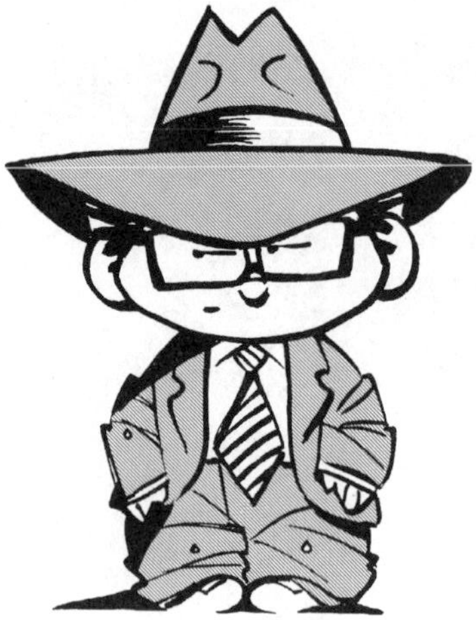

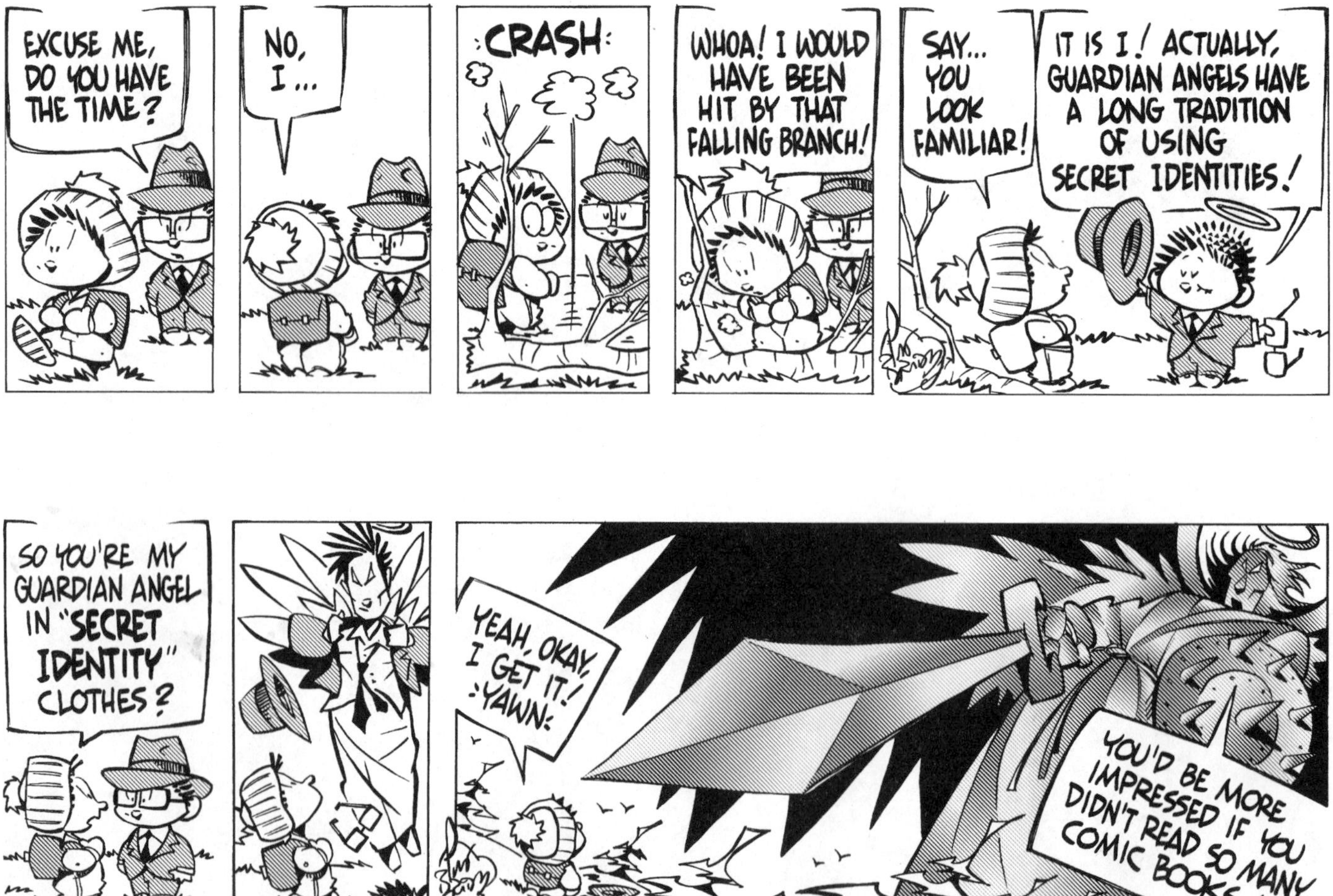
EXCUSE ME, DO YOU HAVE THE TIME?
NO, I...
CRASH
WHOA! I WOULD HAVE BEEN HIT BY THAT FALLING BRANCH!
SAY... YOU LOOK FAMILIAR!
IT IS I! ACTUALLY, GUARDIAN ANGELS HAVE A LONG TRADITION OF USING SECRET IDENTITIES!
SO YOU'RE MY GUARDIAN ANGEL IN "SECRET IDENTITY" CLOTHES?
YEAH, OKAY, I GET IT! YAWN
YOU'D BE MORE IMPRESSED IF YOU DIDN'T READ SO MANY COMIC BOOKS!

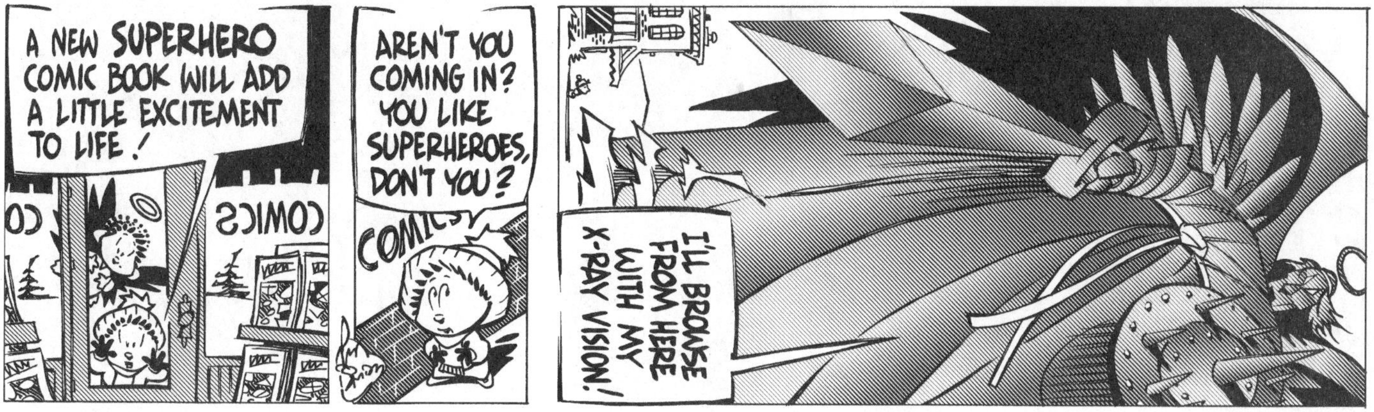
A NEW SUPERHERO COMIC BOOK WILL ADD A LITTLE EXCITEMENT TO LIFE!
COMICS
AREN'T YOU COMING IN? YOU LIKE SUPERHEROES, DON'T YOU?
COMICS
I'LL BROWSE FROM HERE WITH MY X-RAY VISION!

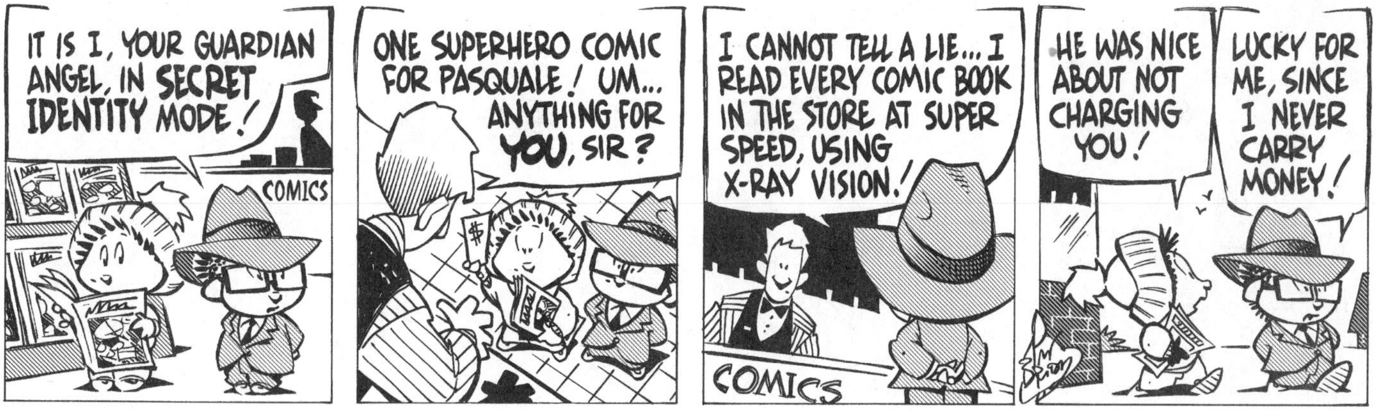
IT IS I, YOUR GUARDIAN ANGEL, IN SECRET IDENTITY MODE!
COMICS
ONE SUPERHERO COMIC FOR PASQUALE! UM... ANYTHING FOR YOU, SIR?
I CANNOT TELL A LIE... I READ EVERY COMIC BOOK IN THE STORE AT SUPER SPEED, USING X-RAY VISION!
COMICS
HE WAS NICE ABOUT NOT CHARGING YOU!
LUCKY FOR ME, SINCE I NEVER CARRY MONEY!

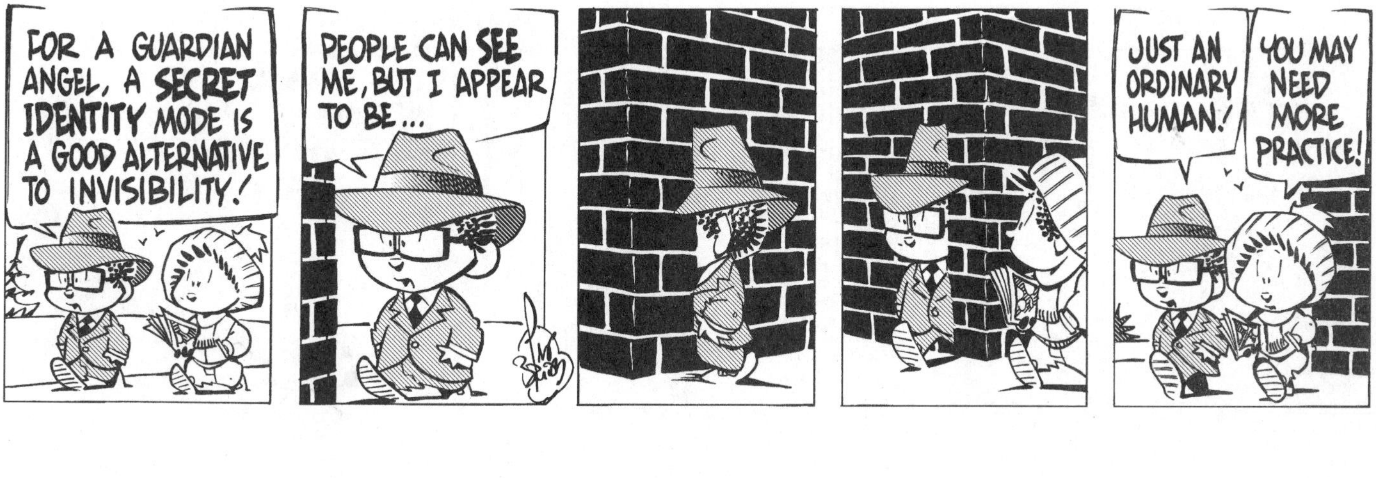
FOR A GUARDIAN ANGEL, A SECRET IDENTITY MODE IS A GOOD ALTERNATIVE TO INVISIBILITY!
PEOPLE CAN SEE ME, BUT I APPEAR TO BE...
JUST AN ORDINARY HUMAN!
YOU MAY NEED MORE PRACTICE!

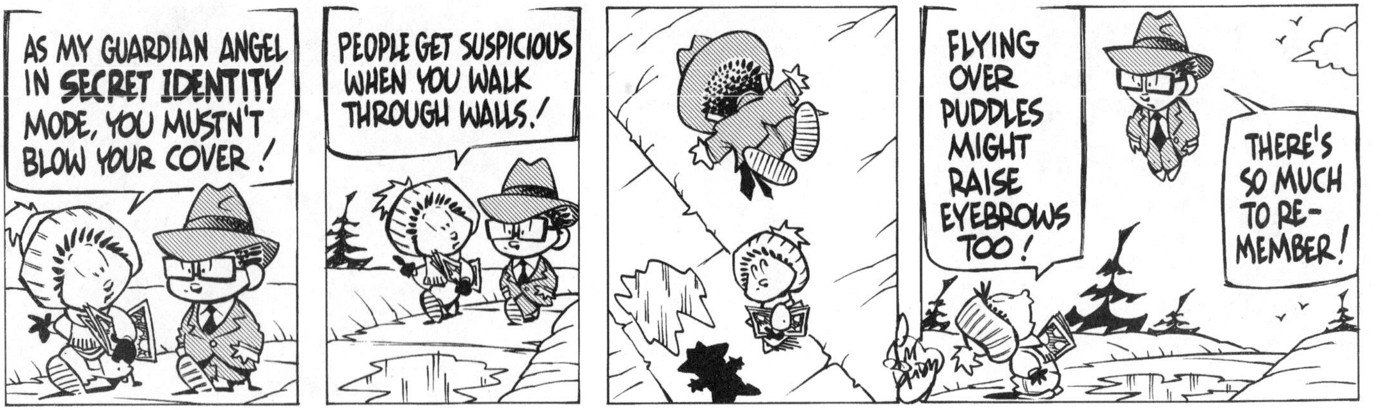
AS MY GUARDIAN ANGEL IN SECRET IDENTITY MODE, YOU MUSTN'T BLOW YOUR COVER!
PEOPLE GET SUSPICIOUS WHEN YOU WALK THROUGH WALLS!
FLYING OVER PUDDLES MIGHT RAISE EYEBROWS TOO!
THERE'S SO MUCH TO RE-MEMBER!

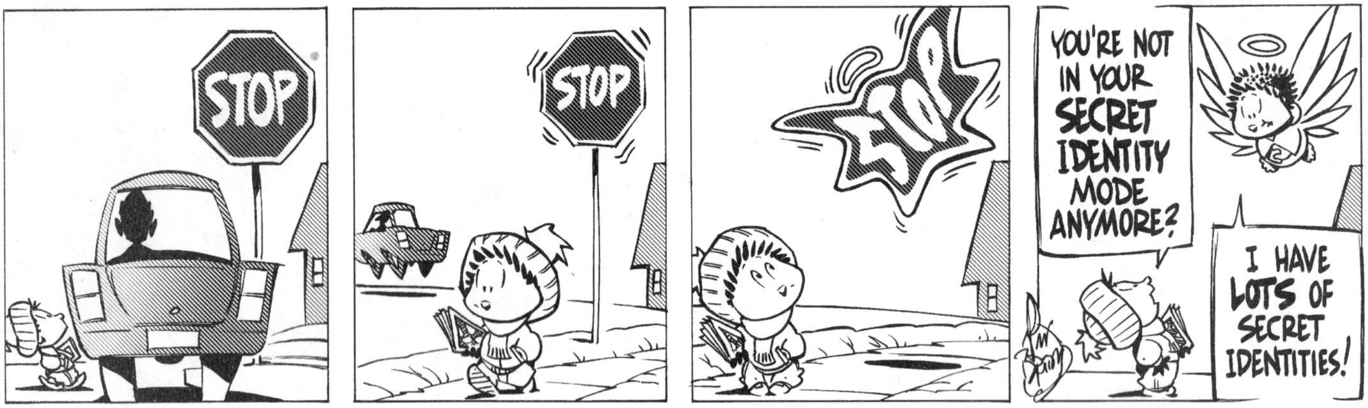
STOP
STOP
STOP
YOU'RE NOT IN YOUR SECRET IDENTITY MODE ANYMORE?
I HAVE LOTS OF SECRET IDENTITIES!

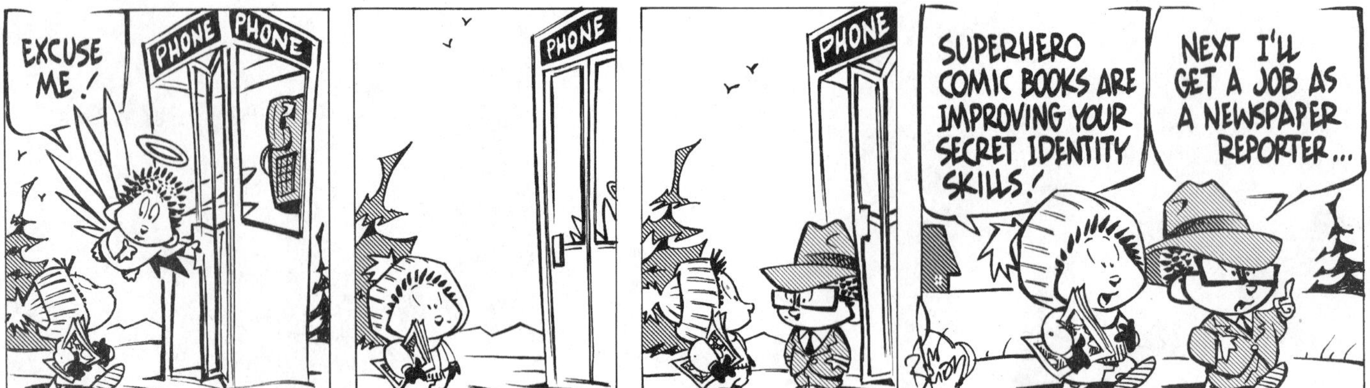
EXCUSE ME!
PHONE PHONE
PHONE
PHONE
SUPERHERO COMIC BOOKS ARE IMPROVING YOUR SECRET IDENTITY SKILLS!
NEXT I'LL GET A JOB AS A NEWSPAPER REPORTER...

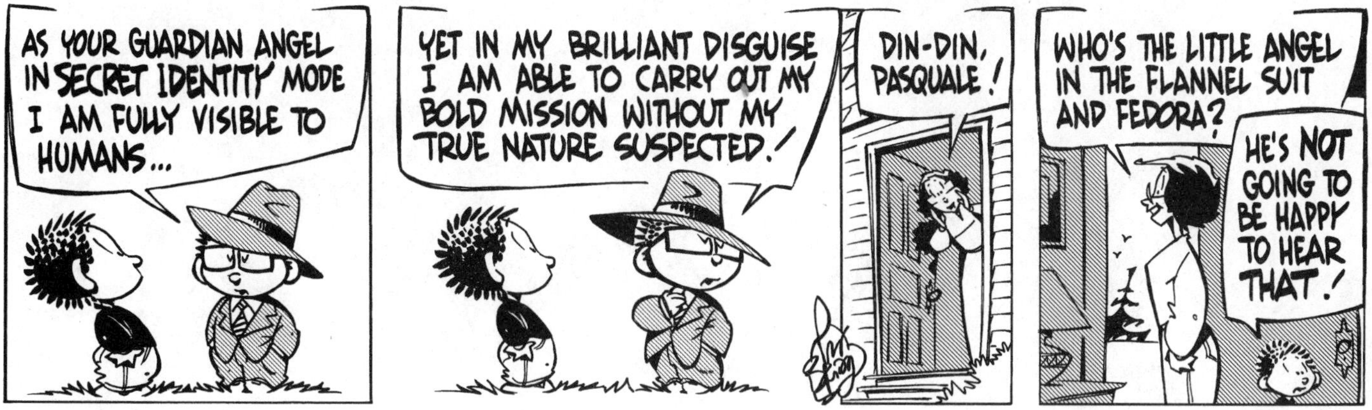
AS YOUR GUARDIAN ANGEL IN SECRET IDENTITY MODE I AM FULLY VISIBLE TO HUMANS...
YET IN MY BRILLIANT DISGUISE I AM ABLE TO CARRY OUT MY BOLD MISSION WITHOUT MY TRUE NATURE SUSPECTED!
DIN-DIN, PASQUALE!
WHO'S THE LITTLE ANGEL IN THE FLANNEL SUIT AND FEDORA?
HE'S NOT GOING TO BE HAPPY TO HEAR THAT!

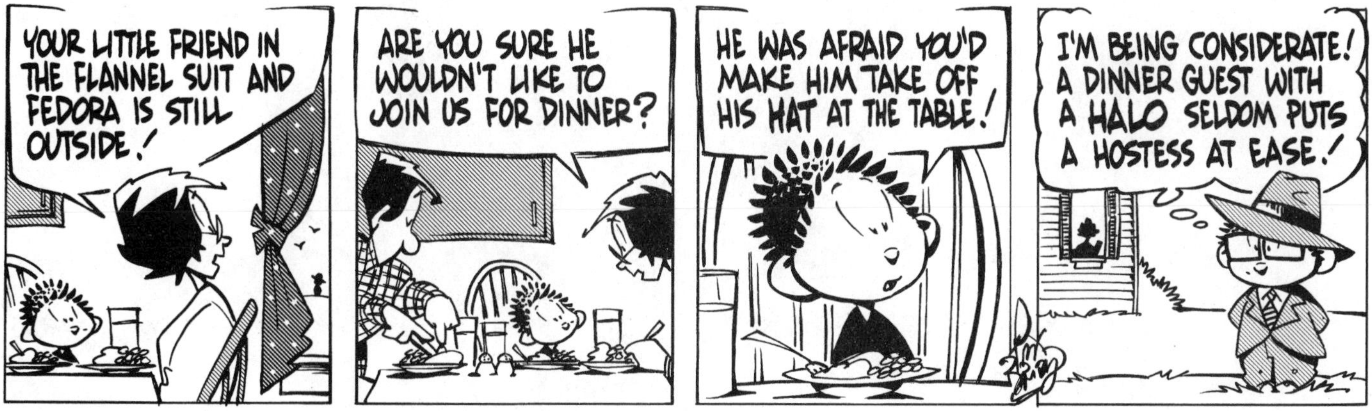
YOUR LITTLE FRIEND IN THE FLANNEL SUIT AND FEDORA IS STILL OUTSIDE!
ARE YOU SURE HE WOULDN'T LIKE TO JOIN US FOR DINNER?
HE WAS AFRAID YOU'D MAKE HIM TAKE OFF HIS HAT AT THE TABLE!
I'M BEING CONSIDERATE! A DINNER GUEST WITH A HALO SELDOM PUTS A HOSTESS AT EASE!

"Don't forget to be kind to strangers,
for some who have done this
have entertained angels without realizing it."

–Hebrews 13:2

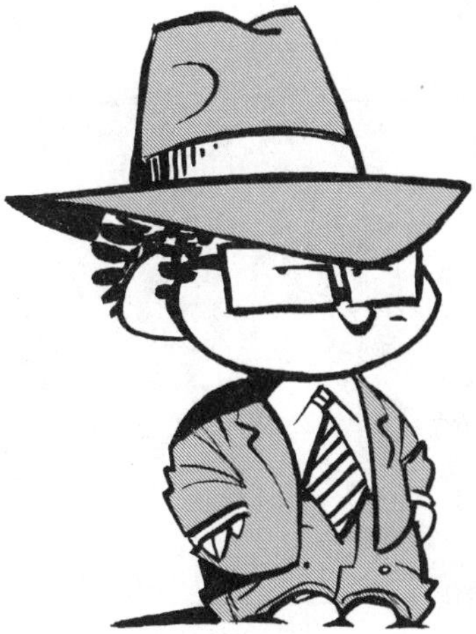

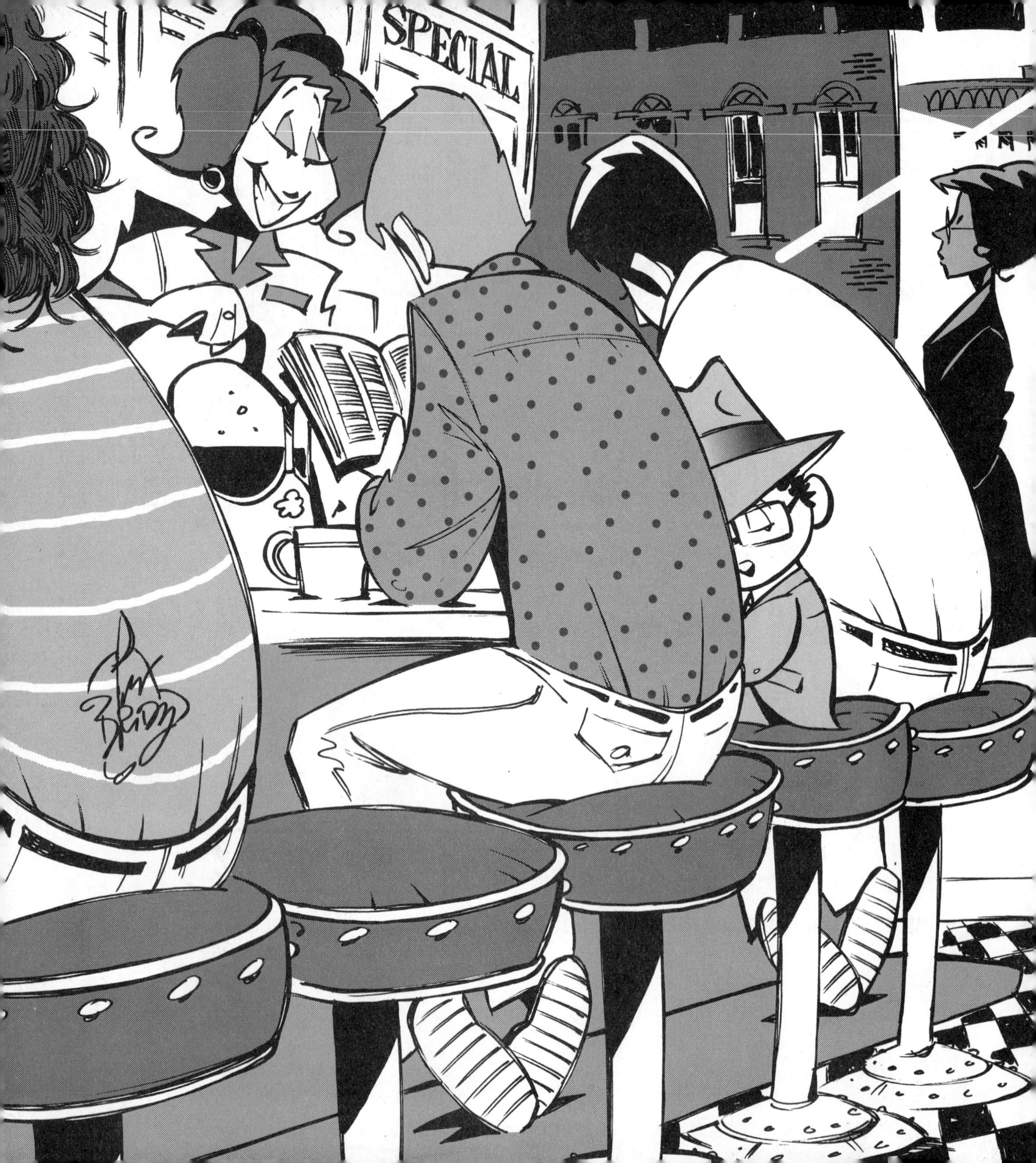
SPECIAL

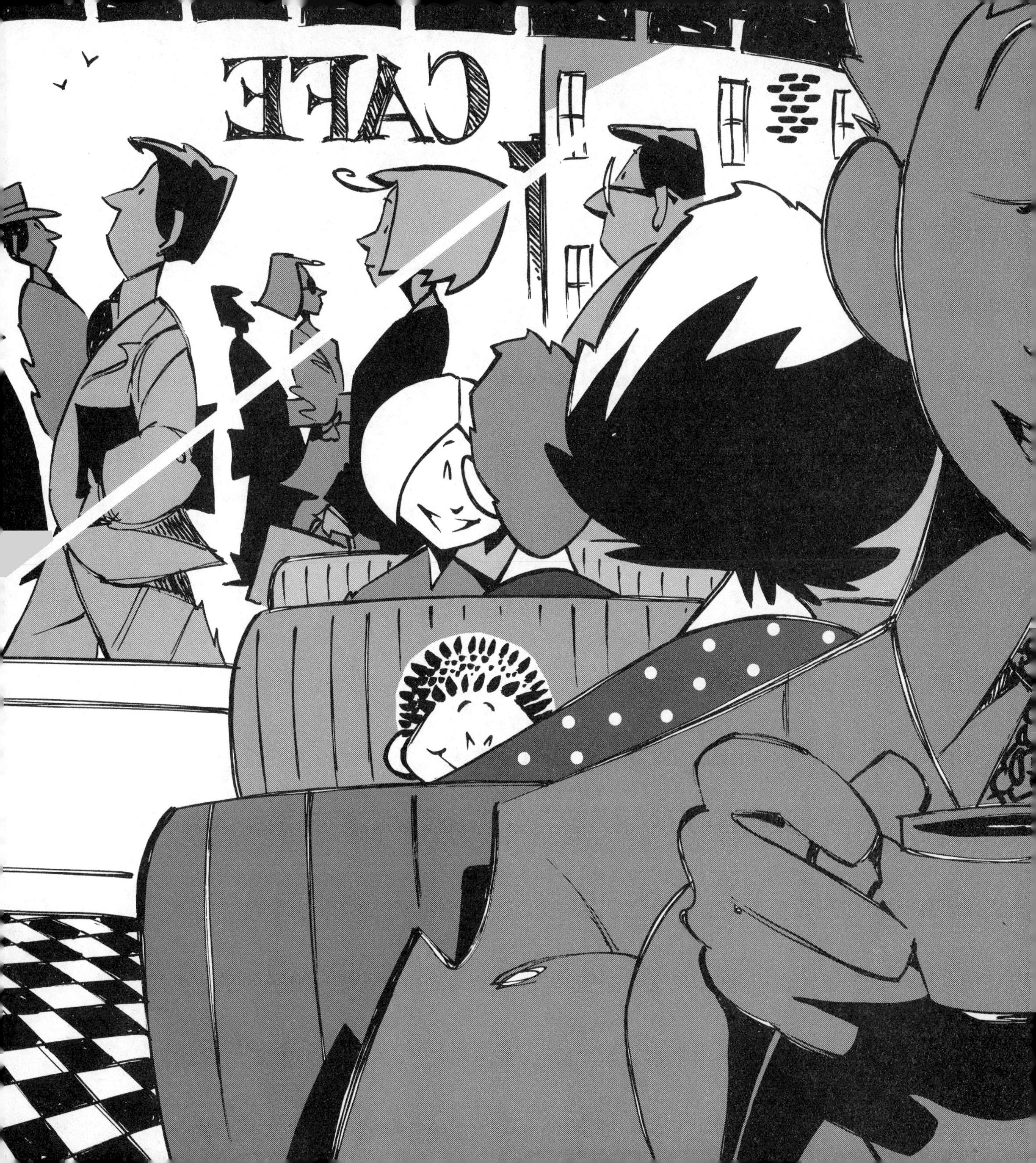
CAFE

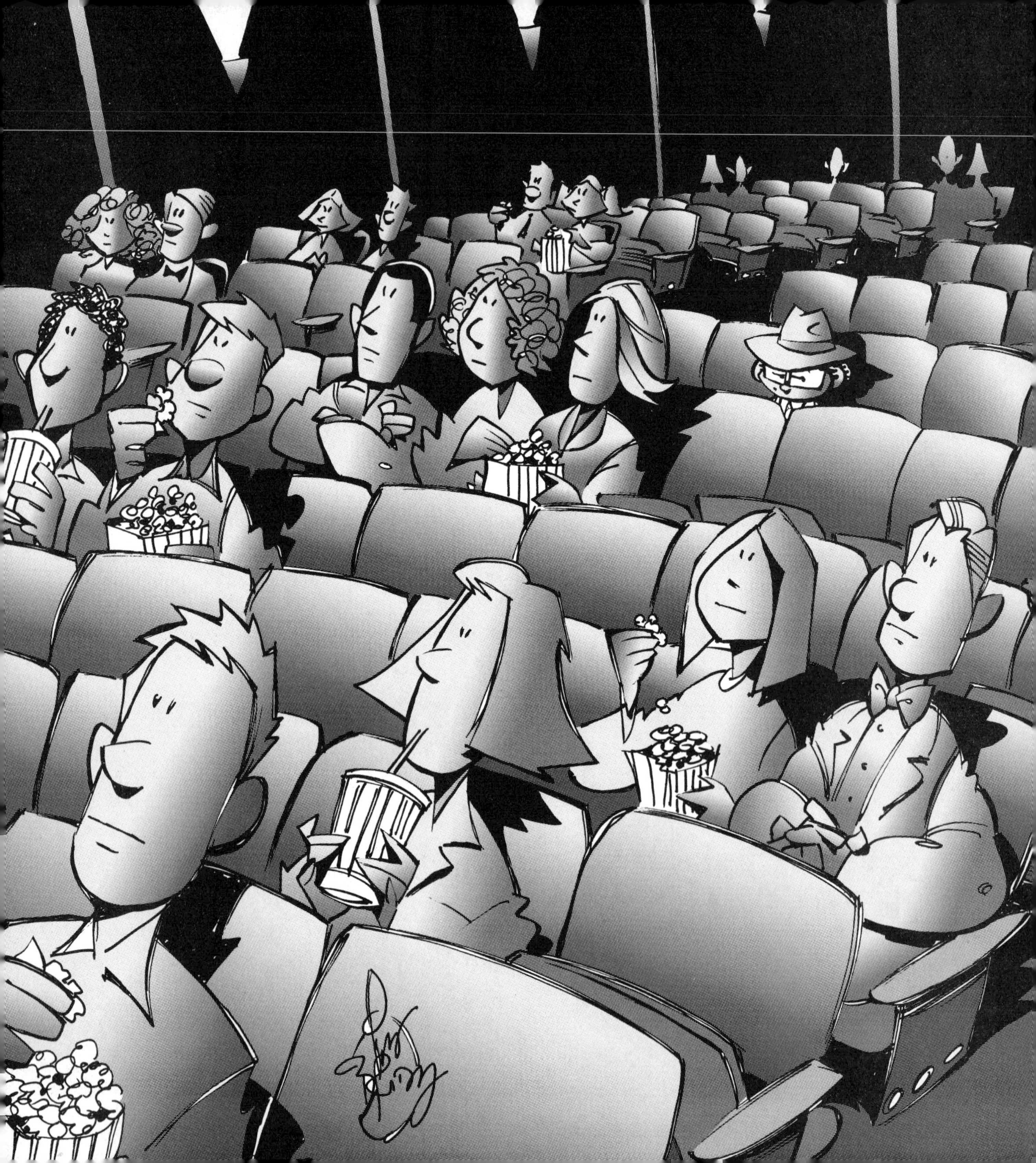

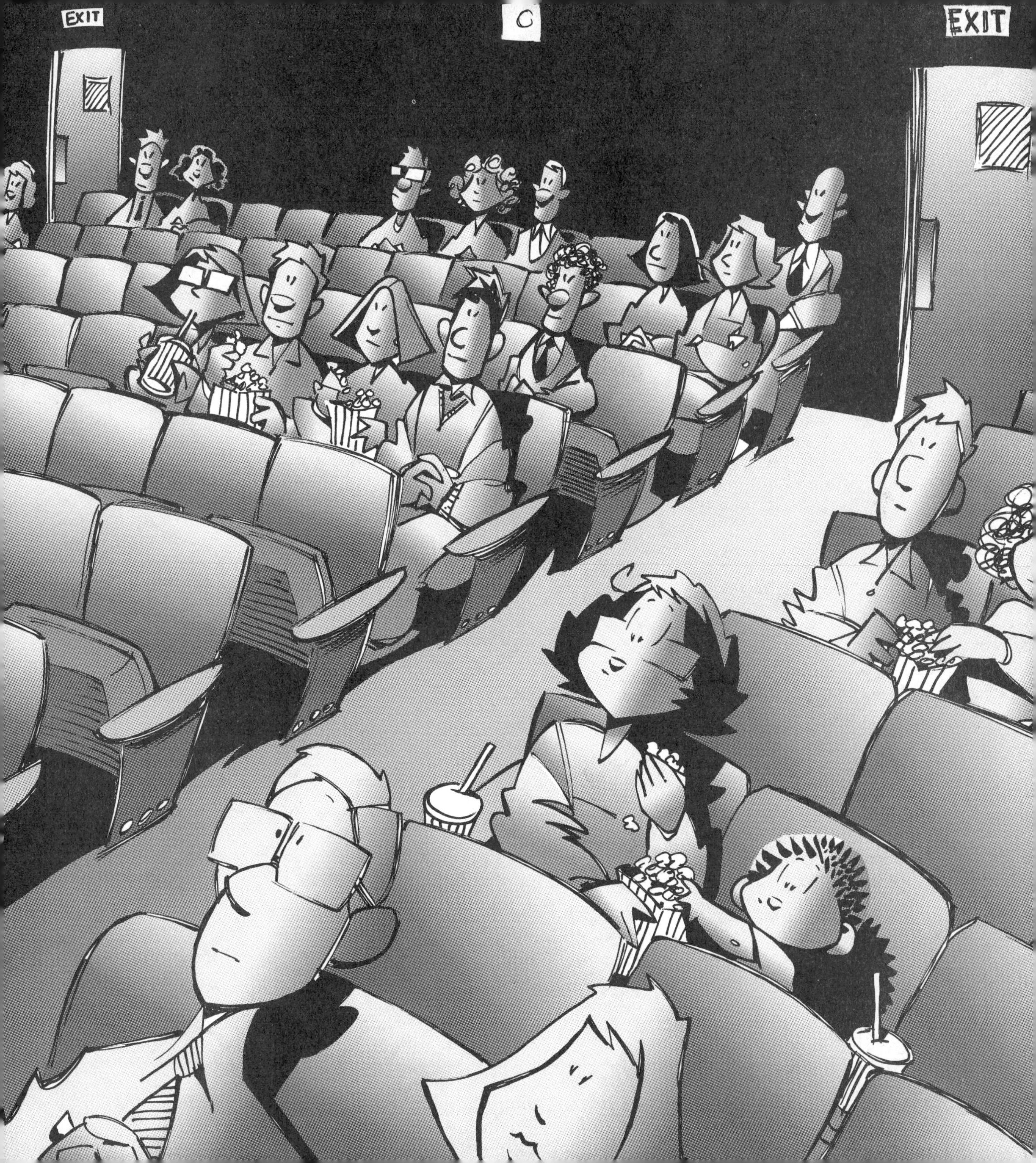
EXIT
C
EXIT

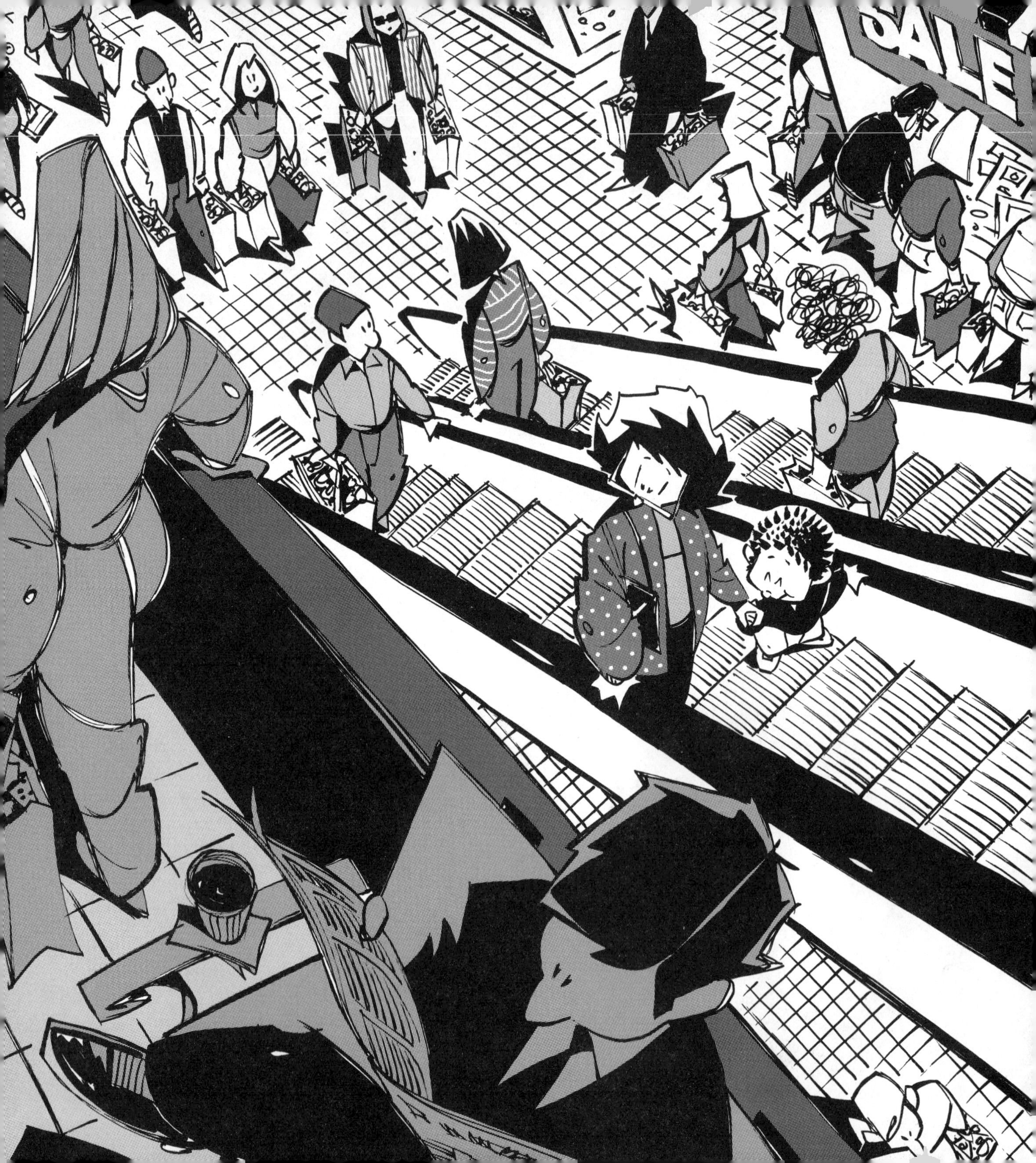
SALE

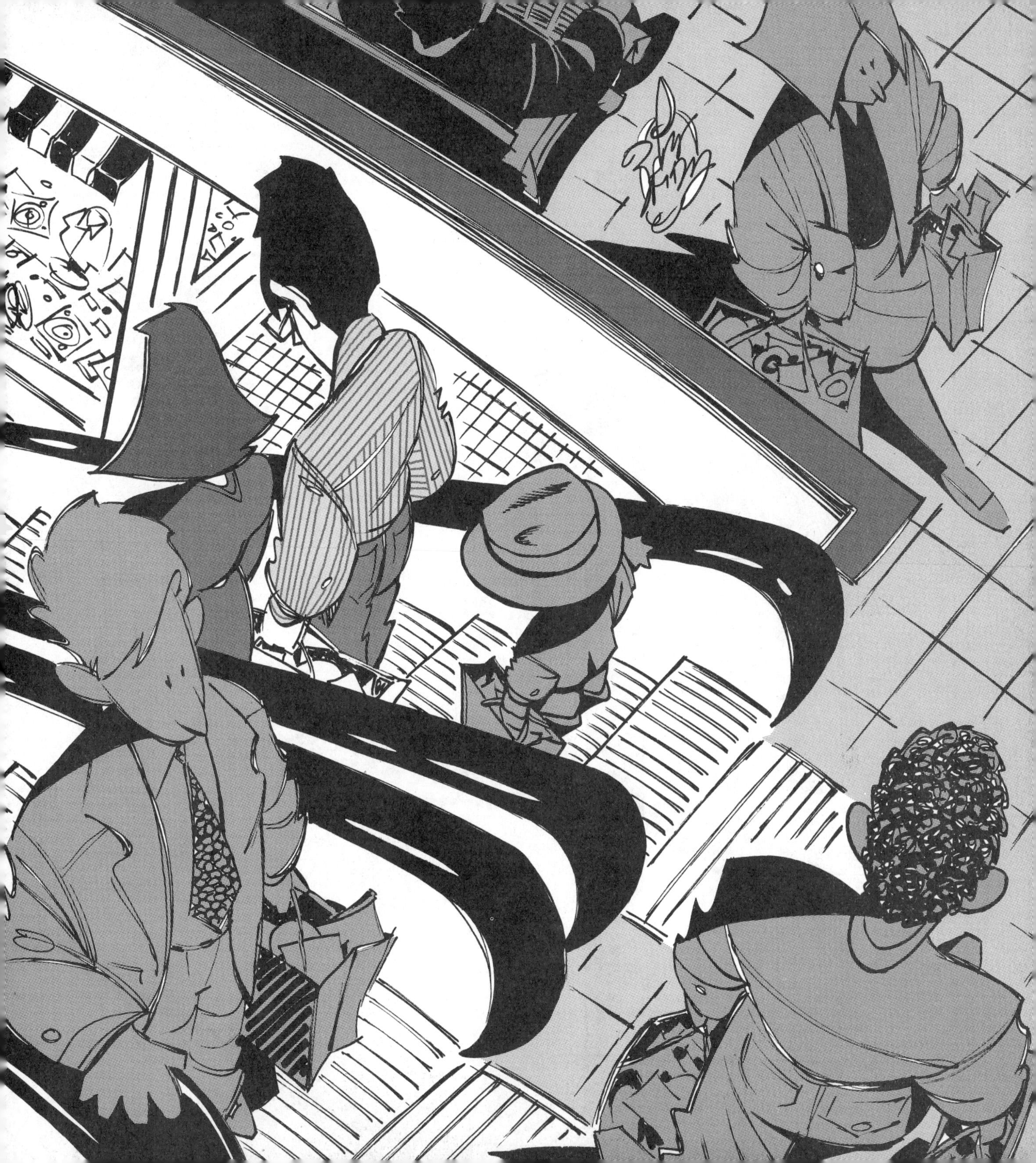

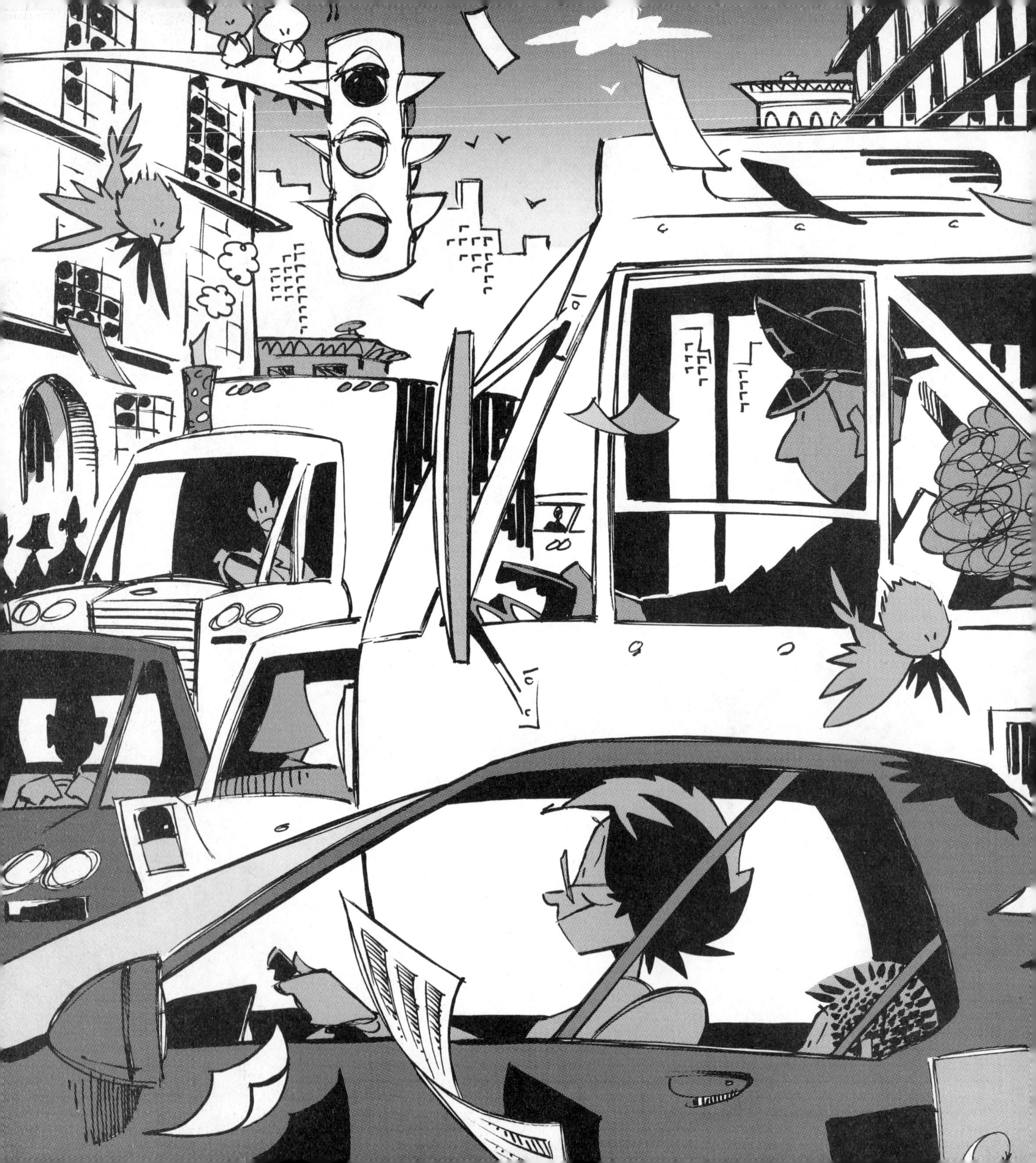

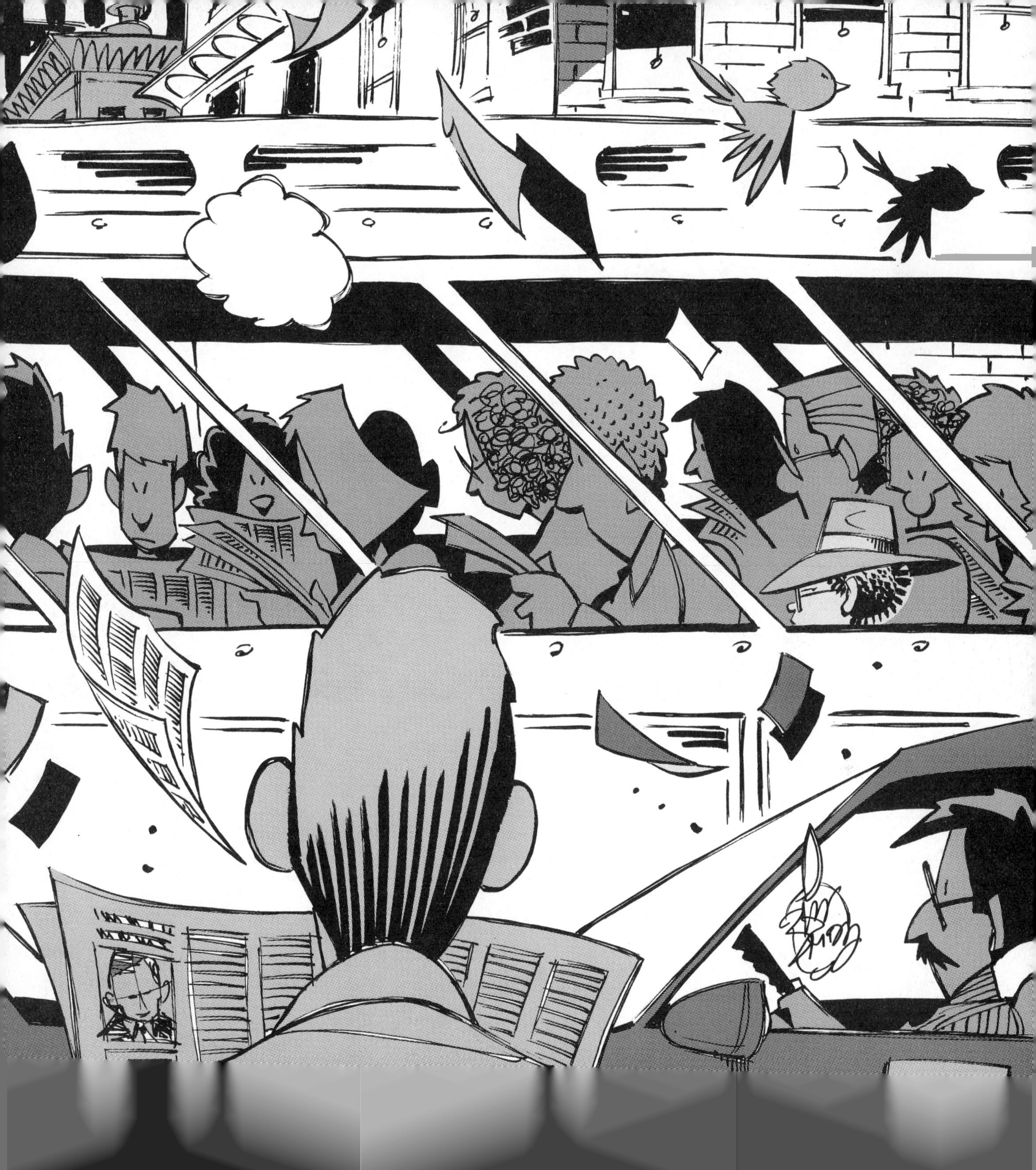

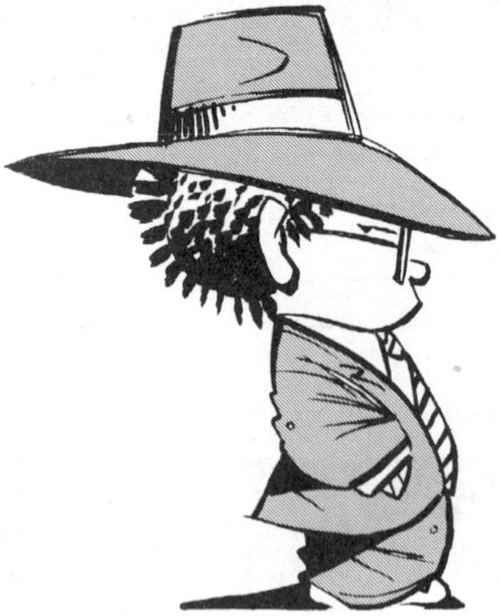

"To be on the safe side,
just deal with strangers
who are two feet tall."

–Pasquale's Guardian Angel

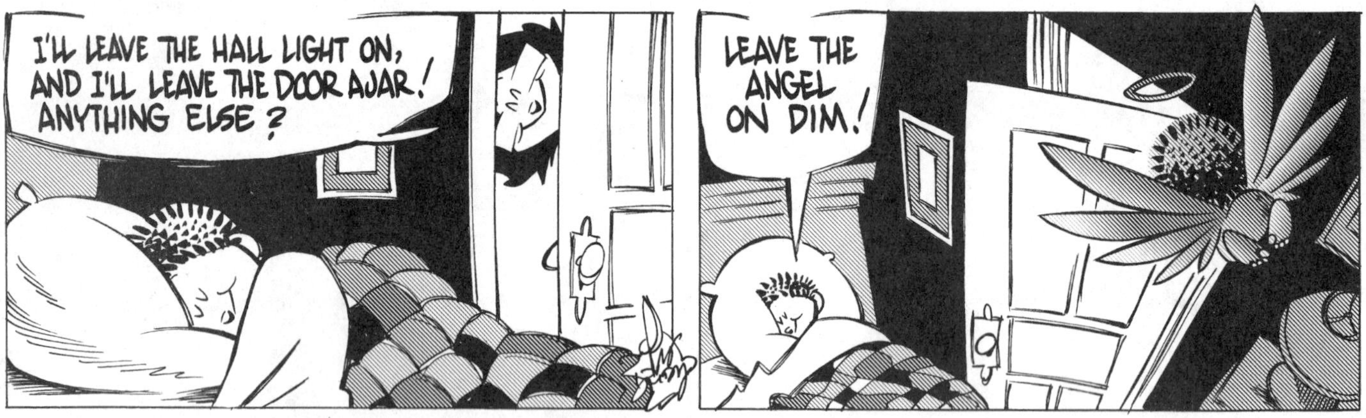
I'LL LEAVE THE HALL LIGHT ON, AND I'LL LEAVE THE DOOR AJAR! ANYTHING ELSE?
LEAVE THE ANGEL ON DIM!

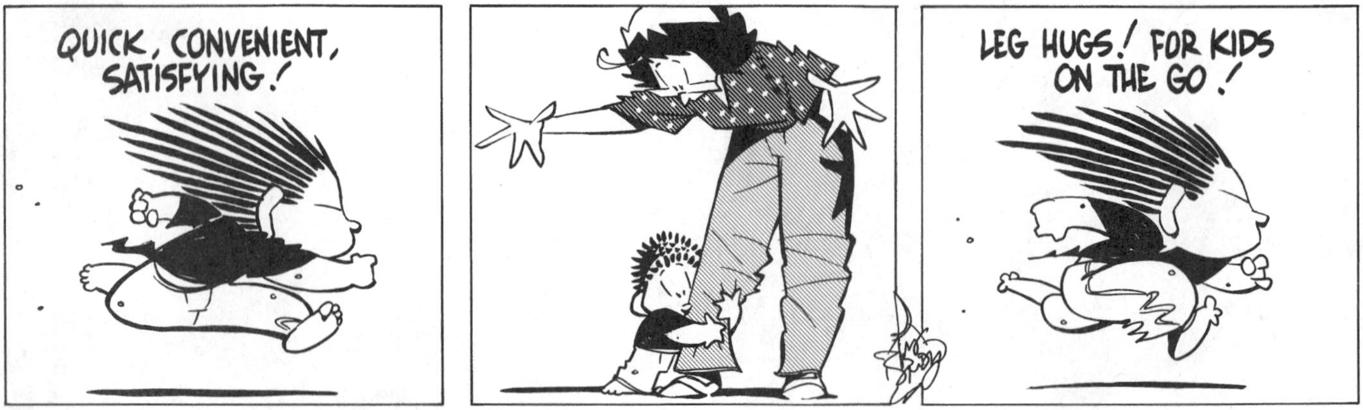
QUICK, CONVENIENT, SATISFYING!
LEG HUGS! FOR KIDS ON THE GO!

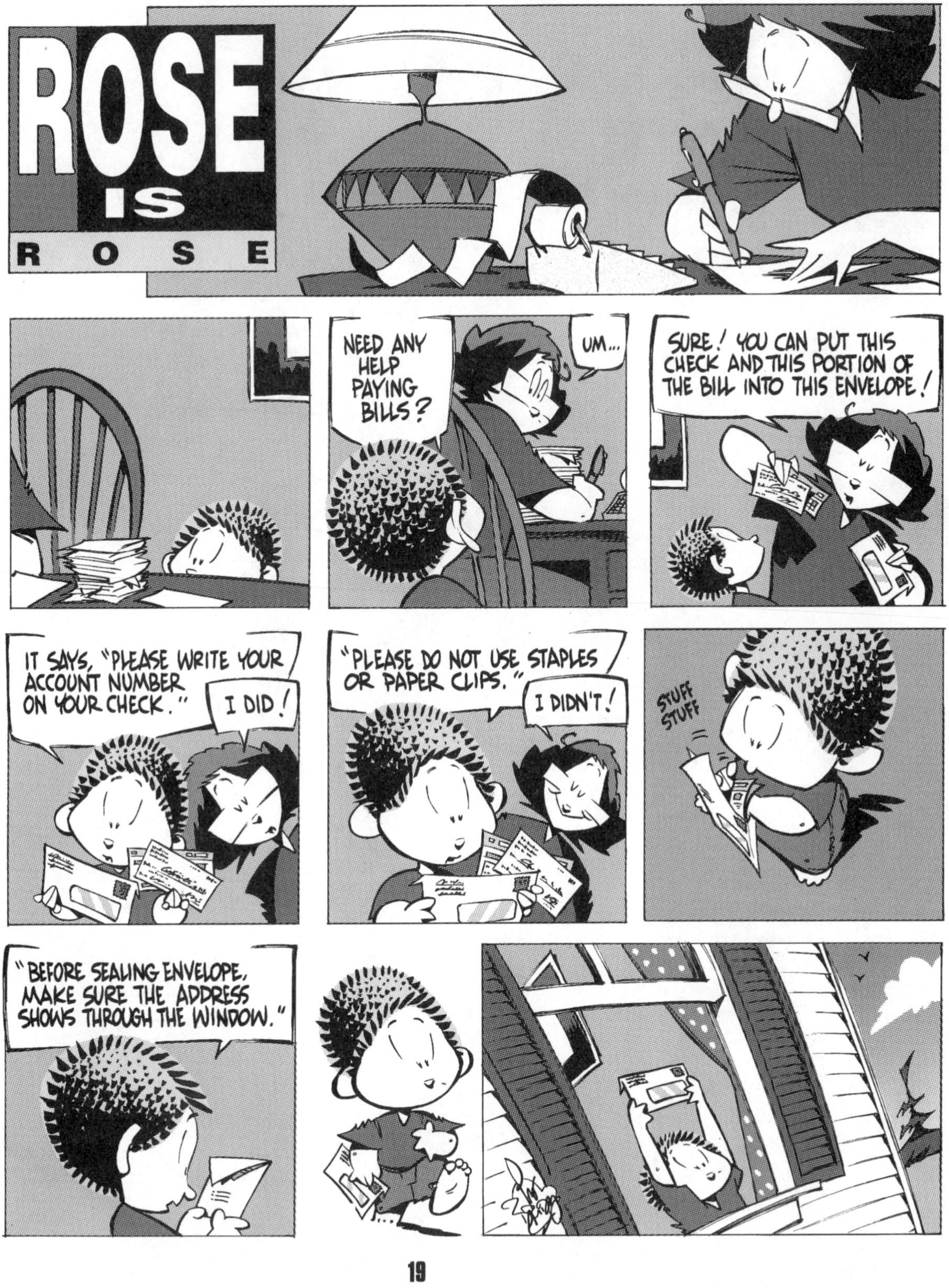
ROSE IS ROSE
NEED ANY HELP PAYING BILLS?
UM...
SURE! YOU CAN PUT THIS CHECK AND THIS PORTION OF THE BILL INTO THIS ENVELOPE!
IT SAYS, "PLEASE WRITE YOUR ACCOUNT NUMBER ON YOUR CHECK."
I DID!
"PLEASE DO NOT USE STAPLES OR PAPER CLIPS."
I DIDN'T!
STUFF STUFF
"BEFORE SEALING ENVELOPE, MAKE SURE THE ADDRESS SHOWS THROUGH THE WINDOW."

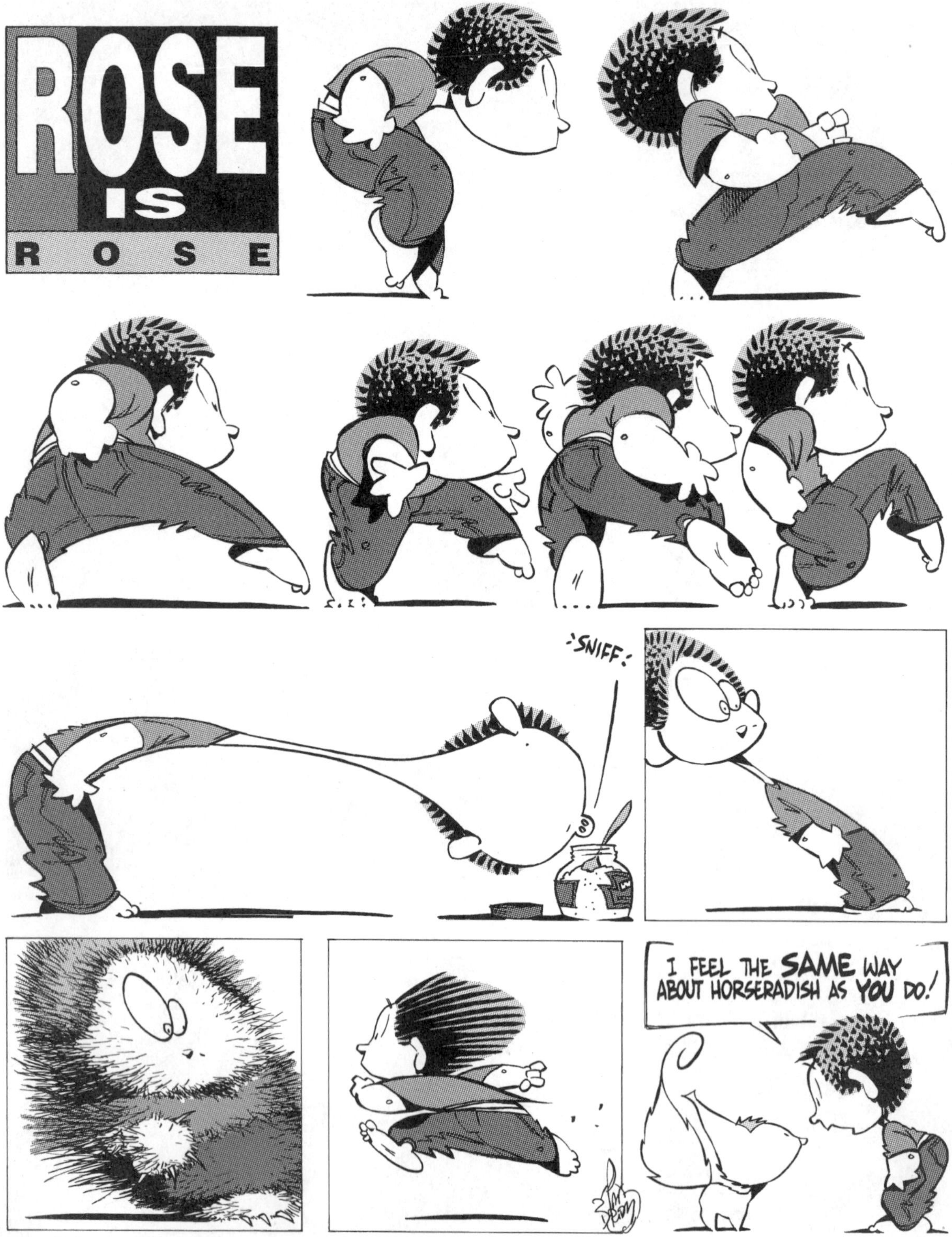
ROSE IS ROSE
SNIFF
I FEEL THE SAME WAY ABOUT HORSERADISH AS YOU DO!

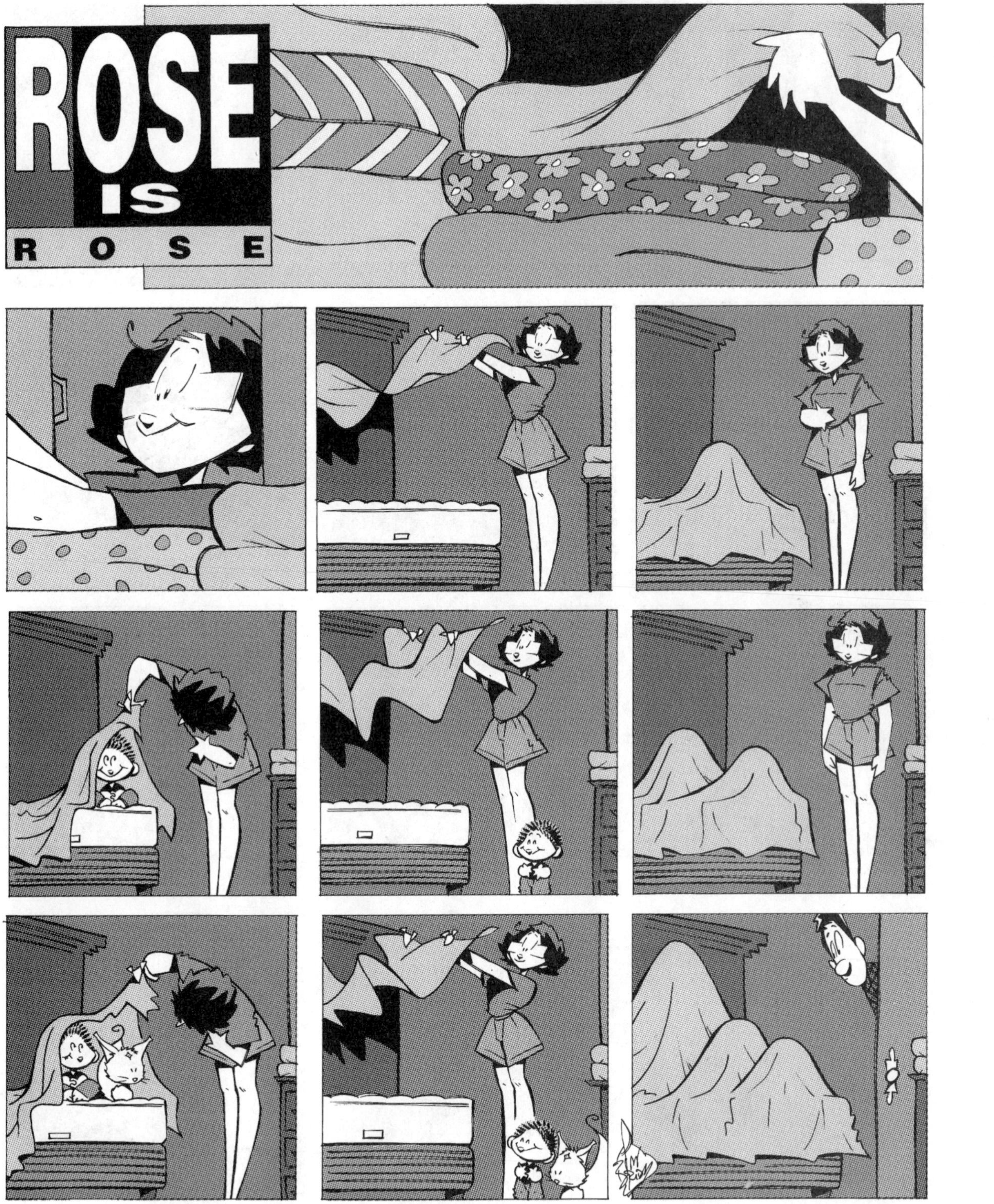
ROSE
IS
ROSE

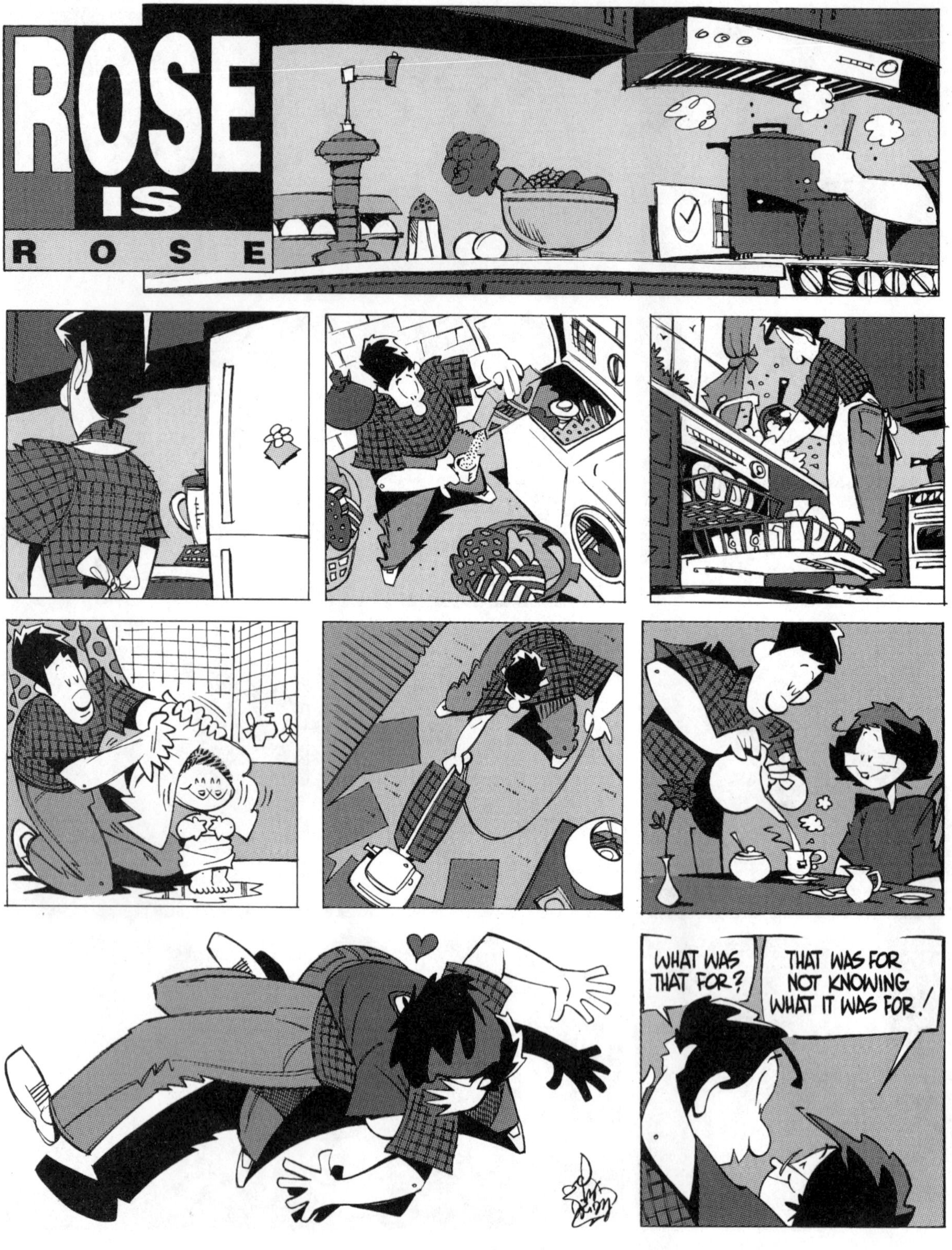
ROSE IS ROSE
WHAT WAS THAT FOR?
THAT WAS FOR NOT KNOWING WHAT IT WAS FOR!

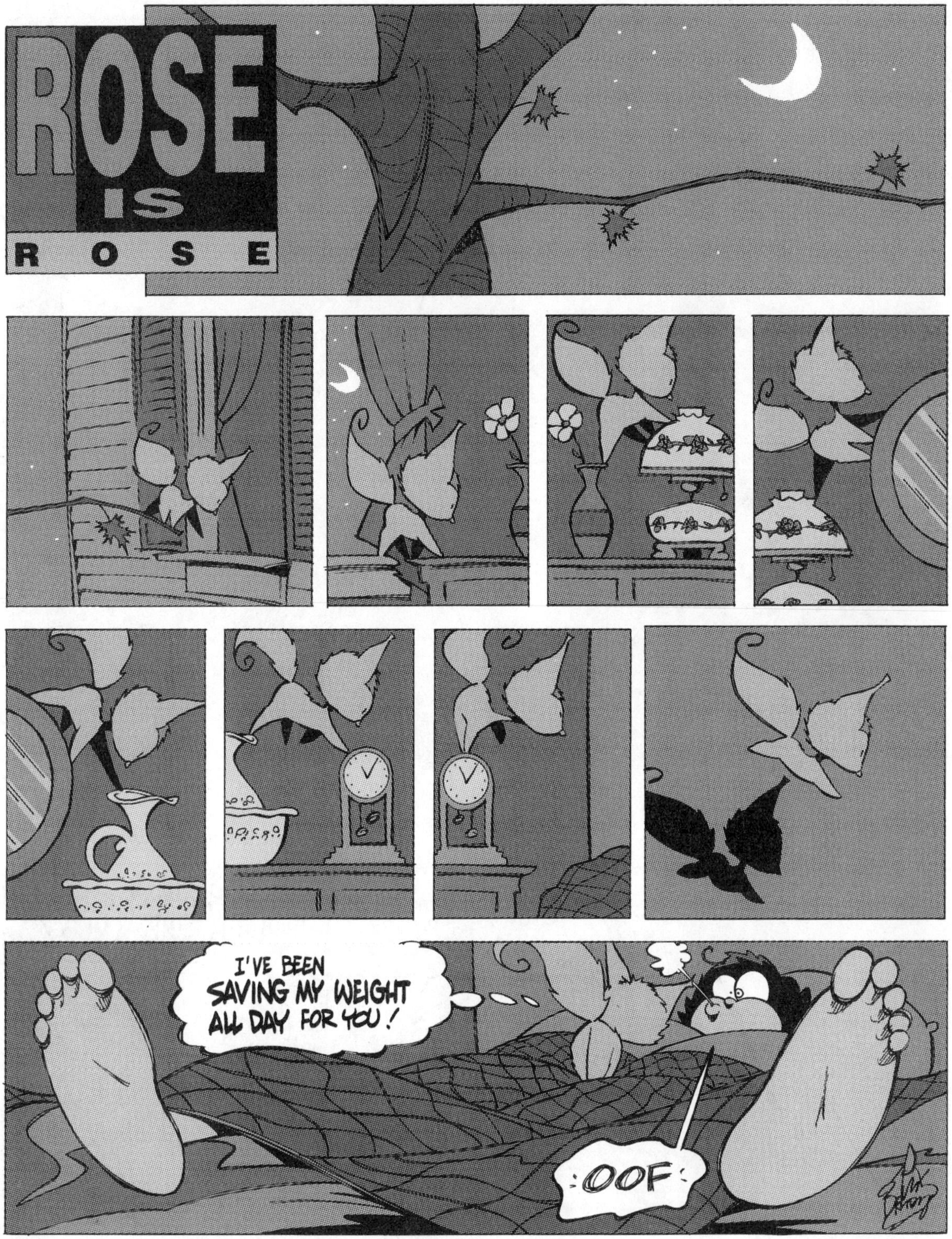
ROSE IS ROSE
I'VE BEEN SAVING MY WEIGHT ALL DAY FOR YOU!
OOF

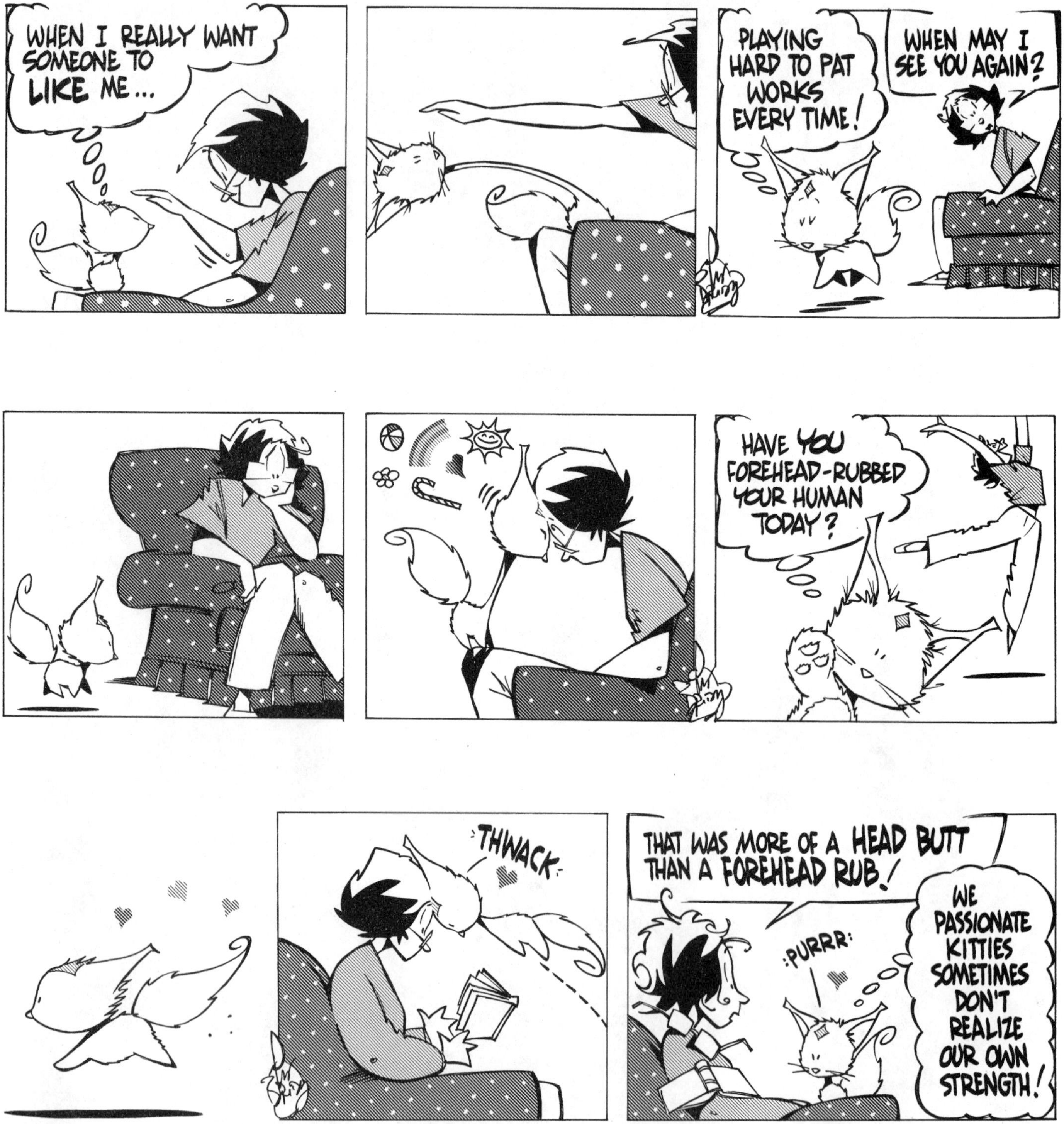
WHEN I REALLY WANT SOMEONE TO LIKE ME...
PLAYING HARD TO PAT WORKS EVERY TIME!
WHEN MAY I SEE YOU AGAIN?
HAVE YOU FOREHEAD-RUBBED YOUR HUMAN TODAY?
THWACK
THAT WAS MORE OF A HEAD BUTT THAN A FOREHEAD RUB!
PURRR
WE PASSIONATE KITTIES SOMETIMES DON'T REALIZE OUR OWN STRENGTH!

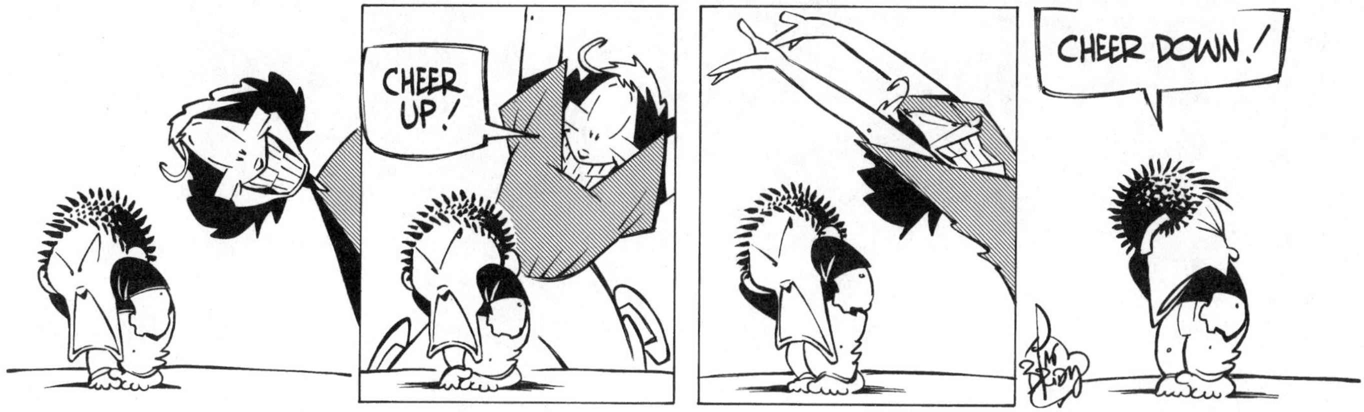
CHEER UP!
CHEER DOWN!

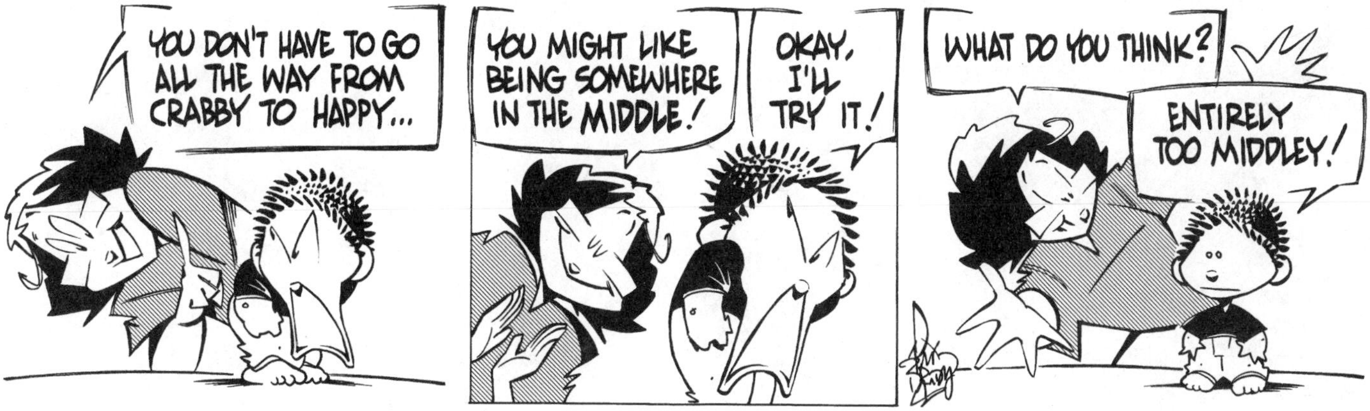
YOU DON'T HAVE TO GO ALL THE WAY FROM CRABBY TO HAPPY...
YOU MIGHT LIKE BEING SOMEWHERE IN THE MIDDLE!
OKAY, I'LL TRY IT!
WHAT DO YOU THINK?
ENTIRELY TOO MIDDLEY!

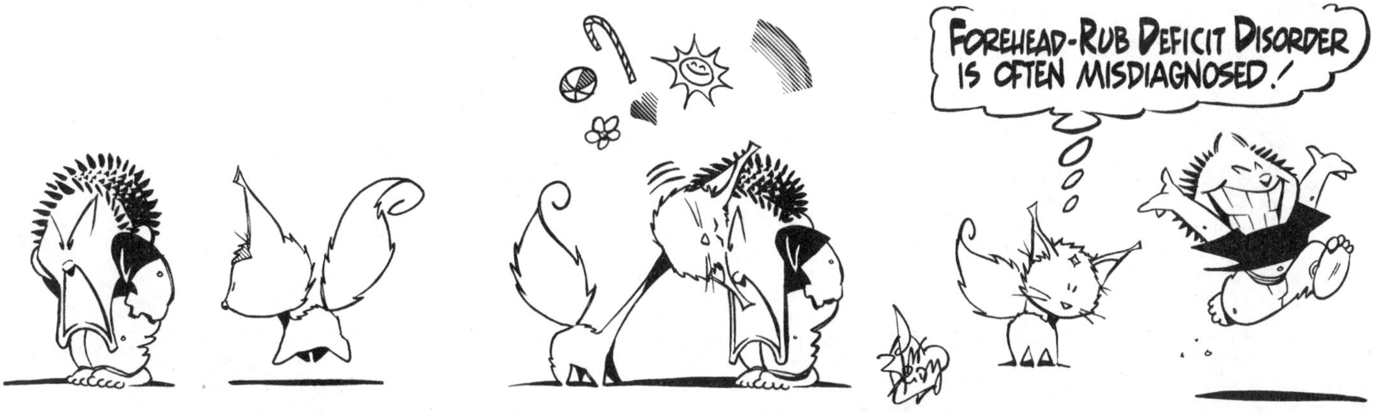
FOREHEAD-RUB DEFICIT DISORDER IS OFTEN MISDIAGNOSED!

AS HUMANS GET OLDER, THEIR MINIMUM DAILY REQUIREMENT OF FOREHEAD-RUBS INCREASES!

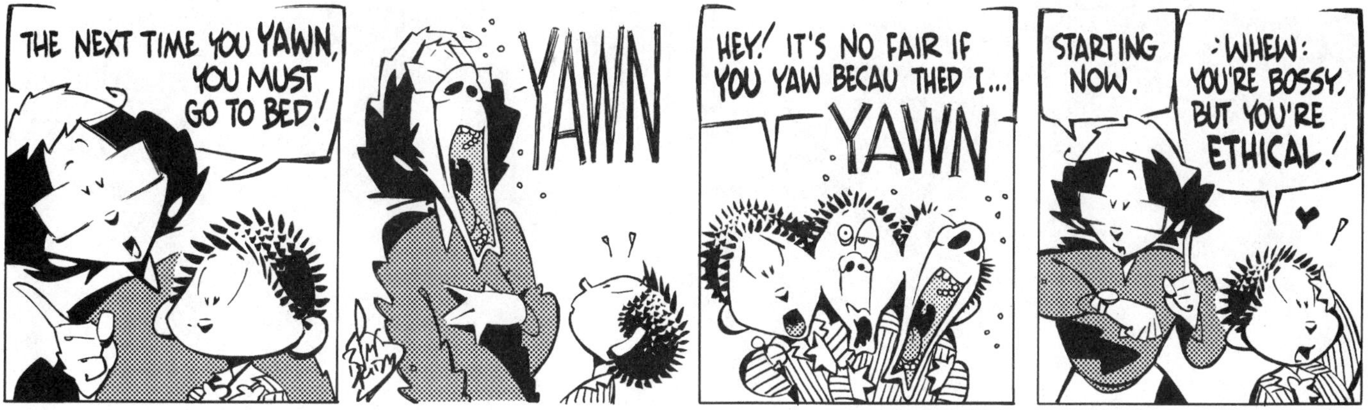
THE NEXT TIME YOU YAWN, YOU MUST GO TO BED!
YAWN
HEY! IT'S NO FAIR IF YOU YAW BECAU THED I...
YAWN
STARTING NOW.
:WHEW: YOU'RE BOSSY, BUT YOU'RE ETHICAL!

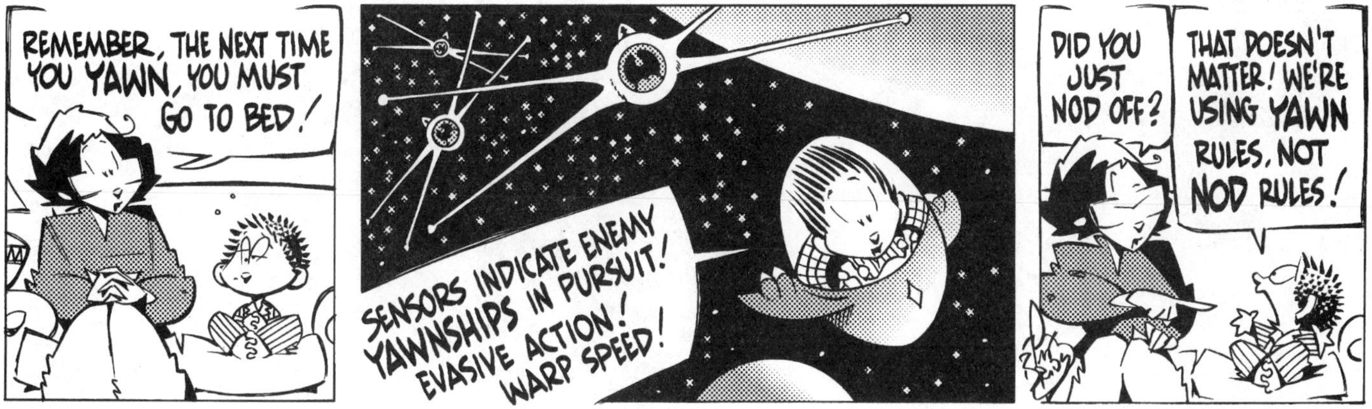
REMEMBER, THE NEXT TIME YOU YAWN, YOU MUST GO TO BED!
SENSORS INDICATE ENEMY YAWNSHIPS IN PURSUIT! EVASIVE ACTION! WARP SPEED!
DID YOU JUST NOD OFF?
THAT DOESN'T MATTER! WE'RE USING YAWN RULES, NOT NOD RULES!

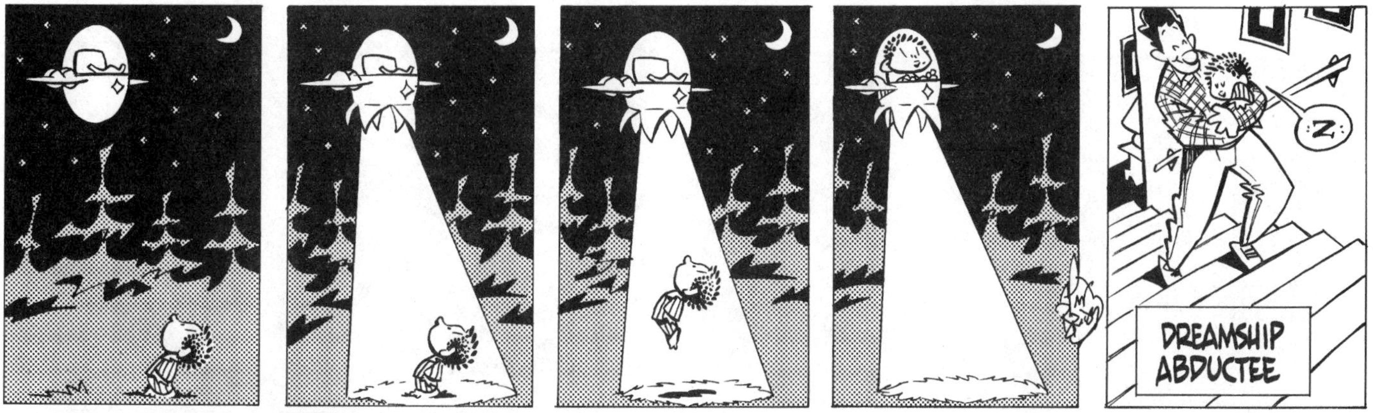
Z
DREAMSHIP ABDUCTEE

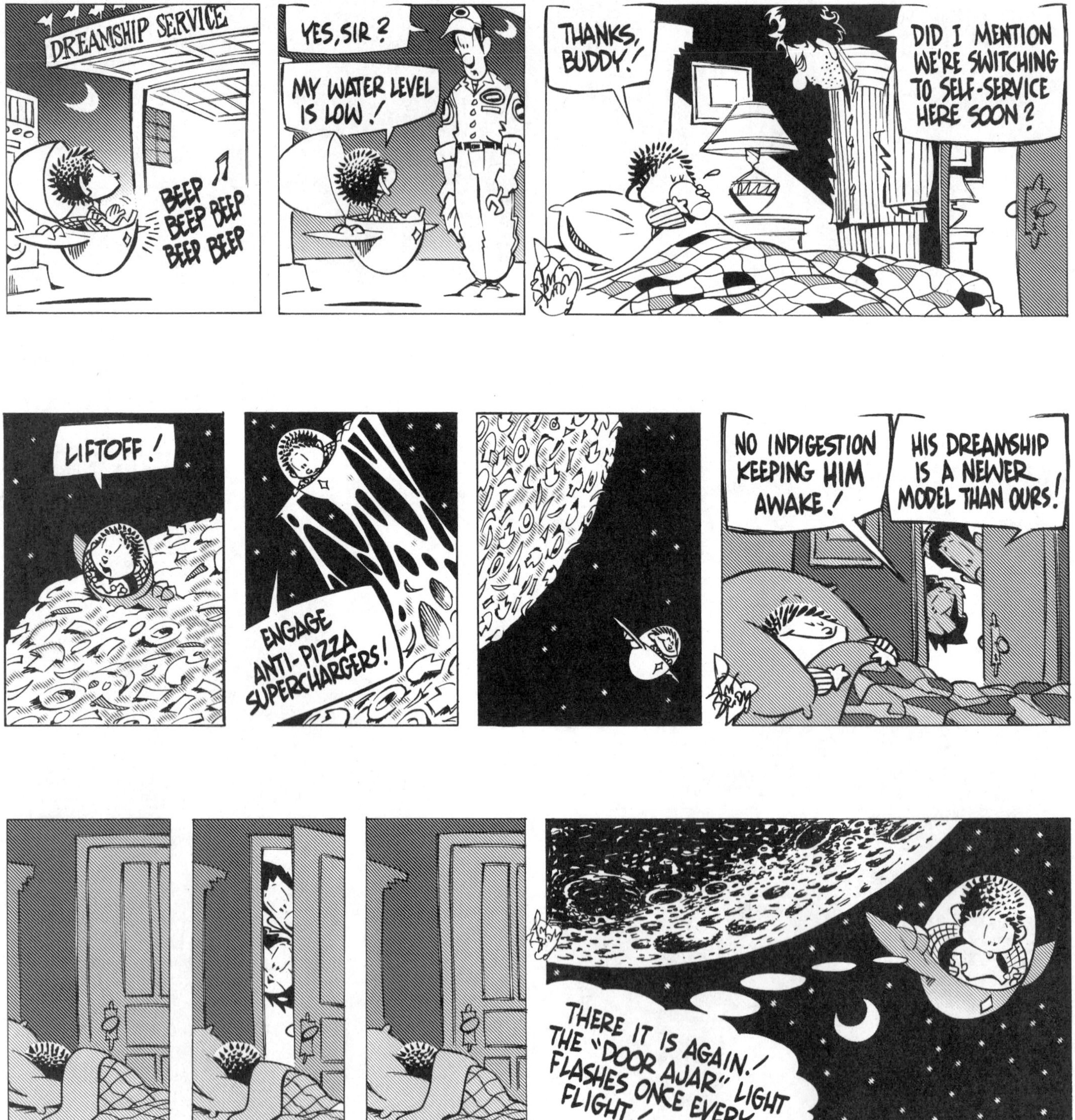
DREAMSHIP SERVICE
BEEP BEEP BEEP BEEP BEEP
YES, SIR?
MY WATER LEVEL IS LOW!
THANKS, BUDDY!
DID I MENTION WE'RE SWITCHING TO SELF-SERVICE HERE SOON?
LIFTOFF!
ENGAGE ANTI-PIZZA SUPERCHARGERS!
NO INDIGESTION KEEPING HIM AWAKE!
HIS DREAMSHIP IS A NEWER MODEL THAN OURS!
THERE IT IS AGAIN! THE "DOOR AJAR" LIGHT FLASHES ONCE EVERY FLIGHT!

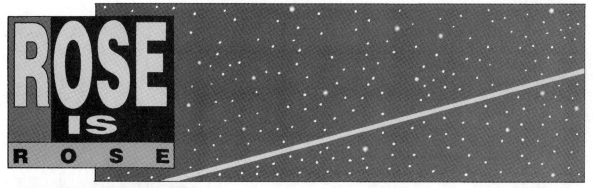

This celestial event occurs once during each rotation of the earth...

It begins with a thin band of light silently splitting the universe...

The band widens until it peaks...

Then it narrows again and quietly disappears.

"The parent check phenomenon"... comforting evidence that we are not alone.

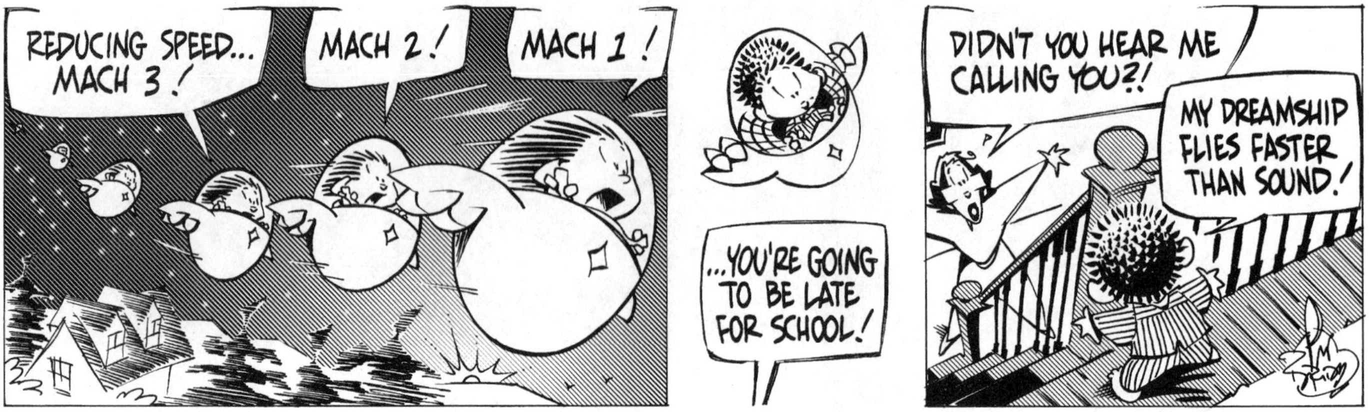
REDUCING SPEED... MACH 3!
MACH 2!
MACH 1!
...YOU'RE GOING TO BE LATE FOR SCHOOL!
DIDN'T YOU HEAR ME CALLING YOU?!
MY DREAMSHIP FLIES FASTER THAN SOUND!

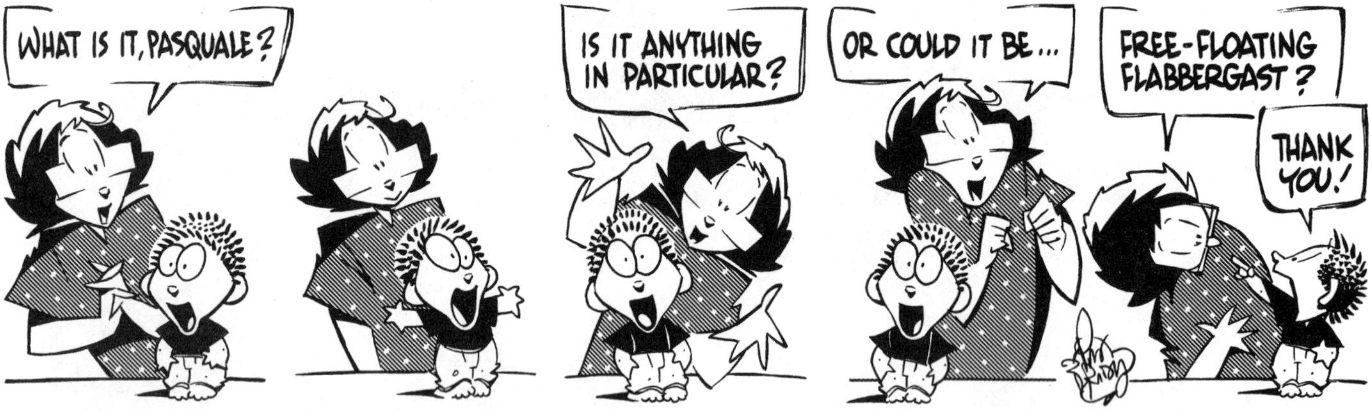
WHAT IS IT, PASQUALE?
IS IT ANYTHING IN PARTICULAR?
OR COULD IT BE...
FREE-FLOATING FLABBERGAST?
THANK YOU!

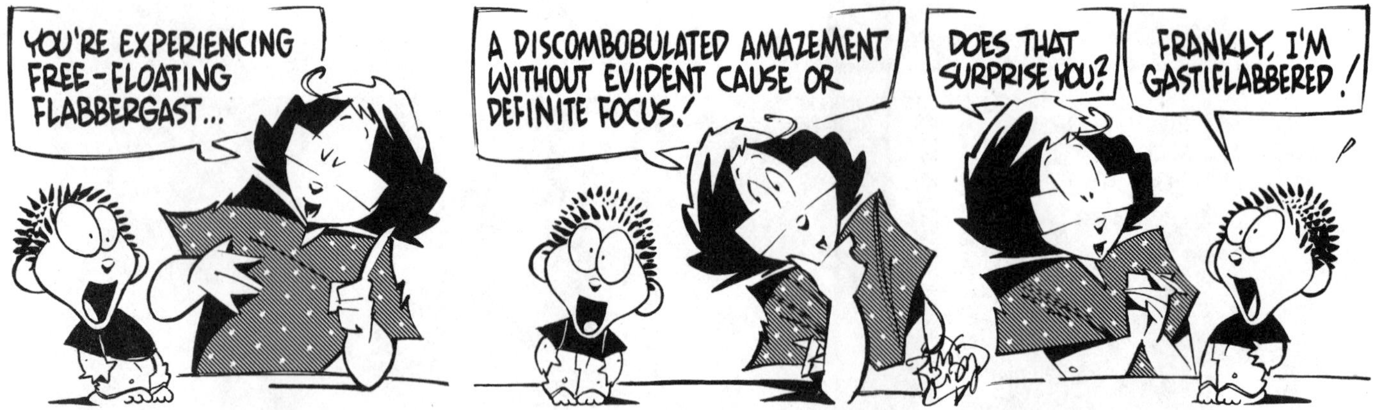
YOU'RE EXPERIENCING FREE-FLOATING FLABBERGAST...
A DISCOMBOBULATED AMAZEMENT WITHOUT EVIDENT CAUSE OR DEFINITE FOCUS!
DOES THAT SURPRISE YOU?
FRANKLY, I'M GASTIFLABBERED!

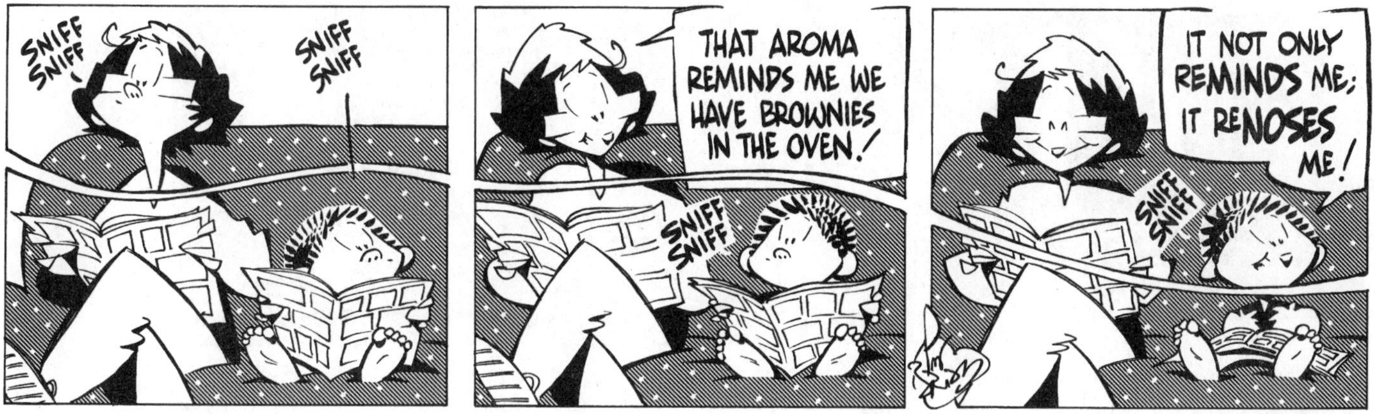
SNIFF SNIFF
SNIFF SNIFF
THAT AROMA REMINDS ME WE HAVE BROWNIES IN THE OVEN!
SNIFF SNIFF
IT NOT ONLY REMINDS ME; IT RENOSES ME!
SNIFF SNIFF

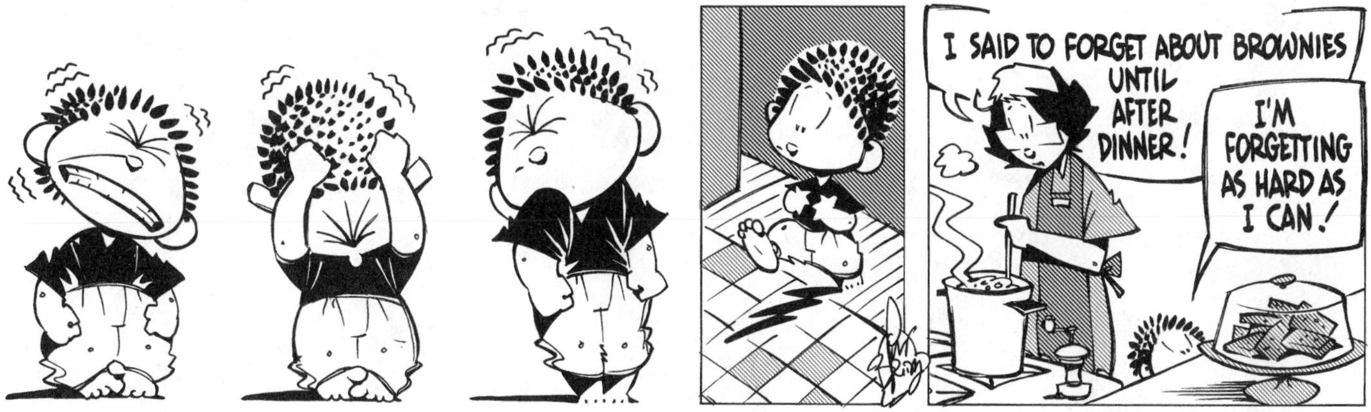
I SAID TO FORGET ABOUT BROWNIES UNTIL AFTER DINNER!
I'M FORGETTING AS HARD AS I CAN!

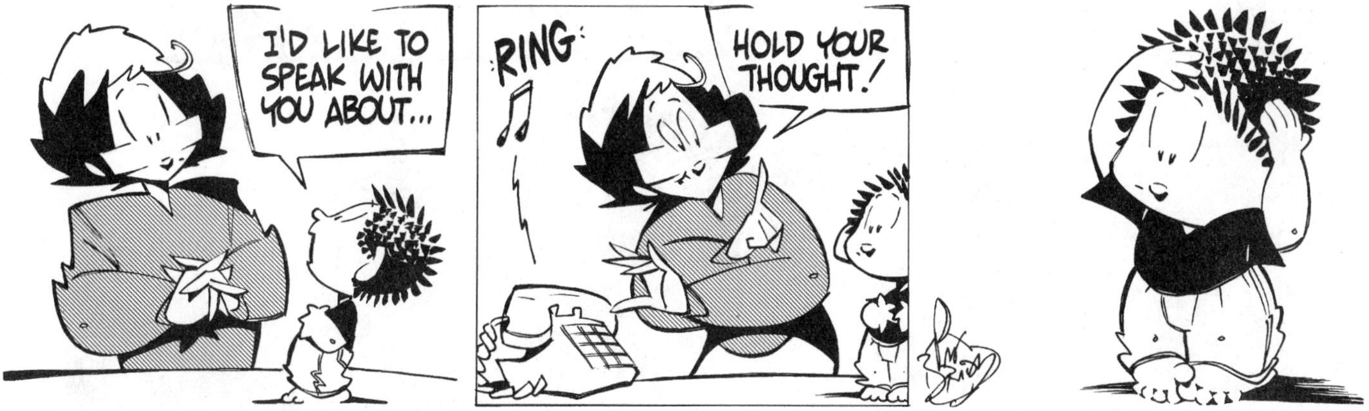
I'D LIKE TO SPEAK WITH YOU ABOUT...
RING
HOLD YOUR THOUGHT!

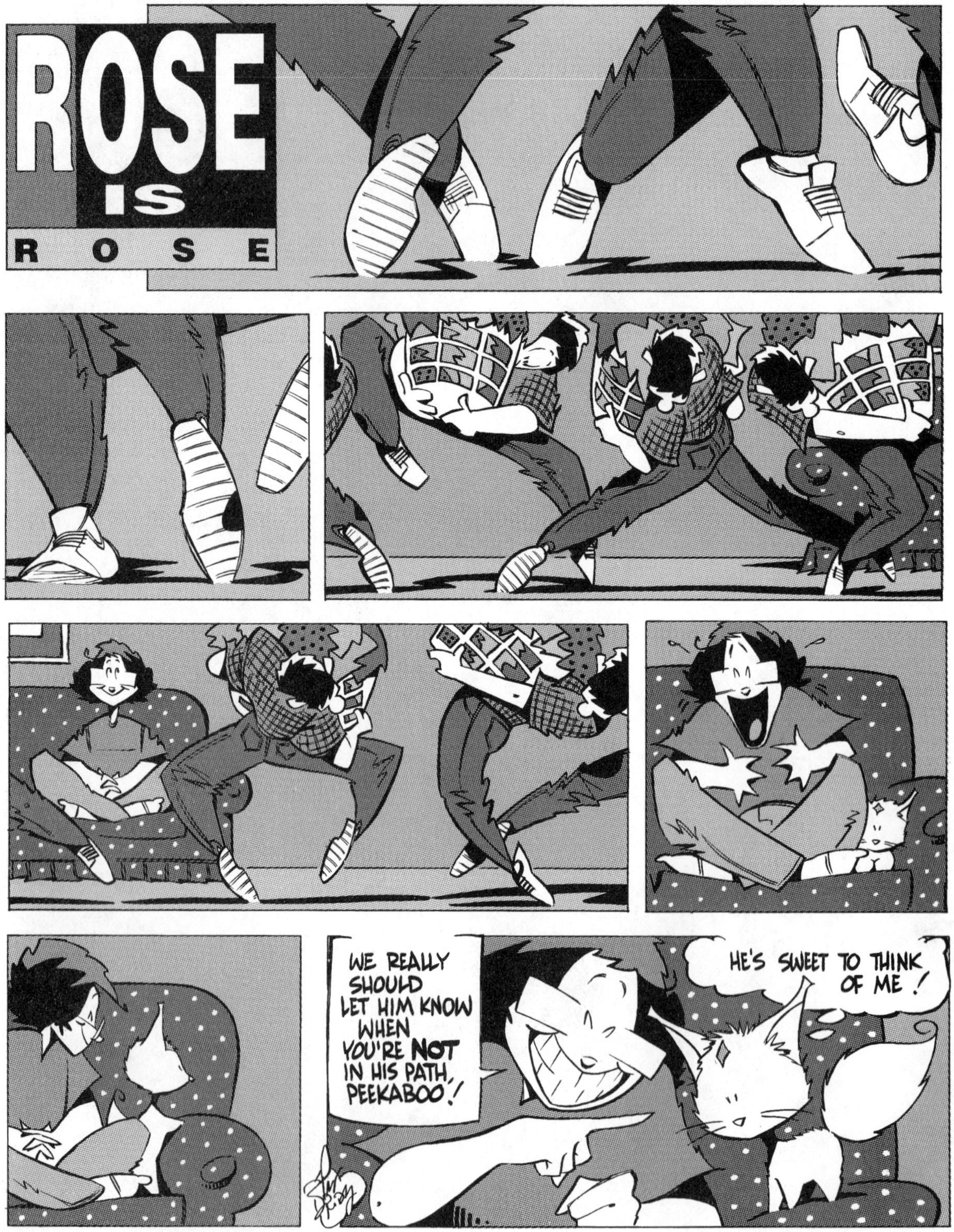
ROSE IS ROSE
WE REALLY SHOULD LET HIM KNOW WHEN YOU'RE **NOT** IN HIS PATH, PEEKABOO!
HE'S SWEET TO THINK OF ME!

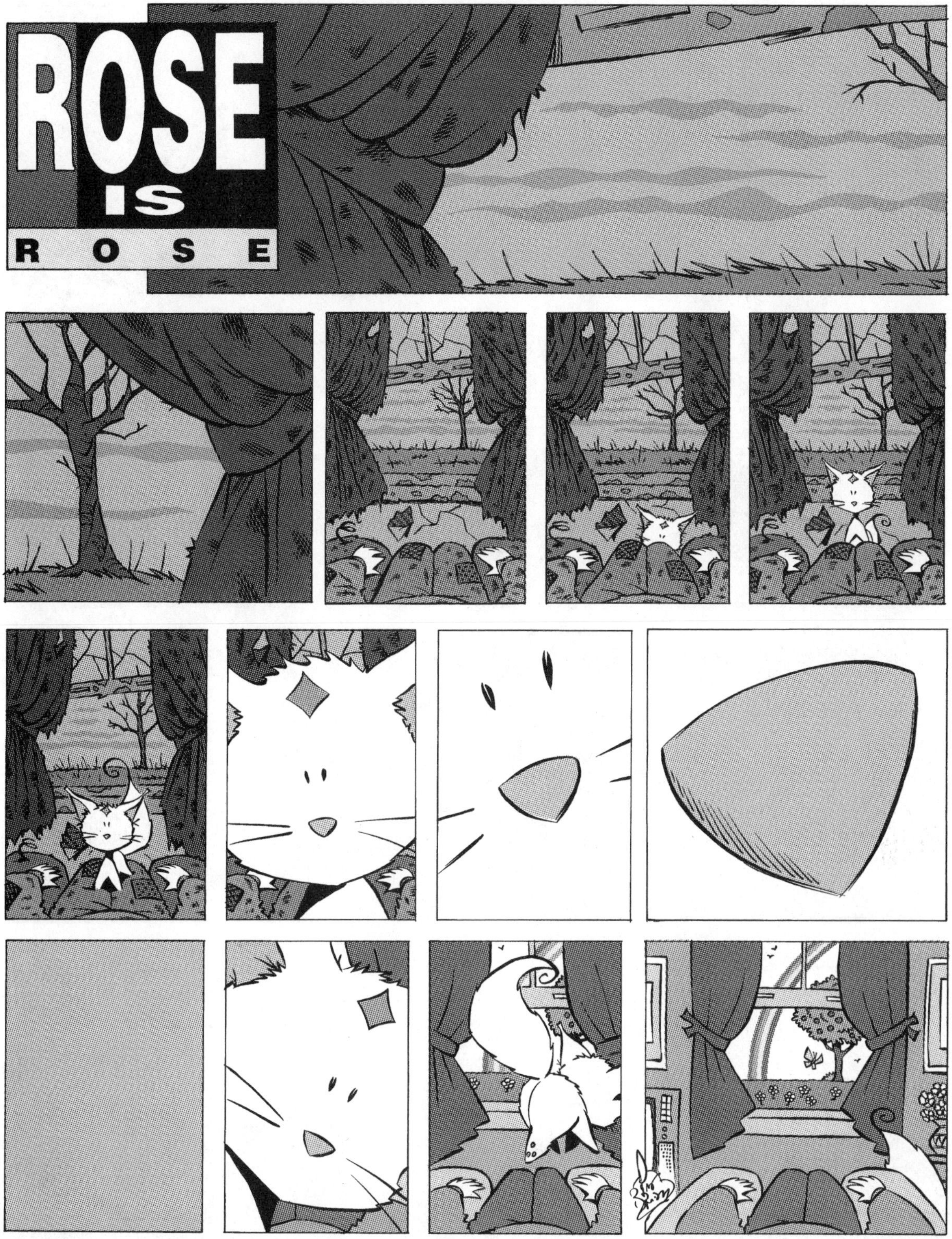
ROSE
IS
ROSE

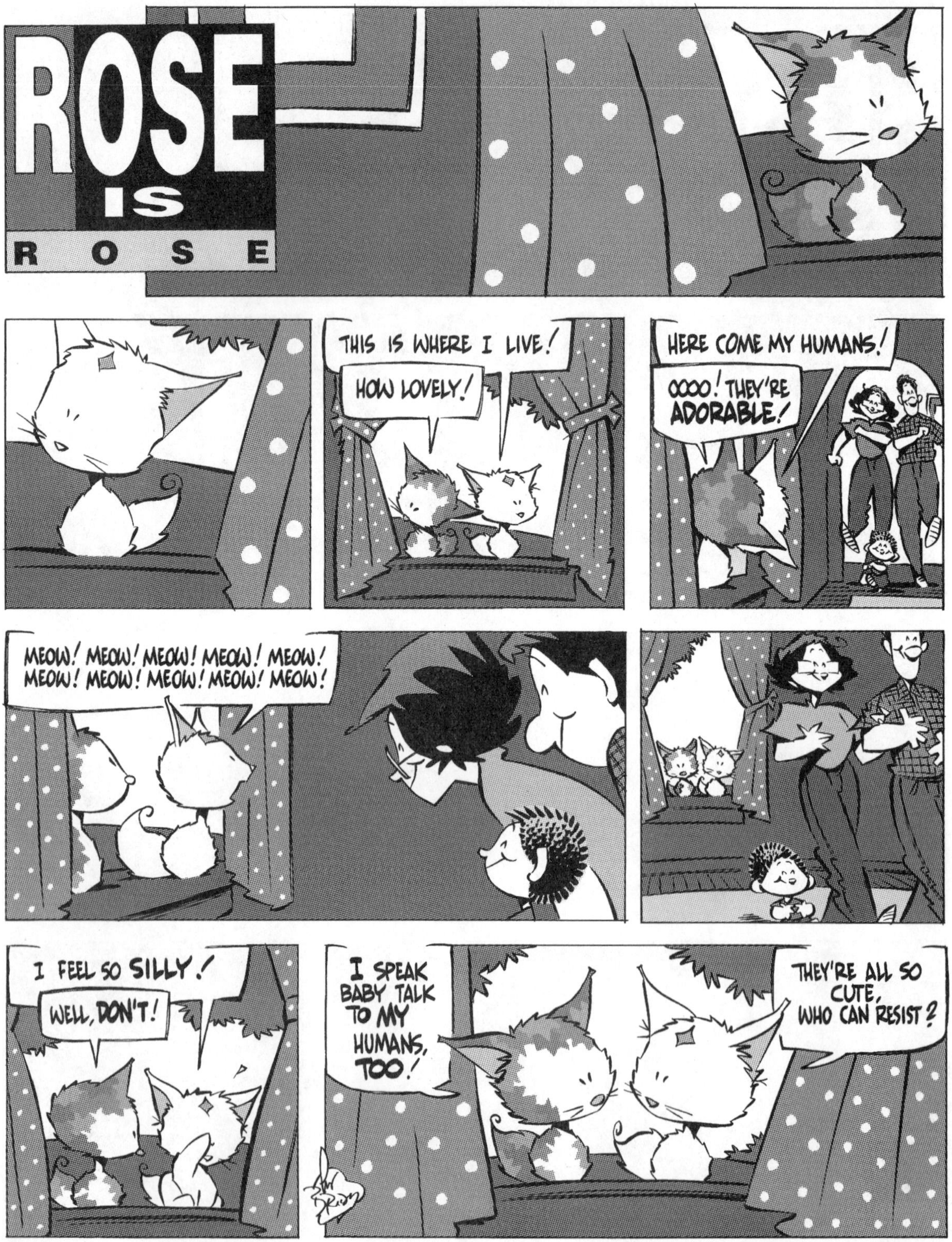
ROSE IS ROSE
THIS IS WHERE I LIVE!
HOW LOVELY!
HERE COME MY HUMANS!
OOOO! THEY'RE ADORABLE!
MEOW! MEOW! MEOW! MEOW! MEOW! MEOW! MEOW! MEOW! MEOW! MEOW!
I FEEL SO SILLY!
WELL, DON'T!
I SPEAK BABY TALK TO MY HUMANS, TOO!
THEY'RE ALL SO CUTE, WHO CAN RESIST?

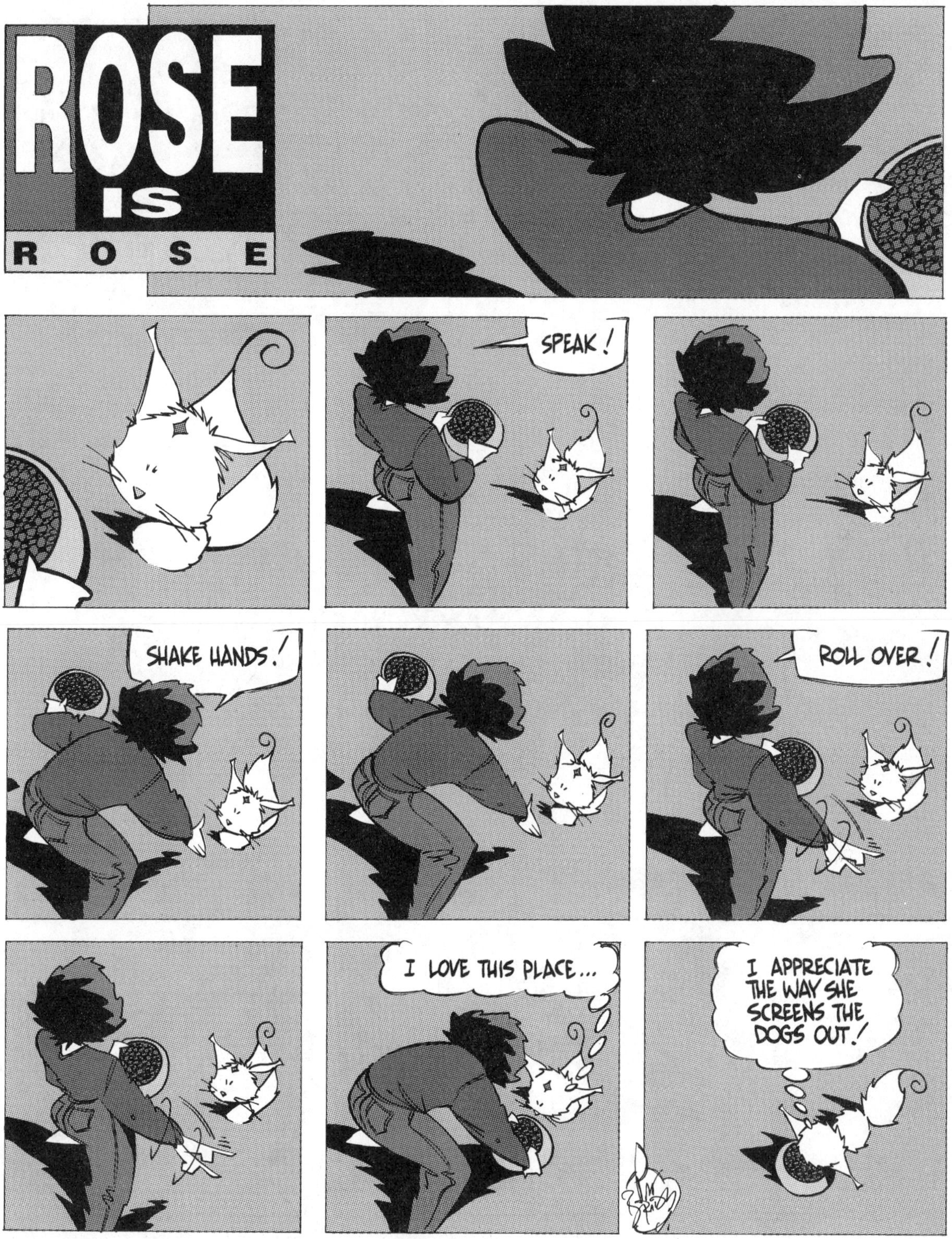
ROSE IS ROSE
SPEAK!
SHAKE HANDS!
ROLL OVER!
I LOVE THIS PLACE...
I APPRECIATE THE WAY SHE SCREENS THE DOGS OUT!

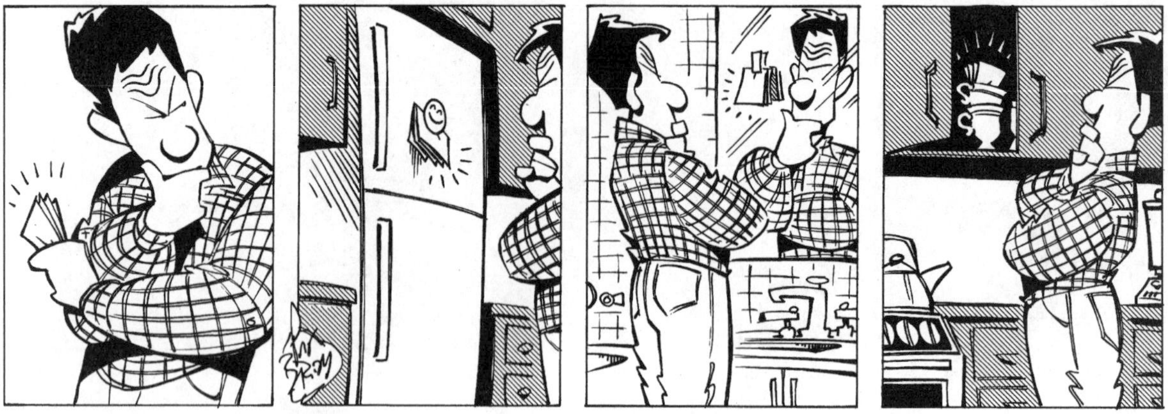

GREAT LOVE NOTE WRITERS AGONIZE OVER THE BEST WAY TO SUBMIT A MANUSCRIPT.

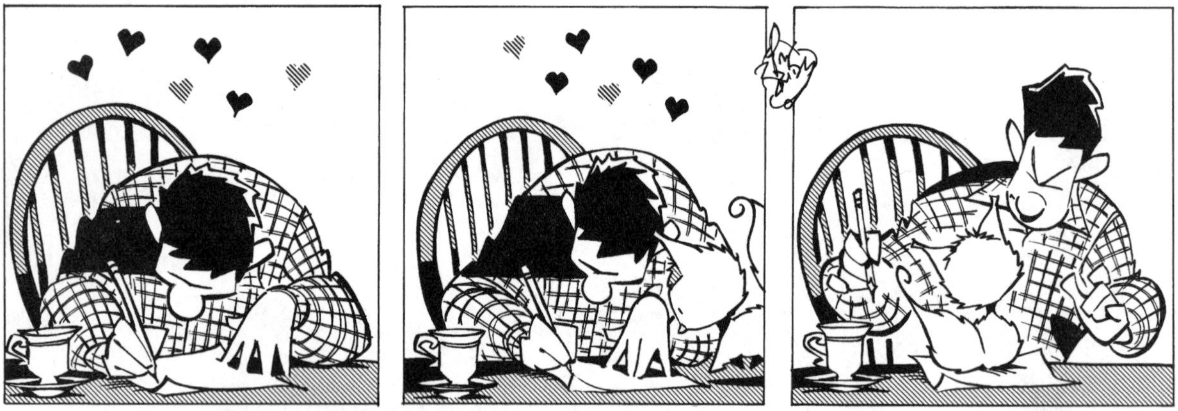

GREAT LOVE NOTE WRITERS OFTEN STRUGGLE UNDER OPPRESSIVE WORKING CONDITIONS.

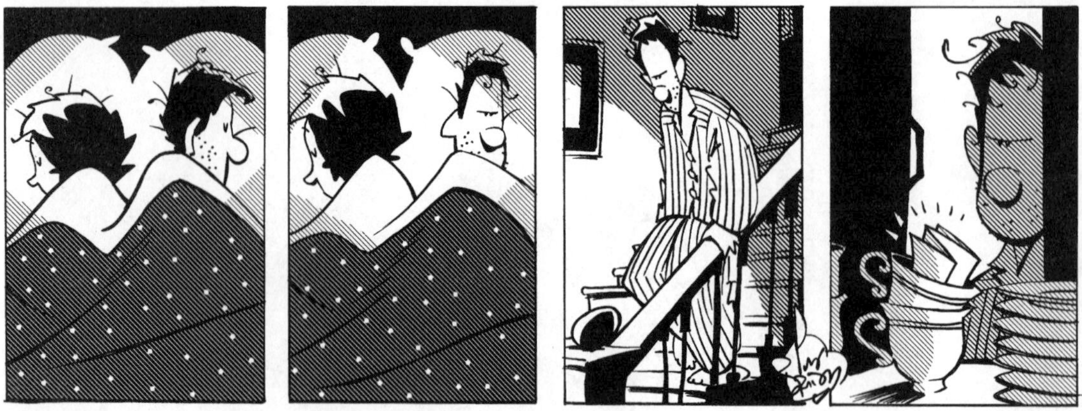

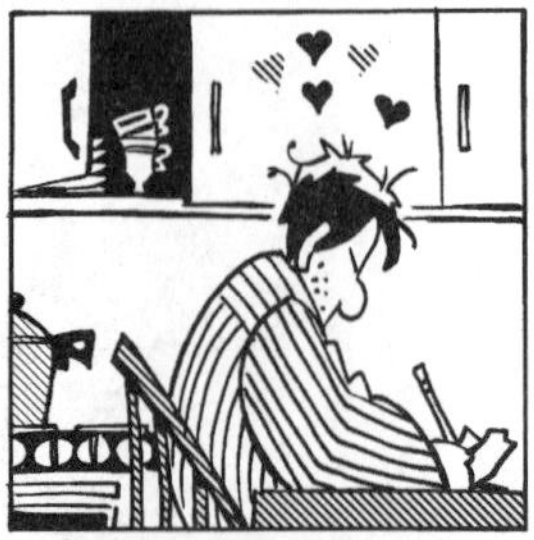

GREAT LOVE NOTE WRITERS SOMETIMES DO REWRITES ALL NIGHT LONG.

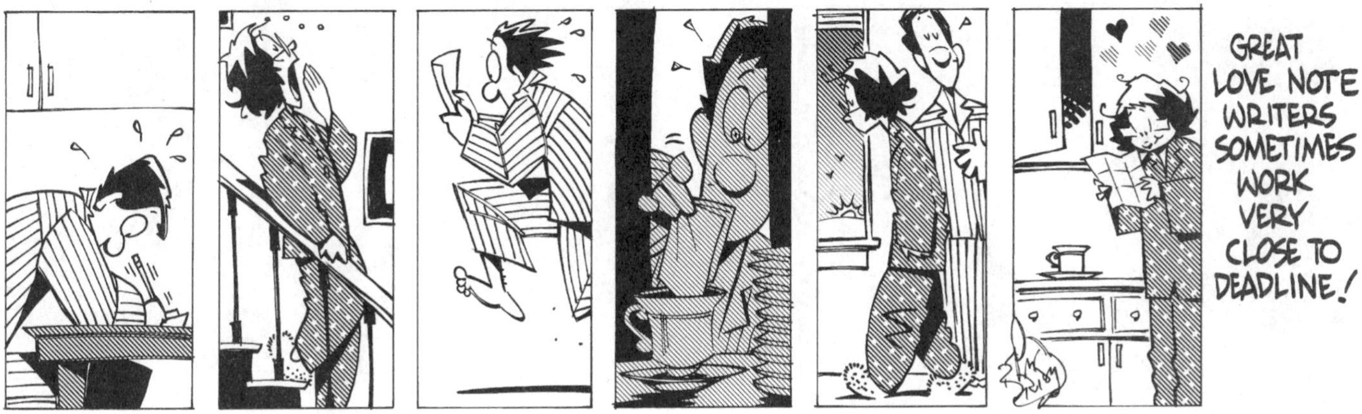
GREAT LOVE NOTE WRITERS SOMETIMES WORK VERY CLOSE TO DEADLINE!

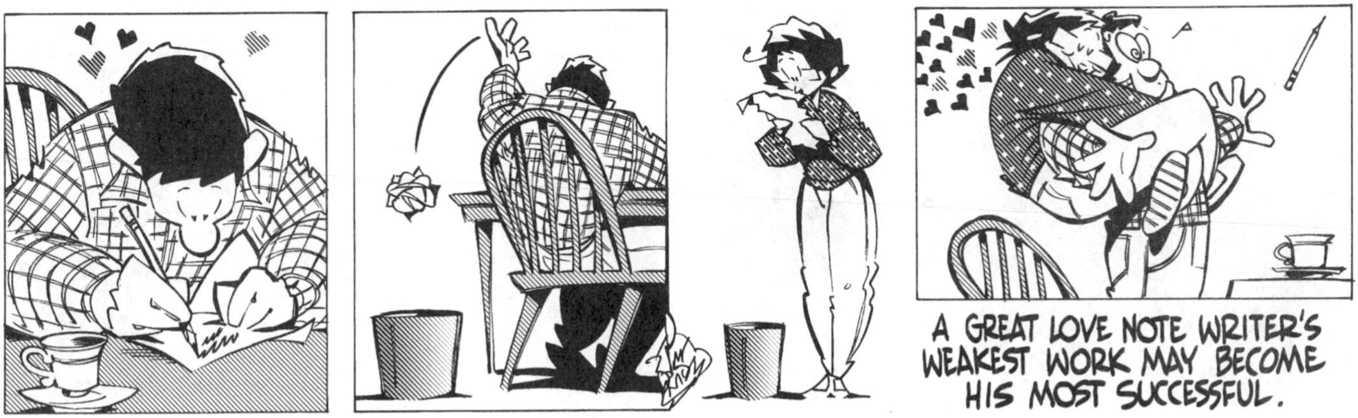
A GREAT LOVE NOTE WRITER'S WEAKEST WORK MAY BECOME HIS MOST SUCCESSFUL.

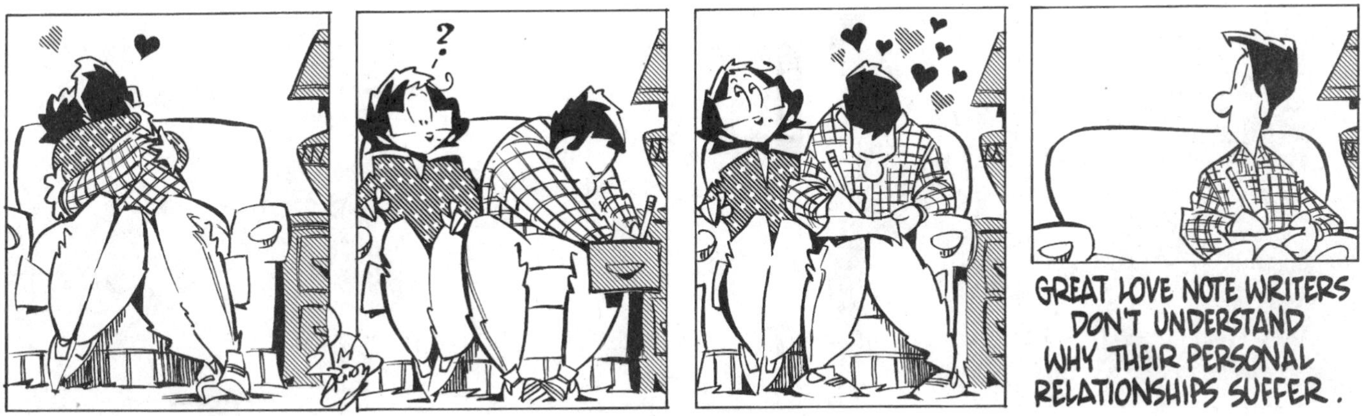
GREAT LOVE NOTE WRITERS DON'T UNDERSTAND WHY THEIR PERSONAL RELATIONSHIPS SUFFER.

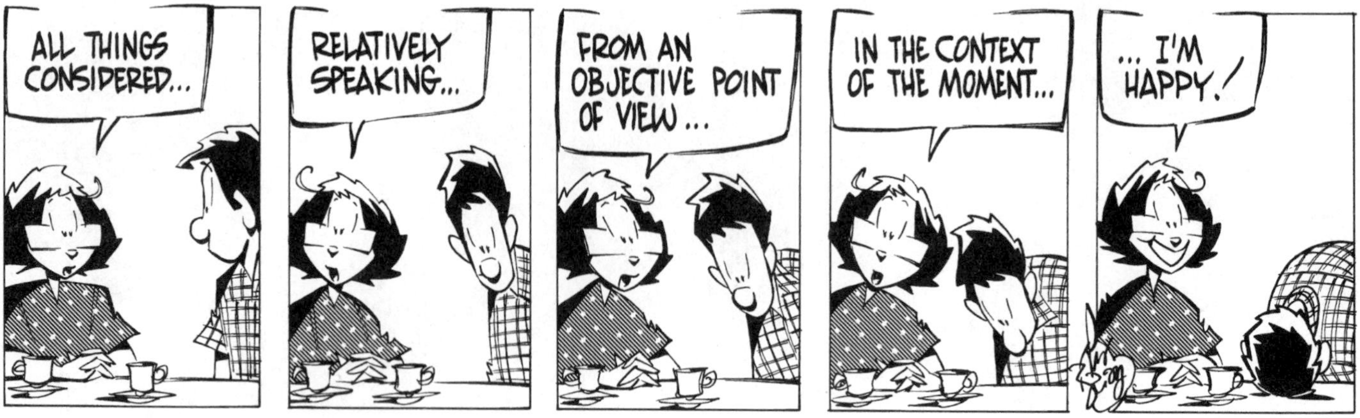
ALL THINGS CONSIDERED...
RELATIVELY SPEAKING...
FROM AN OBJECTIVE POINT OF VIEW...
IN THE CONTEXT OF THE MOMENT...
... I'M HAPPY!

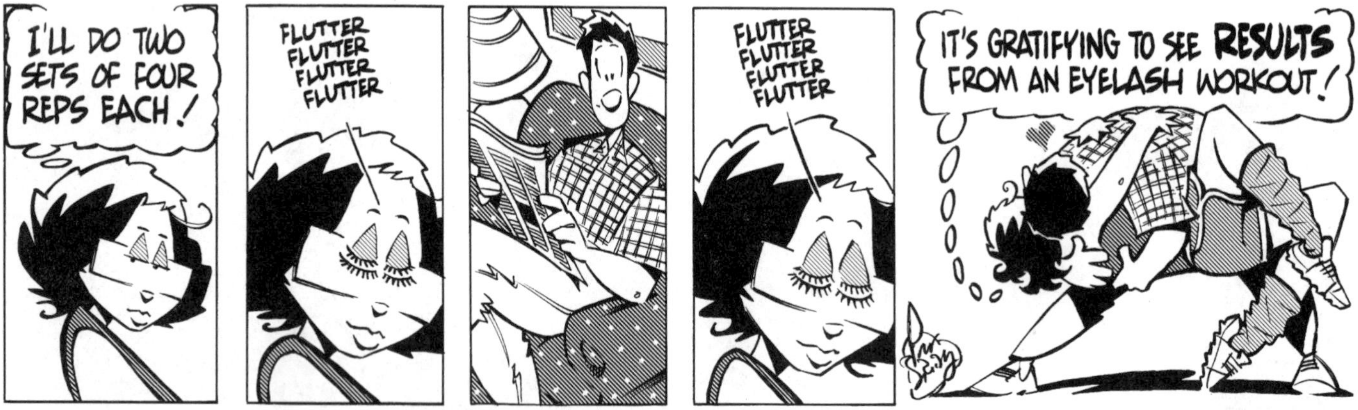
I'LL DO TWO SETS OF FOUR REPS EACH!
FLUTTER FLUTTER FLUTTER FLUTTER
FLUTTER FLUTTER FLUTTER FLUTTER
IT'S GRATIFYING TO SEE **RESULTS** FROM AN EYELASH WORKOUT!

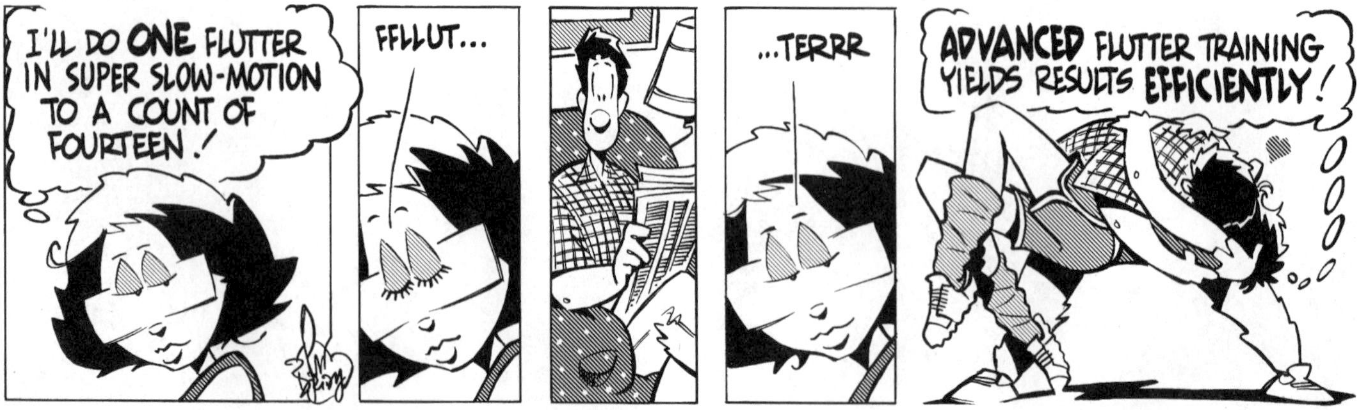
I'LL DO **ONE** FLUTTER IN SUPER SLOW-MOTION TO A COUNT OF FOURTEEN!
FFLLUT...
...TERRR
ADVANCED FLUTTER TRAINING YIELDS RESULTS **EFFICIENTLY**!

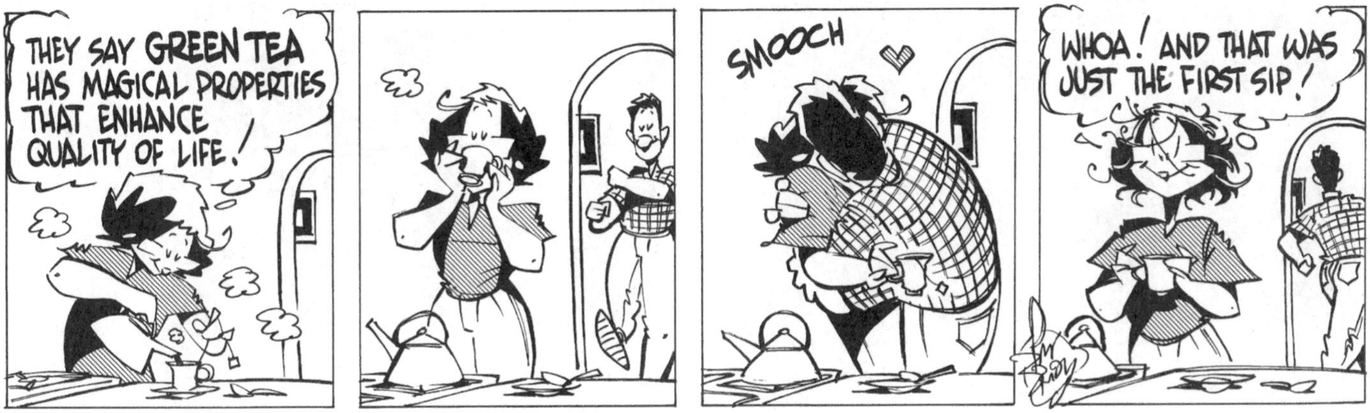
THEY SAY GREEN TEA HAS MAGICAL PROPERTIES THAT ENHANCE QUALITY OF LIFE!
SMOOCH
WHOA! AND THAT WAS JUST THE FIRST SIP!

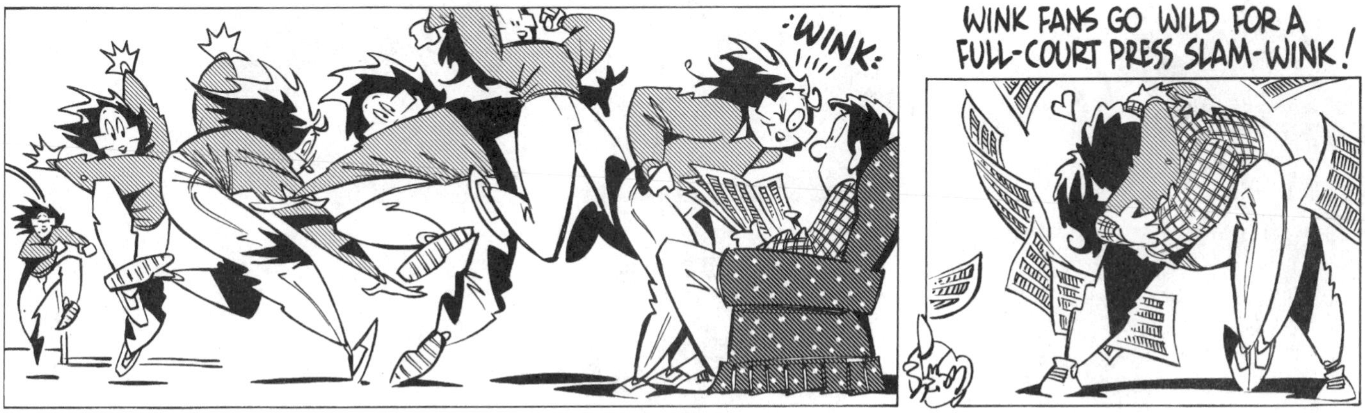
:WINK:
WINK FANS GO WILD FOR A FULL-COURT PRESS SLAM-WINK!

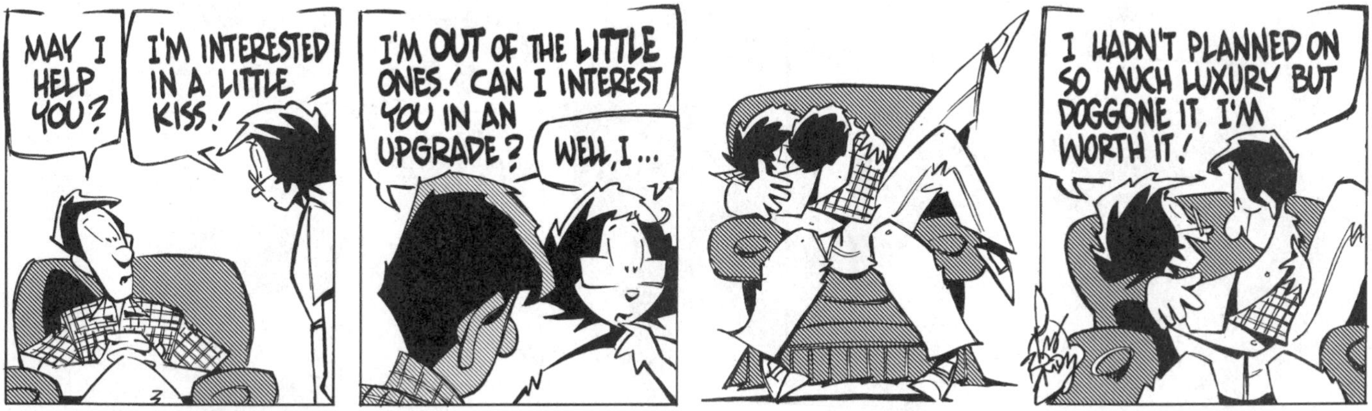
MAY I HELP YOU?
I'M INTERESTED IN A LITTLE KISS!
I'M OUT OF THE LITTLE ONES! CAN I INTEREST YOU IN AN UPGRADE?
WELL, I...
I HADN'T PLANNED ON SO MUCH LUXURY BUT DOGGONE IT, I'M WORTH IT!

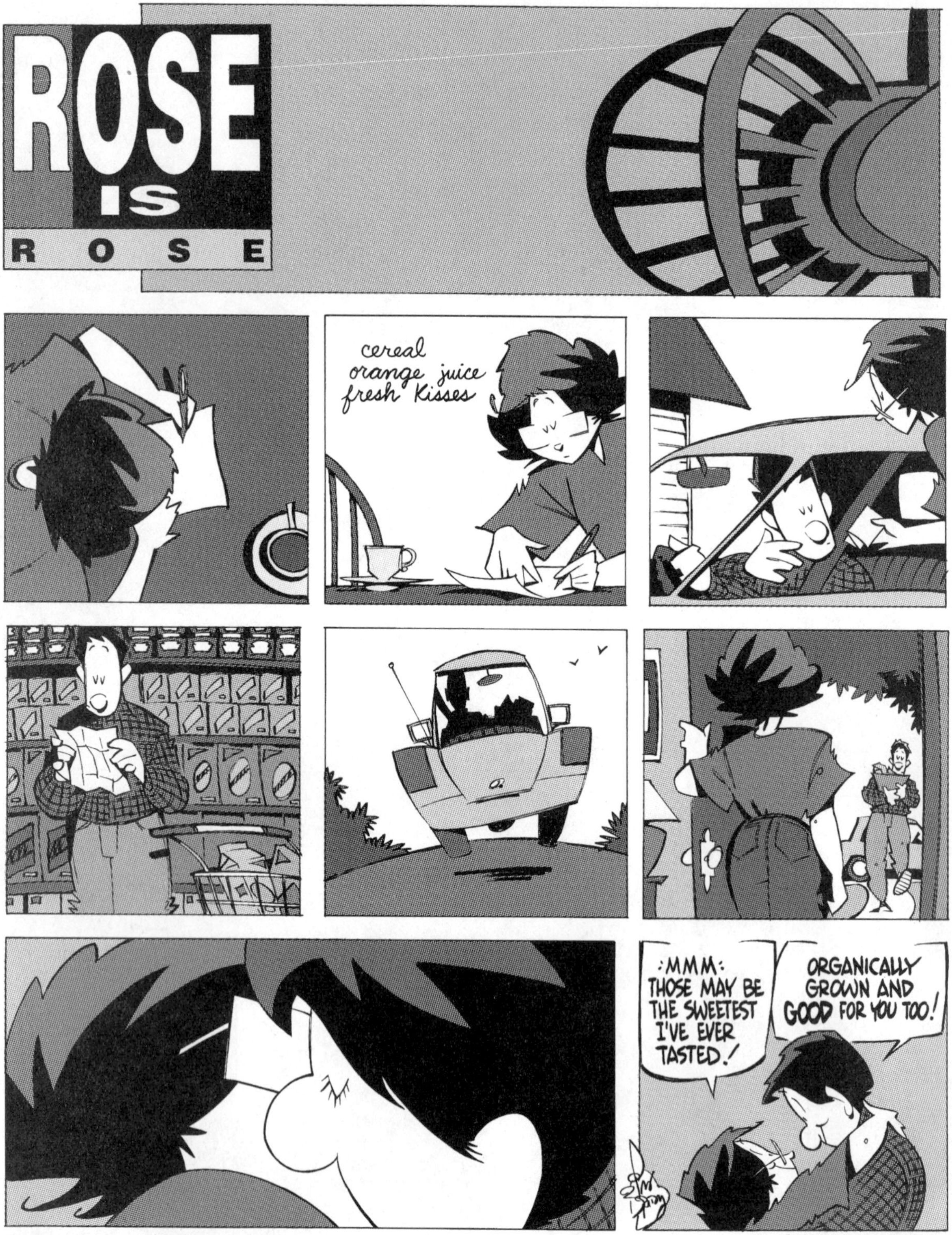
ROSE IS ROSE
cereal
orange juice
fresh Kisses
:MMM: THOSE MAY BE THE SWEETEST I'VE EVER TASTED!
ORGANICALLY GROWN AND GOOD FOR YOU TOO!

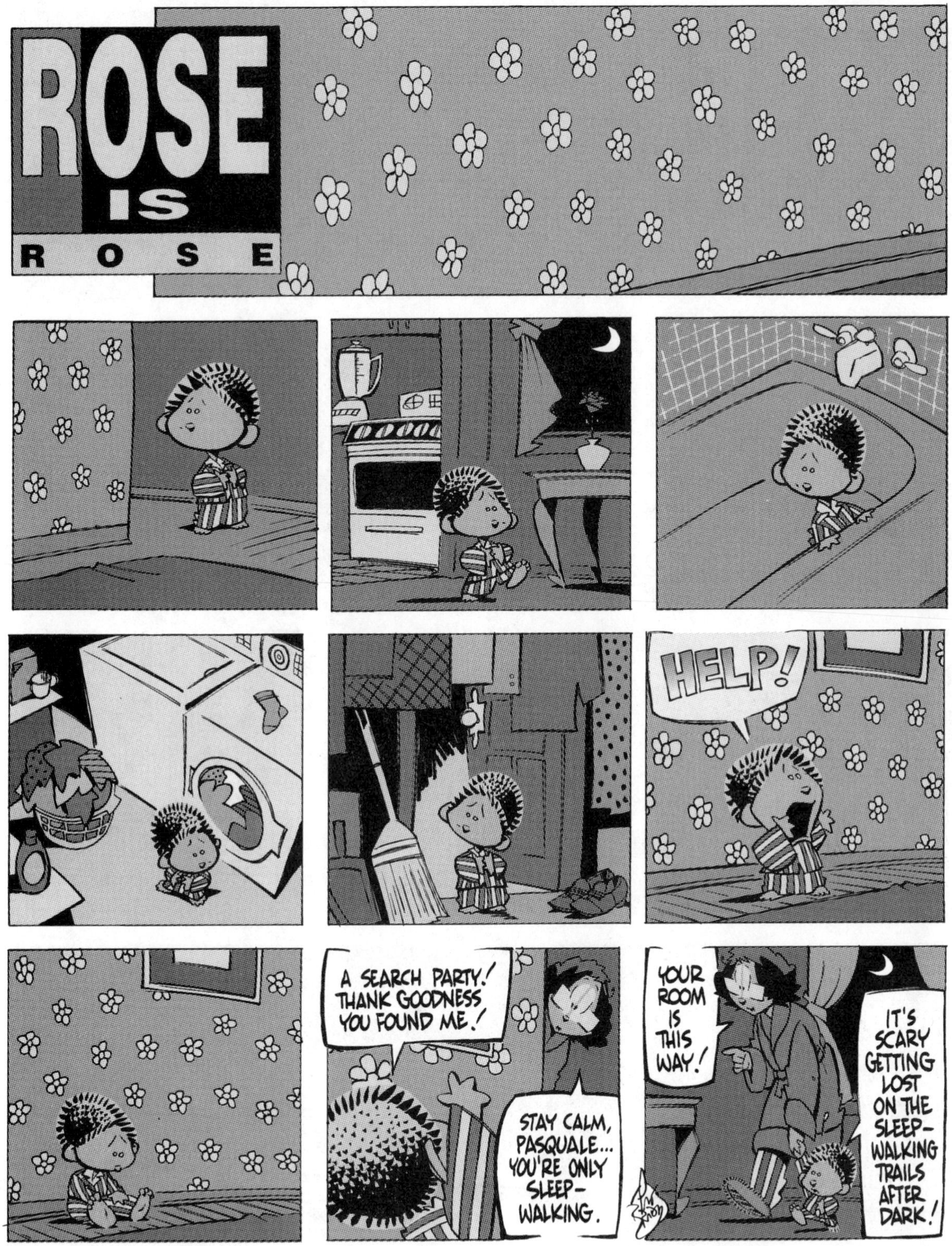
ROSE IS ROSE
HELP!
A SEARCH PARTY! THANK GOODNESS YOU FOUND ME!
STAY CALM, PASQUALE... YOU'RE ONLY SLEEP-WALKING.
YOUR ROOM IS THIS WAY!
IT'S SCARY GETTING LOST ON THE SLEEP-WALKING TRAILS AFTER DARK!

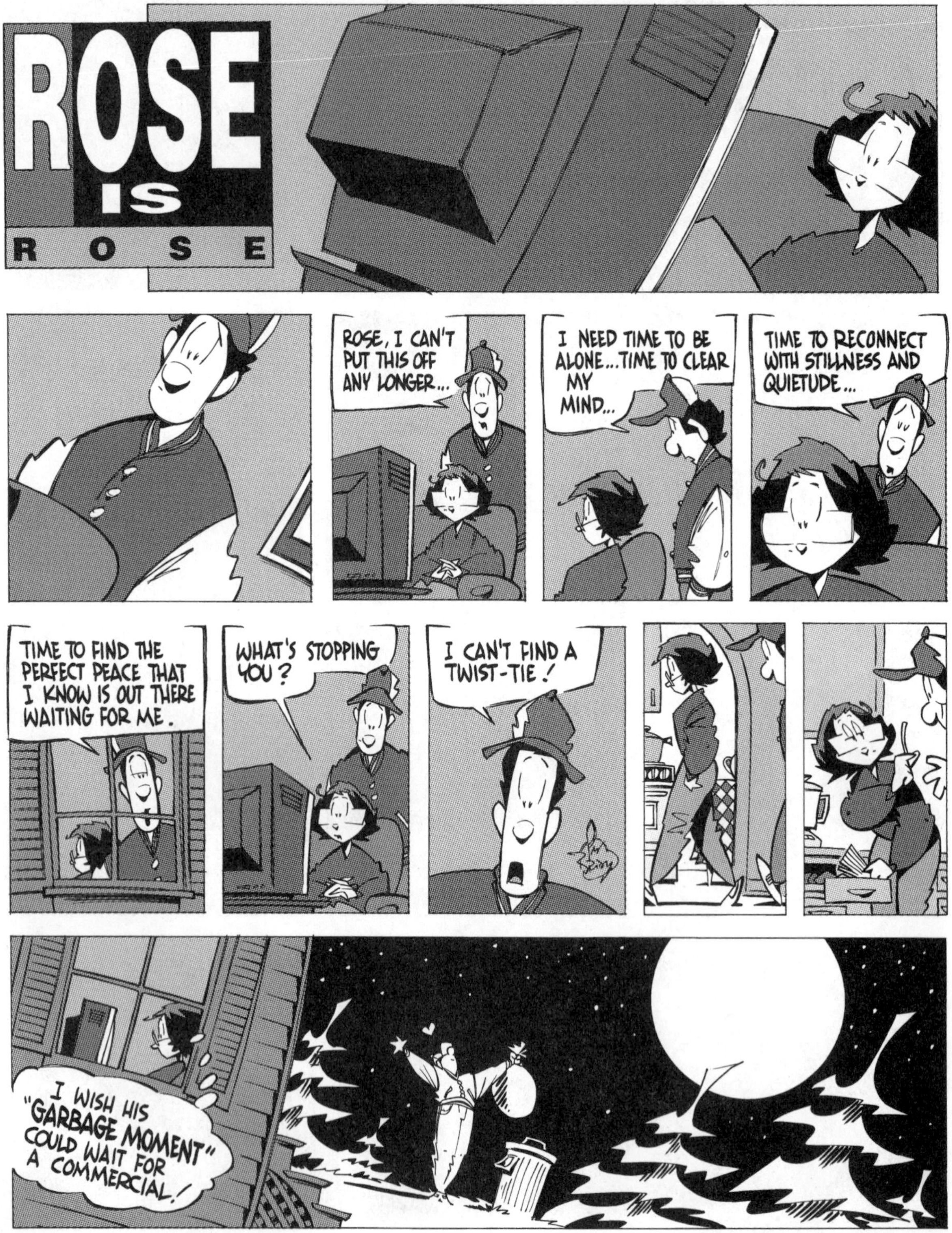
ROSE IS ROSE
ROSE, I CAN'T PUT THIS OFF ANY LONGER...
I NEED TIME TO BE ALONE... TIME TO CLEAR MY MIND...
TIME TO RECONNECT WITH STILLNESS AND QUIETUDE...
TIME TO FIND THE PERFECT PEACE THAT I KNOW IS OUT THERE WAITING FOR ME.
WHAT'S STOPPING YOU?
I CAN'T FIND A TWIST-TIE!
I WISH HIS "GARBAGE MOMENT" COULD WAIT FOR A COMMERCIAL!

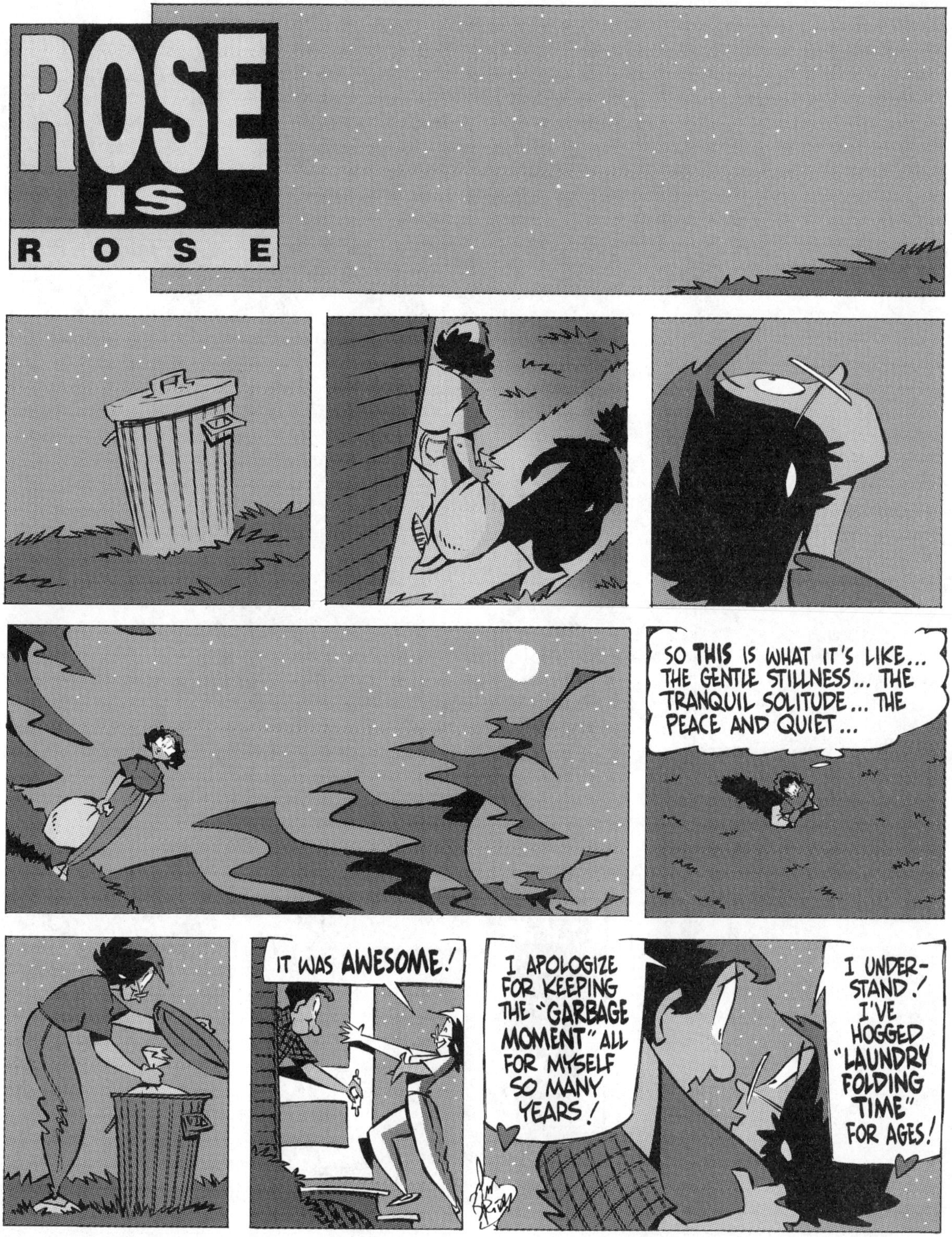
ROSE IS ROSE
SO THIS IS WHAT IT'S LIKE... THE GENTLE STILLNESS... THE TRANQUIL SOLITUDE... THE PEACE AND QUIET...
IT WAS AWESOME!
I APOLOGIZE FOR KEEPING THE "GARBAGE MOMENT" ALL FOR MYSELF SO MANY YEARS!
I UNDER-STAND! I'VE HOGGED "LAUNDRY FOLDING TIME" FOR AGES!

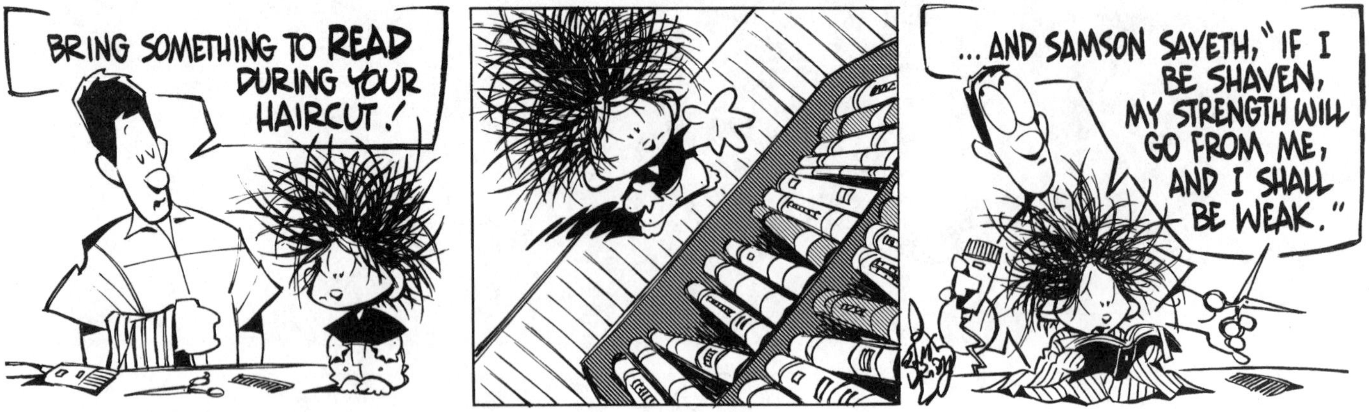
BRING SOMETHING TO READ DURING YOUR HAIRCUT!
... AND SAMSON SAYETH, "IF I BE SHAVEN, MY STRENGTH WILL GO FROM ME, AND I SHALL BE WEAK."

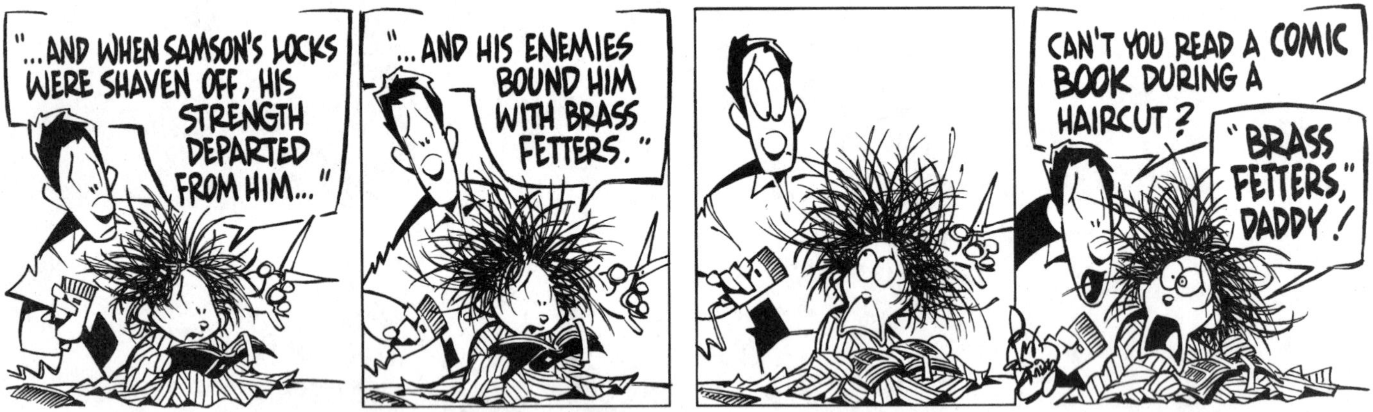
"... AND WHEN SAMSON'S LOCKS WERE SHAVEN OFF, HIS STRENGTH DEPARTED FROM HIM..."
"... AND HIS ENEMIES BOUND HIM WITH BRASS FETTERS."
CAN'T YOU READ A COMIC BOOK DURING A HAIRCUT?
"BRASS FETTERS," DADDY!

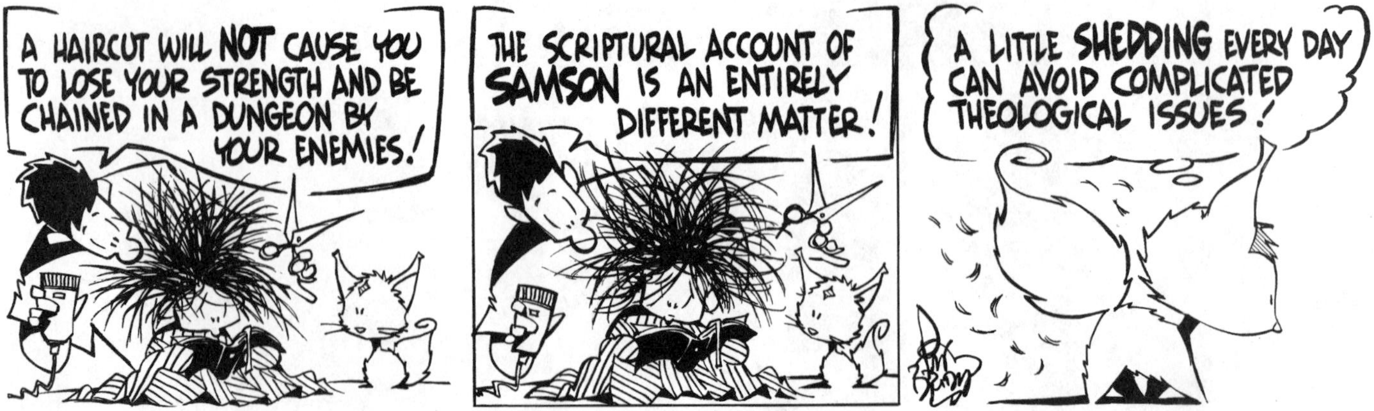
A HAIRCUT WILL NOT CAUSE YOU TO LOSE YOUR STRENGTH AND BE CHAINED IN A DUNGEON BY YOUR ENEMIES!
THE SCRIPTURAL ACCOUNT OF SAMSON IS AN ENTIRELY DIFFERENT MATTER!
A LITTLE SHEDDING EVERY DAY CAN AVOID COMPLICATED THEOLOGICAL ISSUES!

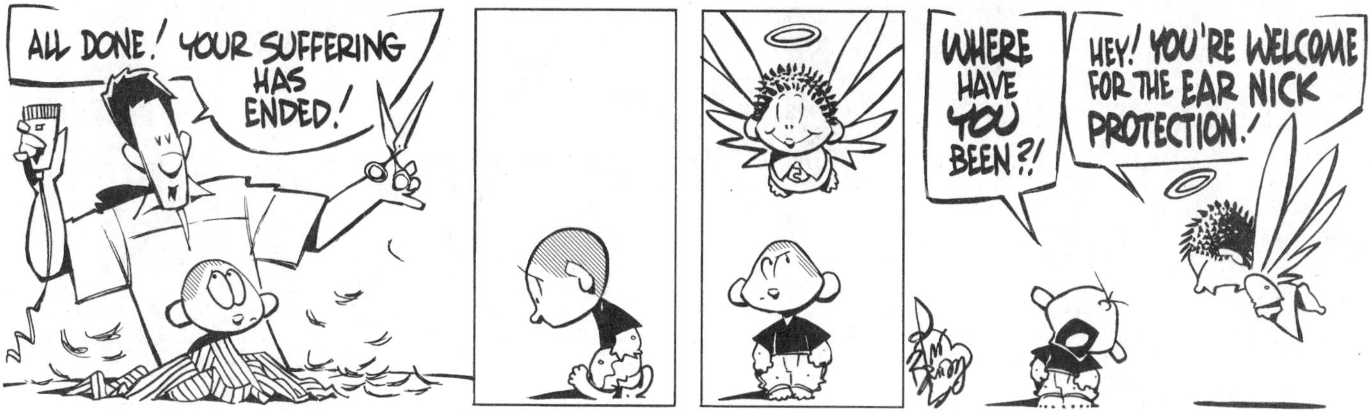
ALL DONE! YOUR SUFFERING HAS ENDED!
WHERE HAVE YOU BEEN?!
HEY! YOU'RE WELCOME FOR THE EAR NICK PROTECTION!

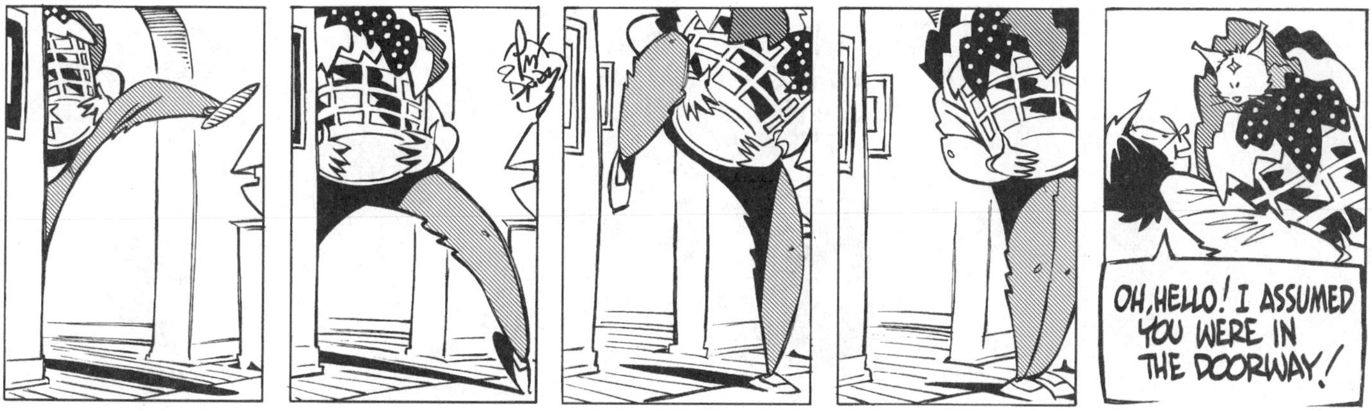
OH, HELLO! I ASSUMED YOU WERE IN THE DOORWAY!

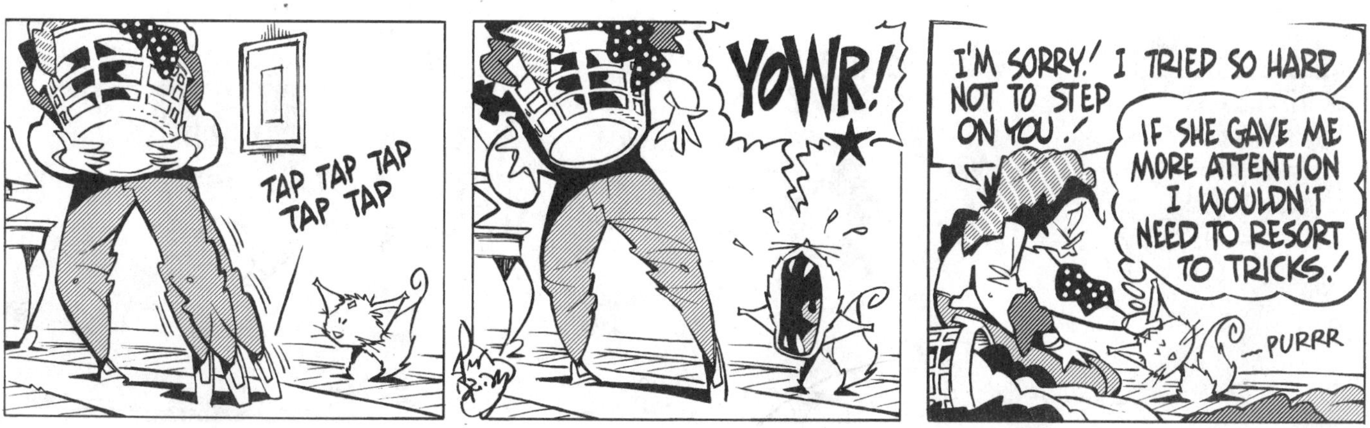
TAP TAP TAP TAP TAP
YOWR!
I'M SORRY! I TRIED SO HARD NOT TO STEP ON YOU!
IF SHE GAVE ME MORE ATTENTION I WOULDN'T NEED TO RESORT TO TRICKS!
PURRR

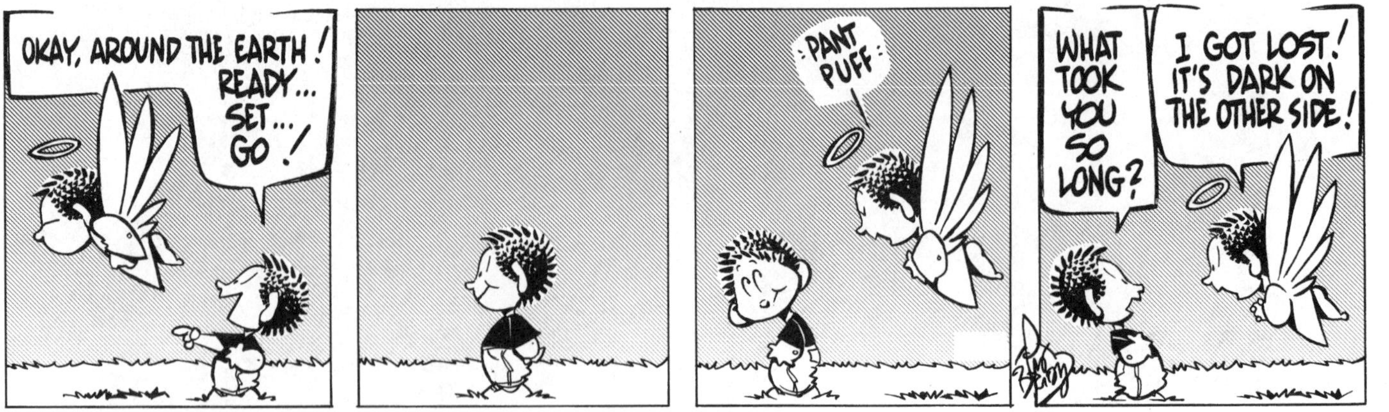
OKAY, AROUND THE EARTH! READY... SET... GO!
PANT PUFF
WHAT TOOK YOU SO LONG?
I GOT LOST! IT'S DARK ON THE OTHER SIDE!

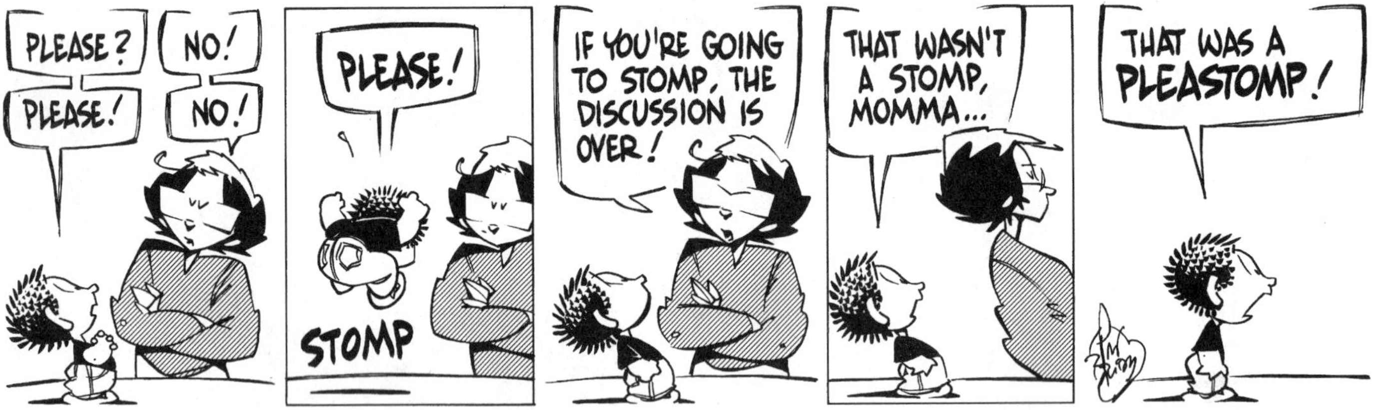
PLEASE?
NO!
PLEASE!
NO!
PLEASE!
STOMP
IF YOU'RE GOING TO STOMP, THE DISCUSSION IS OVER!
THAT WASN'T A STOMP, MOMMA...
THAT WAS A PLEASTOMP!

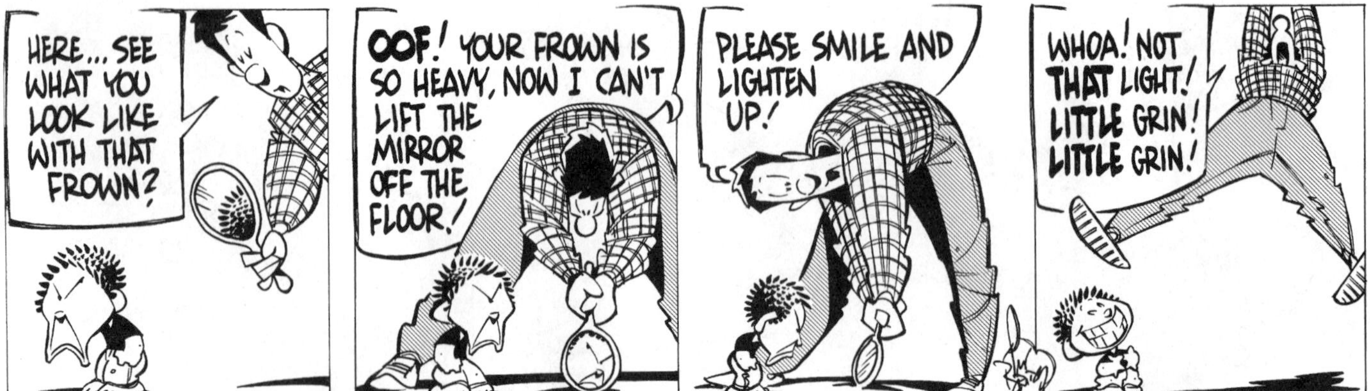
HERE... SEE WHAT YOU LOOK LIKE WITH THAT FROWN?
OOF! YOUR FROWN IS SO HEAVY, NOW I CAN'T LIFT THE MIRROR OFF THE FLOOR!
PLEASE SMILE AND LIGHTEN UP!
WHOA! NOT THAT LIGHT! LITTLE GRIN! LITTLE GRIN!

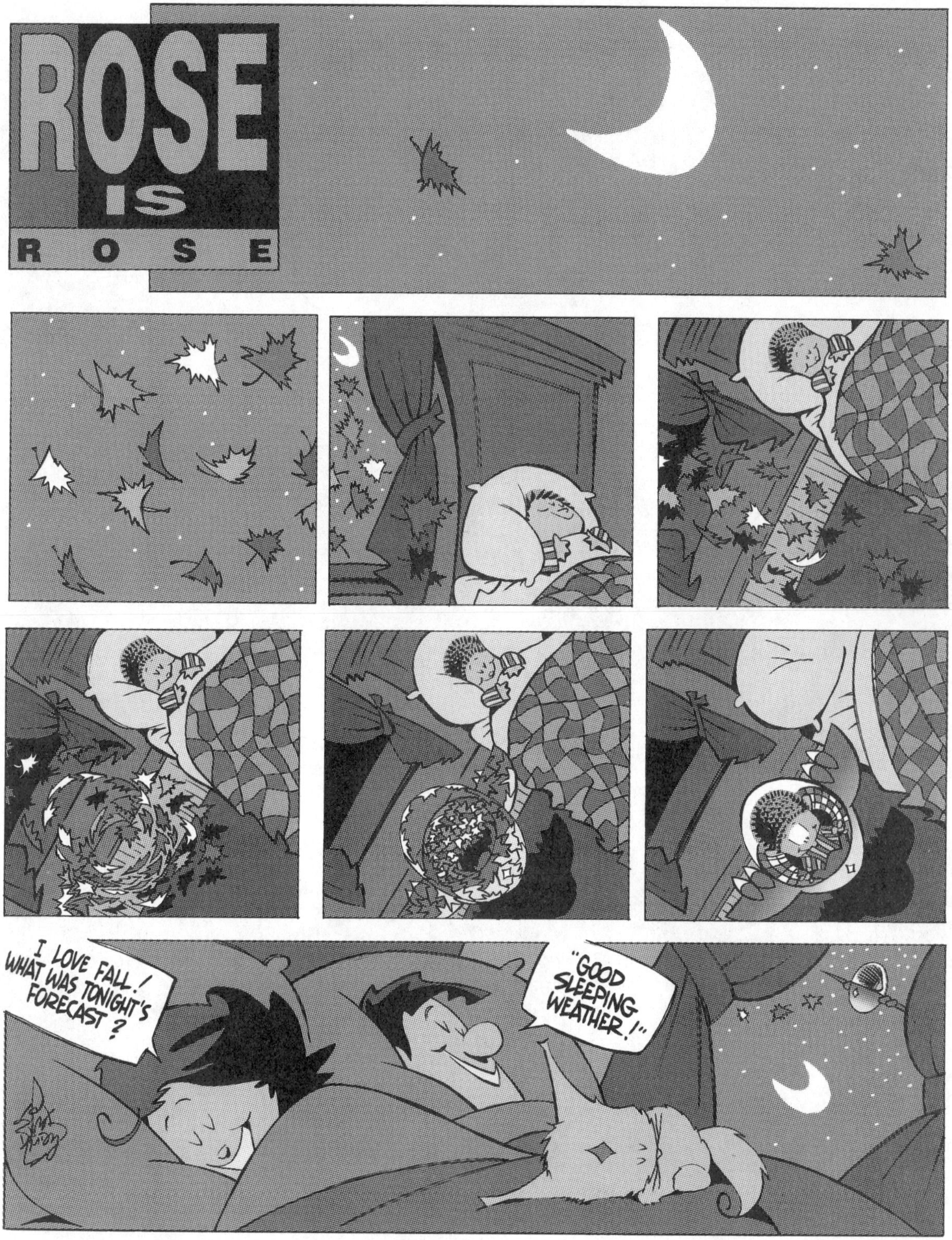
ROSE IS ROSE
I LOVE FALL! WHAT WAS TONIGHT'S FORECAST?
"GOOD SLEEPING WEATHER!"

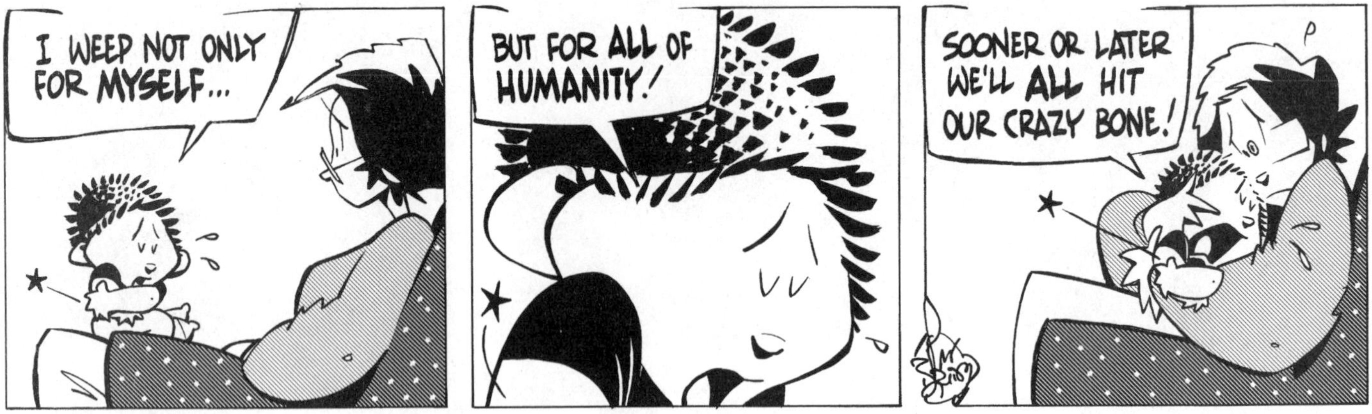
I WEEP NOT ONLY FOR MYSELF...
BUT FOR ALL OF HUMANITY!
SOONER OR LATER WE'LL ALL HIT OUR CRAZY BONE!

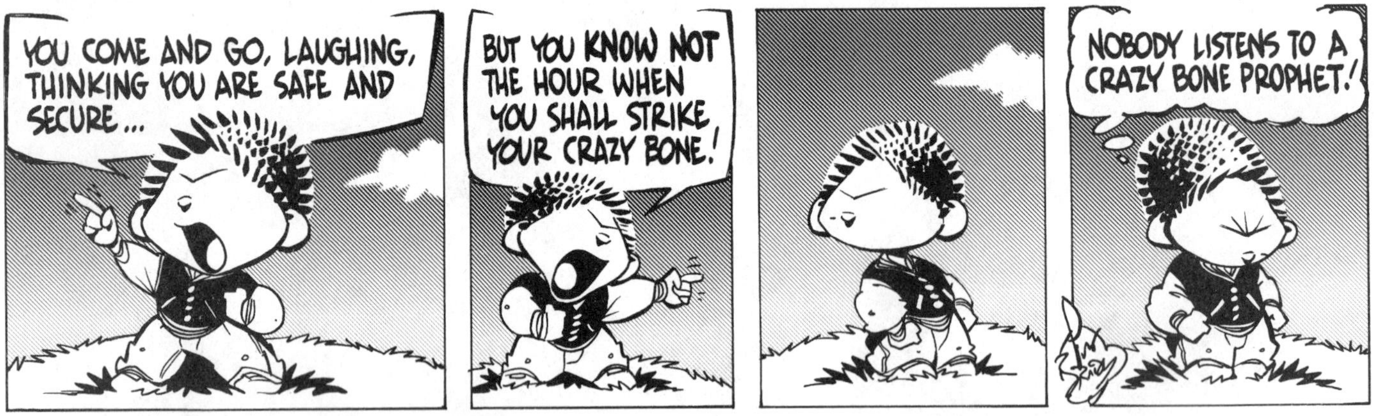
YOU COME AND GO, LAUGHING, THINKING YOU ARE SAFE AND SECURE...
BUT YOU KNOW NOT THE HOUR WHEN YOU SHALL STRIKE YOUR CRAZY BONE!
NOBODY LISTENS TO A CRAZY BONE PROPHET!

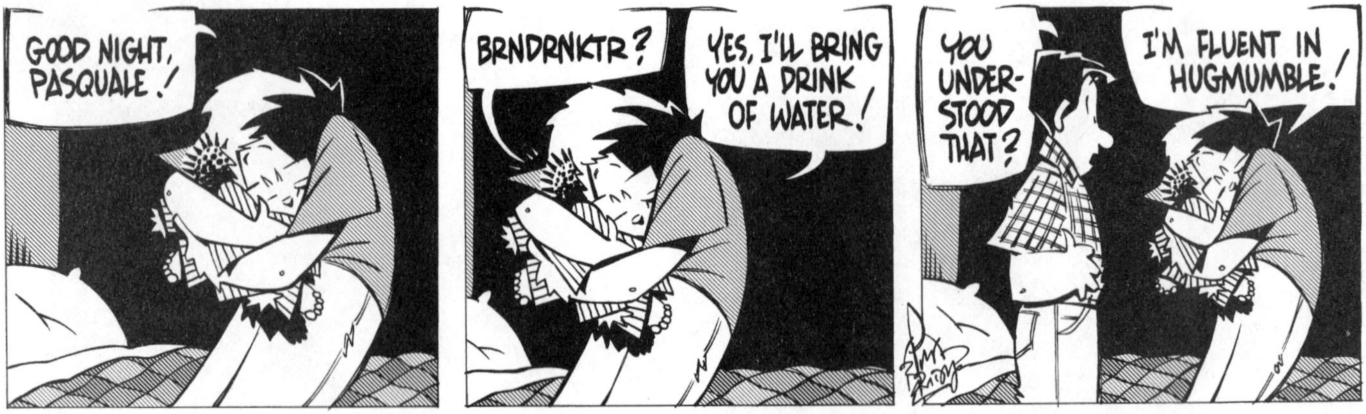
GOOD NIGHT, PASQUALE!
BRNDRNKTR?
YES, I'LL BRING YOU A DRINK OF WATER!
YOU UNDERSTOOD THAT?
I'M FLUENT IN HUGMUMBLE!

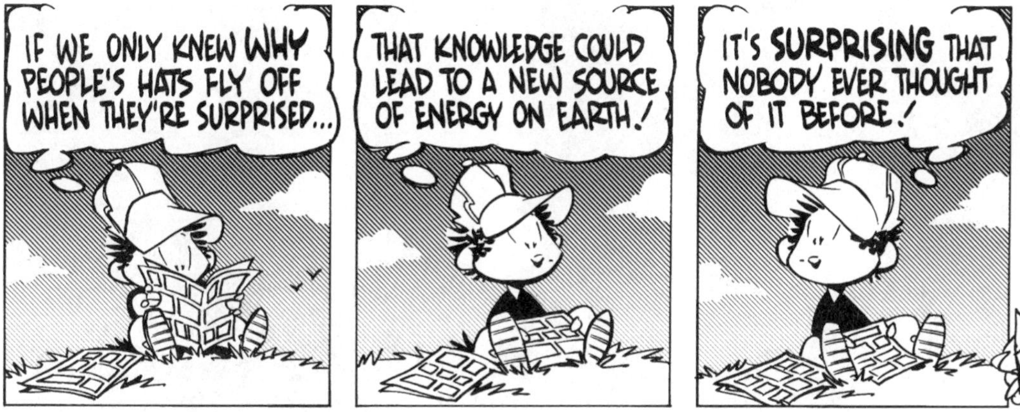
IF WE ONLY KNEW WHY PEOPLE'S HATS FLY OFF WHEN THEY'RE SURPRISED...
THAT KNOWLEDGE COULD LEAD TO A NEW SOURCE OF ENERGY ON EARTH!
IT'S SURPRISING THAT NOBODY EVER THOUGHT OF IT BEFORE!

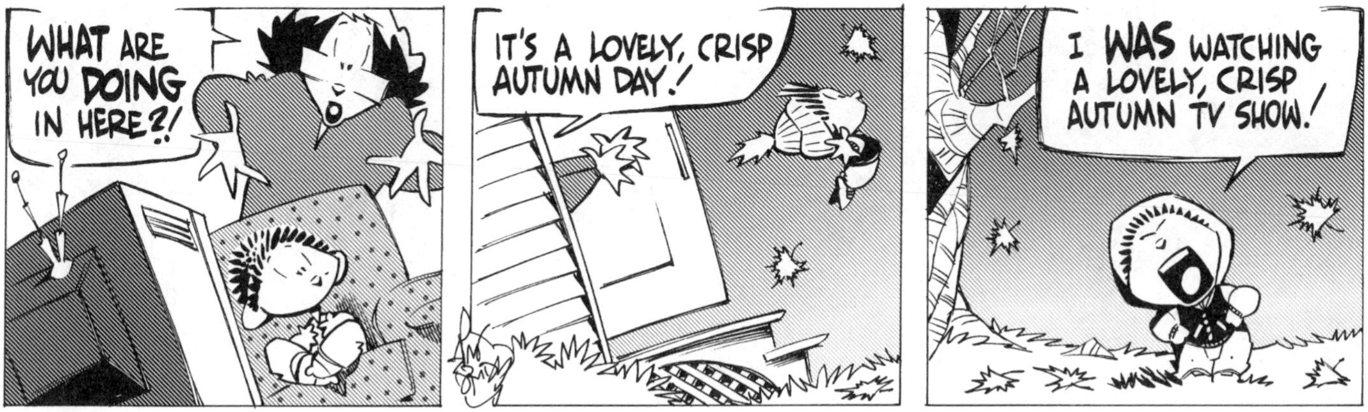
WHAT ARE YOU DOING IN HERE?!
IT'S A LOVELY, CRISP AUTUMN DAY!
I WAS WATCHING A LOVELY, CRISP AUTUMN TV SHOW!

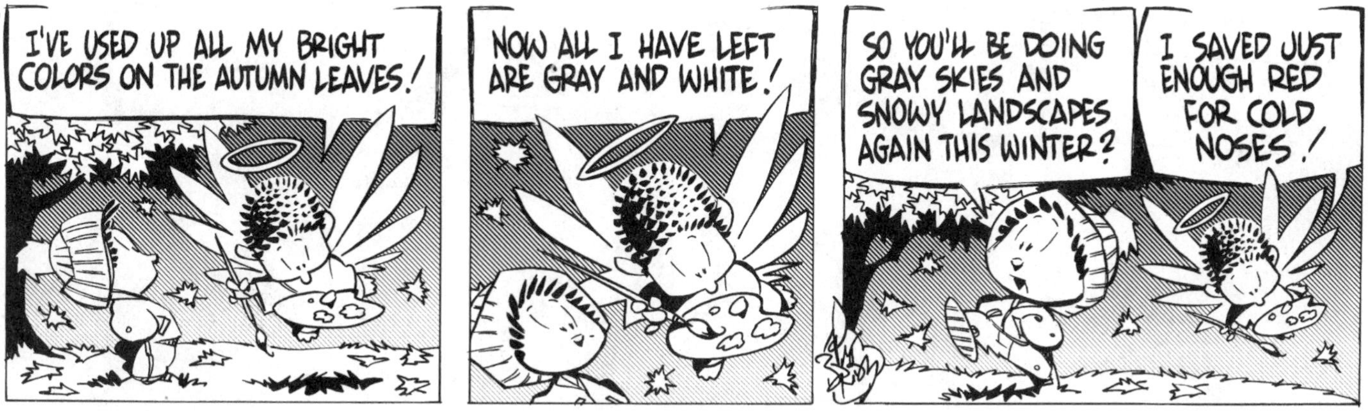
I'VE USED UP ALL MY BRIGHT COLORS ON THE AUTUMN LEAVES!
NOW ALL I HAVE LEFT ARE GRAY AND WHITE!
SO YOU'LL BE DOING GRAY SKIES AND SNOWY LANDSCAPES AGAIN THIS WINTER?
I SAVED JUST ENOUGH RED FOR COLD NOSES!

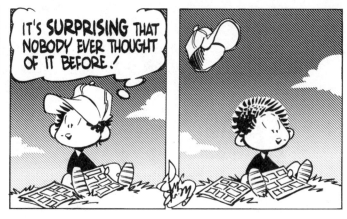

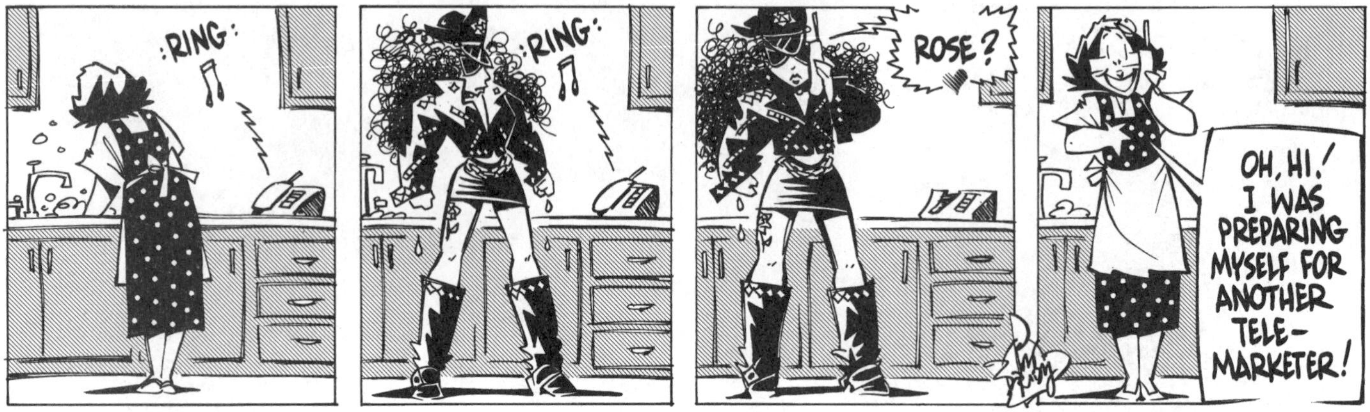
:RING:
:RING:
ROSE?
OH, HI! I WAS PREPARING MYSELF FOR ANOTHER TELE-MARKETER!

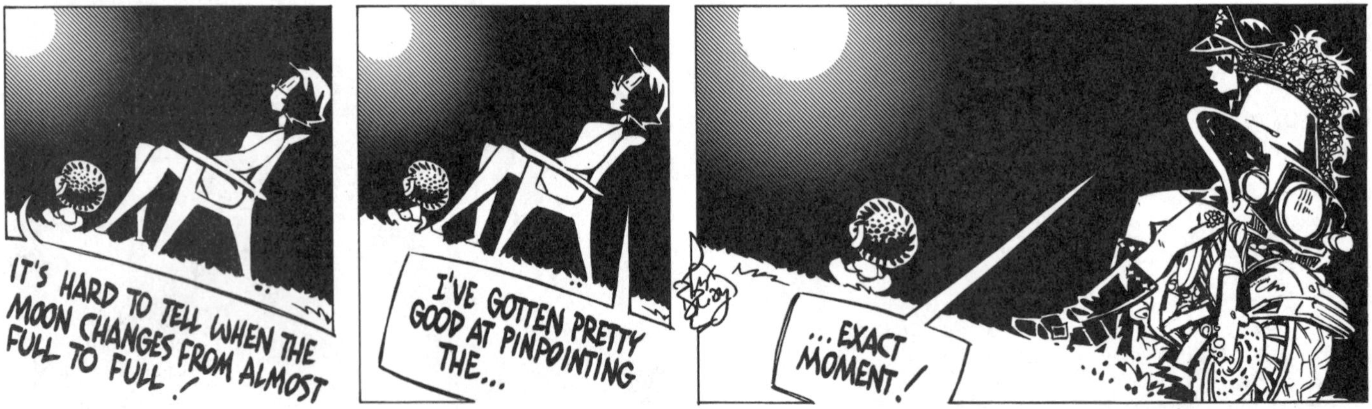
IT'S HARD TO TELL WHEN THE MOON CHANGES FROM ALMOST FULL TO FULL!
I'VE GOTTEN PRETTY GOOD AT PINPOINTING THE...
...EXACT MOMENT!

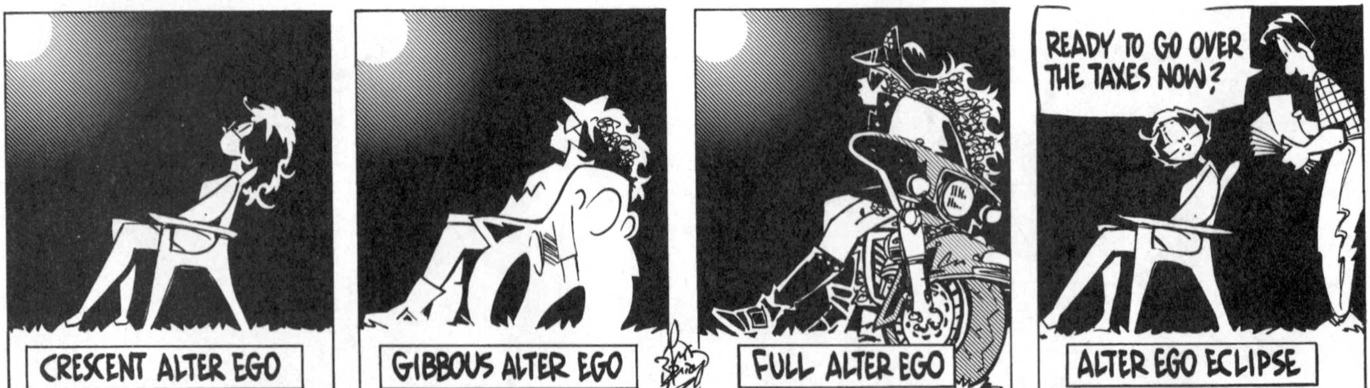
CRESCENT ALTER EGO
GIBBOUS ALTER EGO
FULL ALTER EGO
READY TO GO OVER THE TAXES NOW?
ALTER EGO ECLIPSE

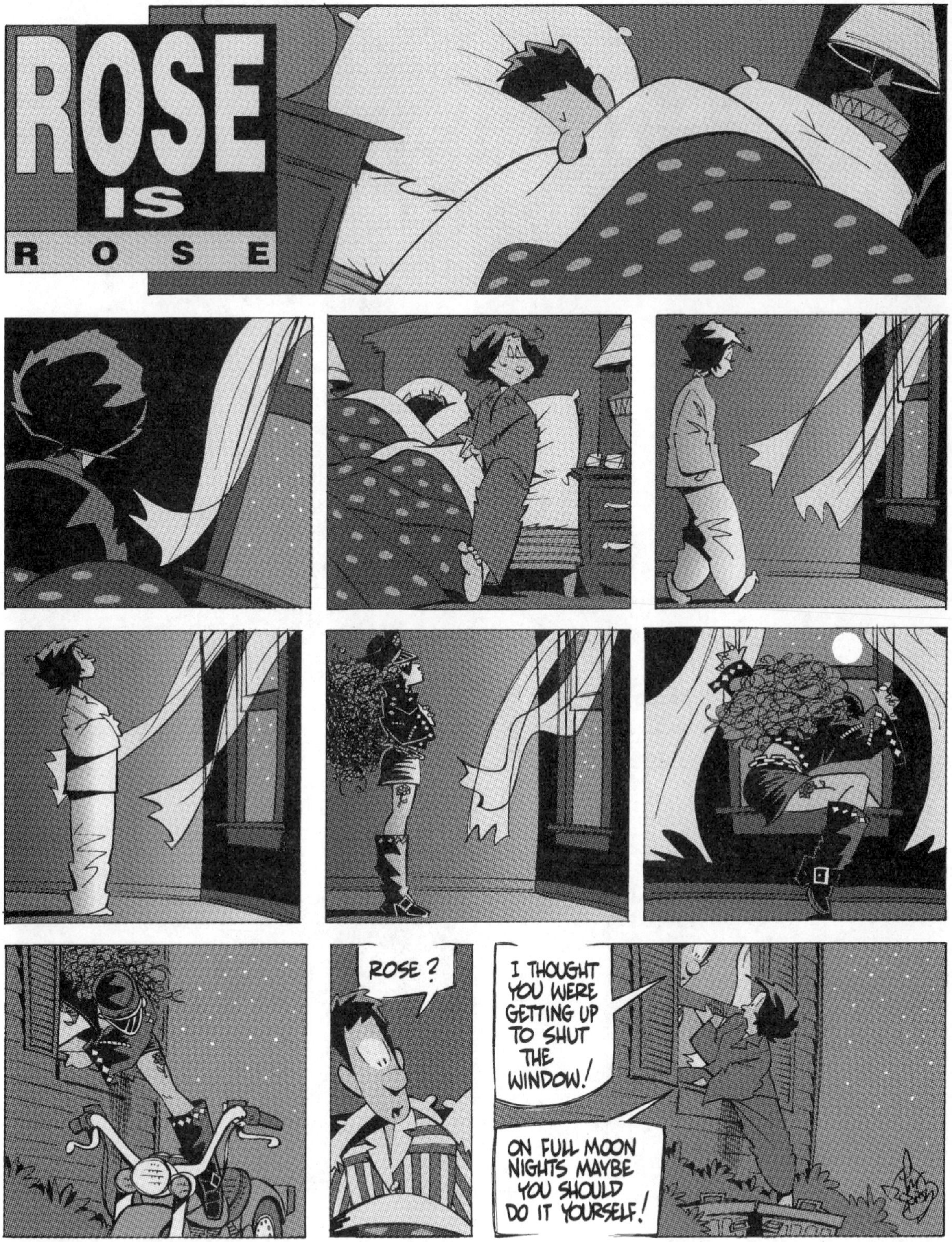
ROSE IS ROSE
ROSE ?
I THOUGHT YOU WERE GETTING UP TO SHUT THE WINDOW!
ON FULL MOON NIGHTS MAYBE YOU SHOULD DO IT YOURSELF!

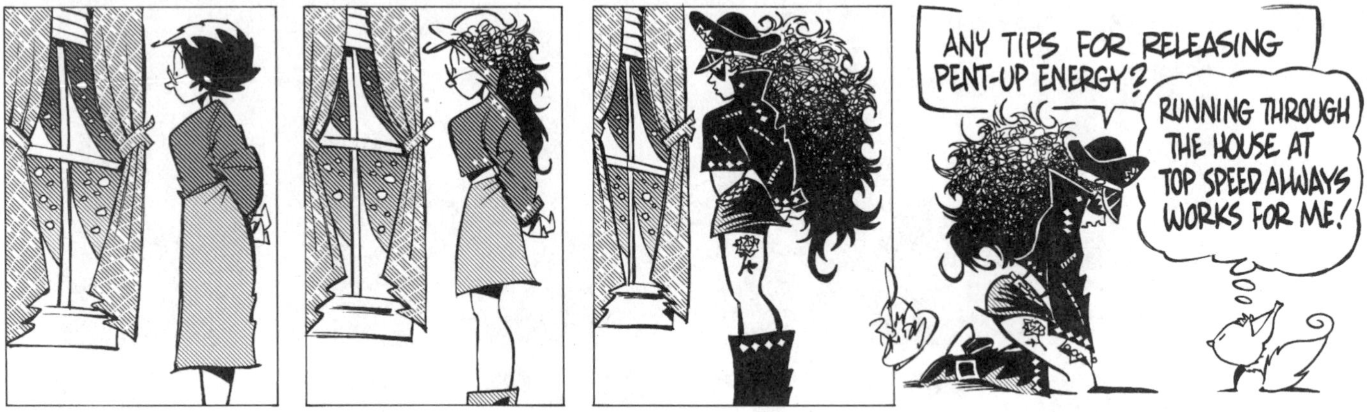
ANY TIPS FOR RELEASING PENT-UP ENERGY?
RUNNING THROUGH THE HOUSE AT TOP SPEED ALWAYS WORKS FOR ME!

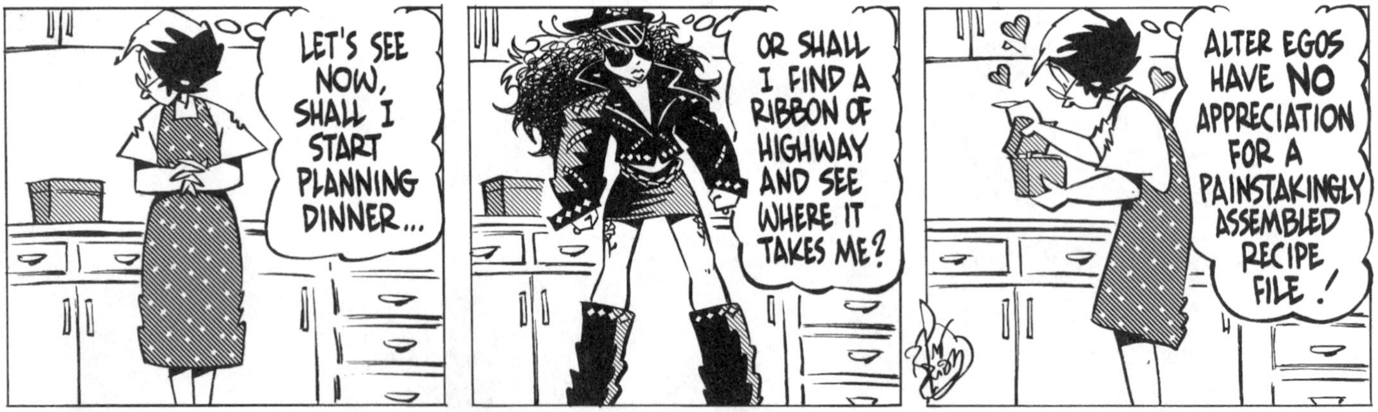
LET'S SEE NOW, SHALL I START PLANNING DINNER...
OR SHALL I FIND A RIBBON OF HIGHWAY AND SEE WHERE IT TAKES ME?
ALTER EGOS HAVE NO APPRECIATION FOR A PAINSTAKINGLY ASSEMBLED RECIPE FILE!

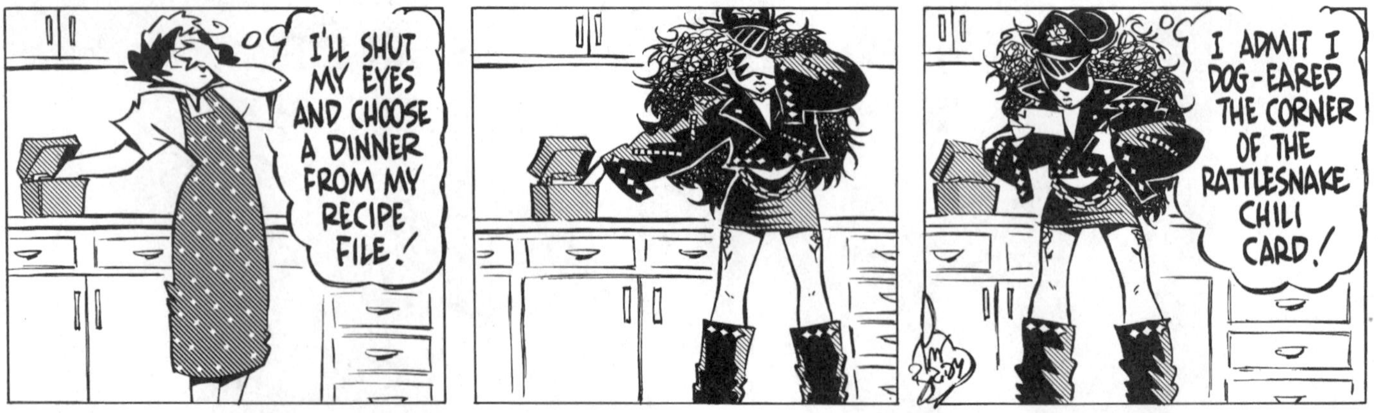
I'LL SHUT MY EYES AND CHOOSE A DINNER FROM MY RECIPE FILE!
I ADMIT I DOG-EARED THE CORNER OF THE RATTLESNAKE CHILI CARD!

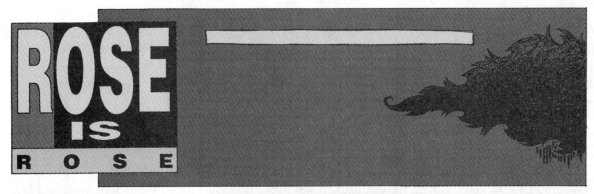

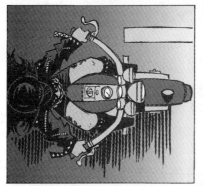

FINDING EVERYTHING YOU NEED, MA'AM?

SHH! DON'T BOTHER MRS. GUMBO WHEN SHE'S GATHERING HER CHILI FIXINGS!

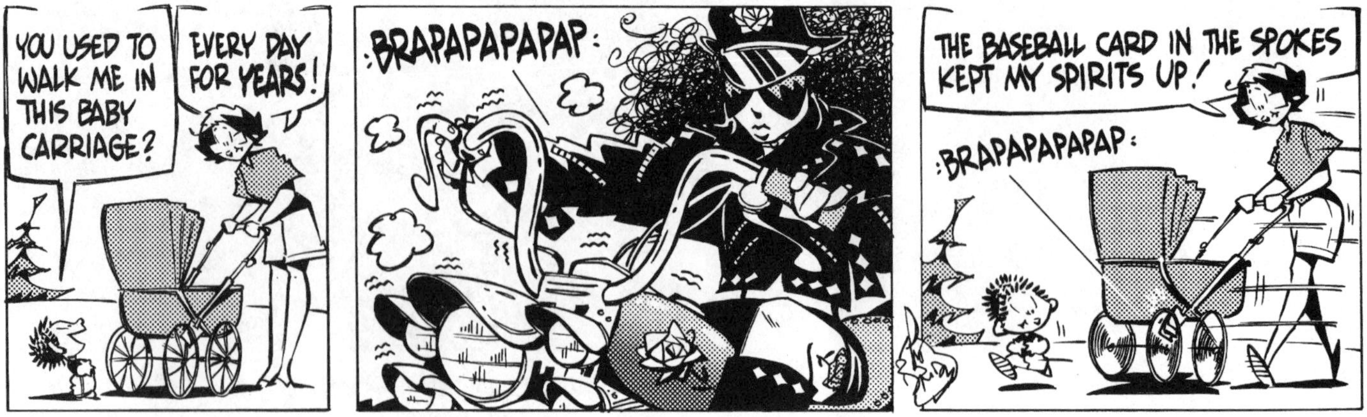
YOU USED TO WALK ME IN THIS BABY CARRIAGE?
EVERY DAY FOR YEARS!
BRAPAPAPAPAP
THE BASEBALL CARD IN THE SPOKES KEPT MY SPIRITS UP!
BRAPAPAPAPAP

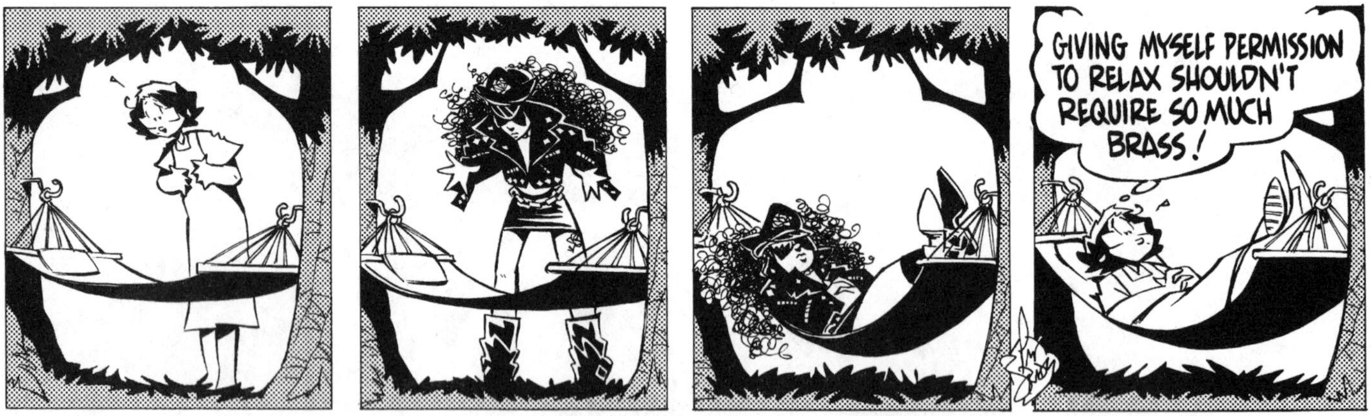
GIVING MYSELF PERMISSION TO RELAX SHOULDN'T REQUIRE SO MUCH BRASS!

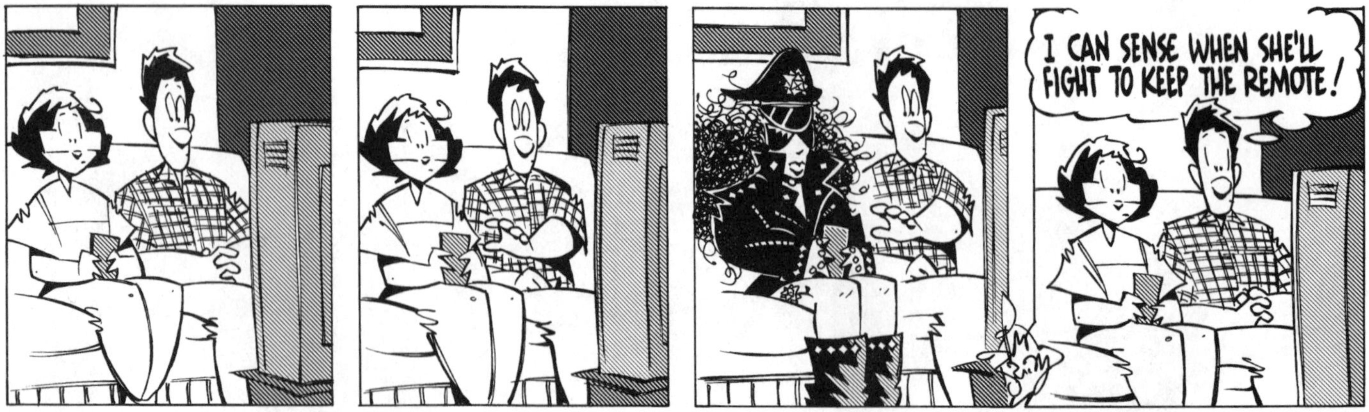
I CAN SENSE WHEN SHE'LL FIGHT TO KEEP THE REMOTE!

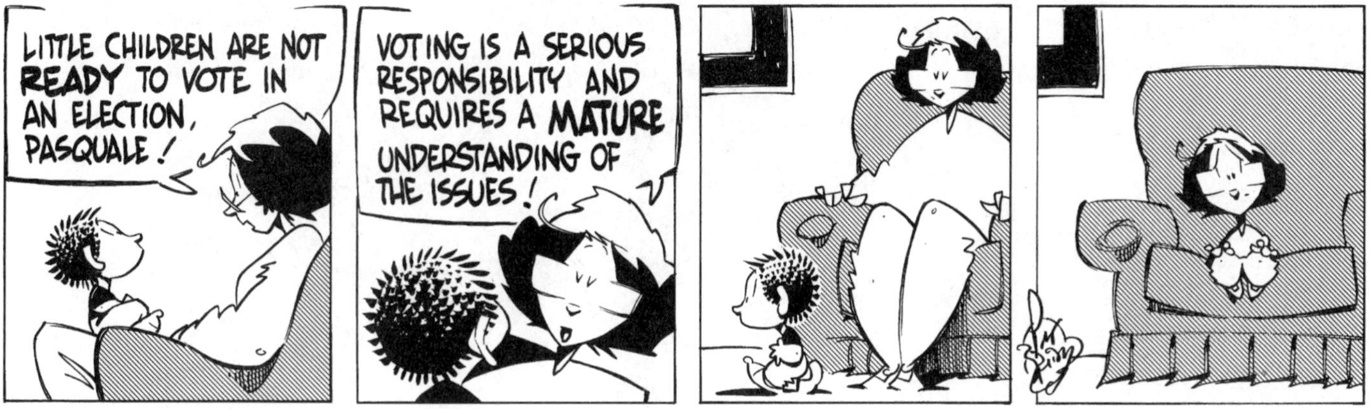
LITTLE CHILDREN ARE NOT READY TO VOTE IN AN ELECTION, PASQUALE!
VOTING IS A SERIOUS RESPONSIBILITY AND REQUIRES A MATURE UNDERSTANDING OF THE ISSUES!

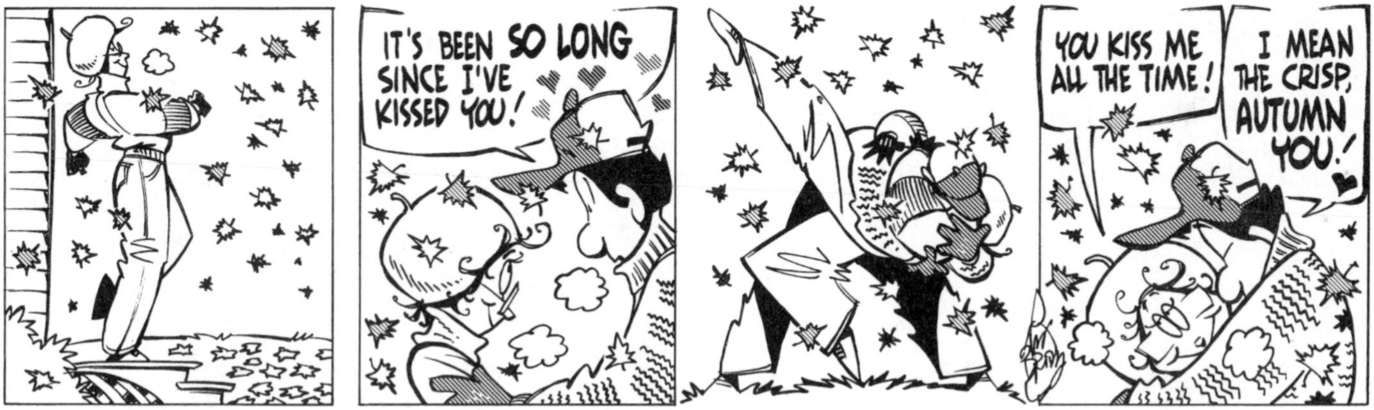
IT'S BEEN SO LONG SINCE I'VE KISSED YOU!
YOU KISS ME ALL THE TIME!
I MEAN THE CRISP, AUTUMN YOU!

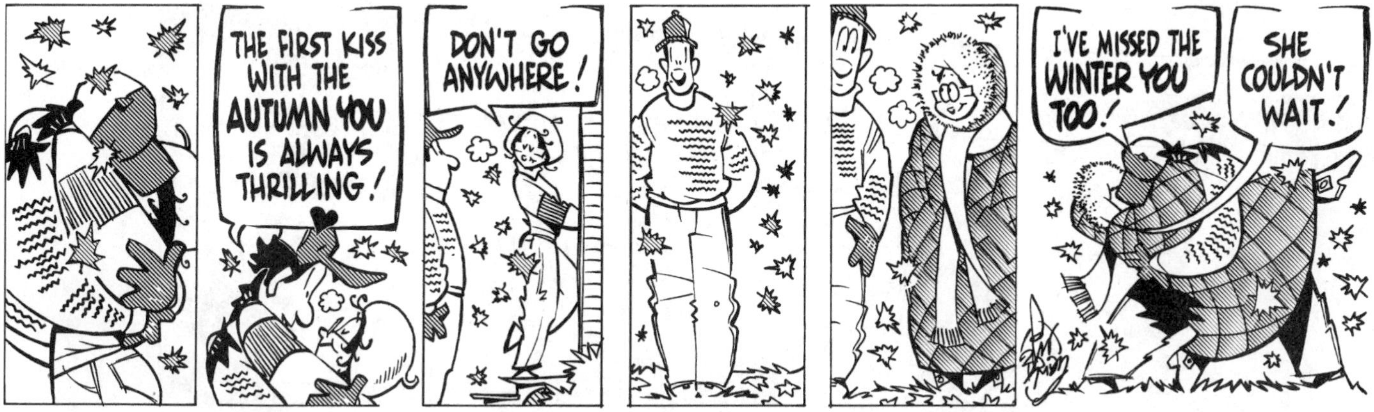
THE FIRST KISS WITH THE AUTUMN YOU IS ALWAYS THRILLING!
DON'T GO ANYWHERE!
I'VE MISSED THE WINTER YOU TOO!
SHE COULDN'T WAIT!

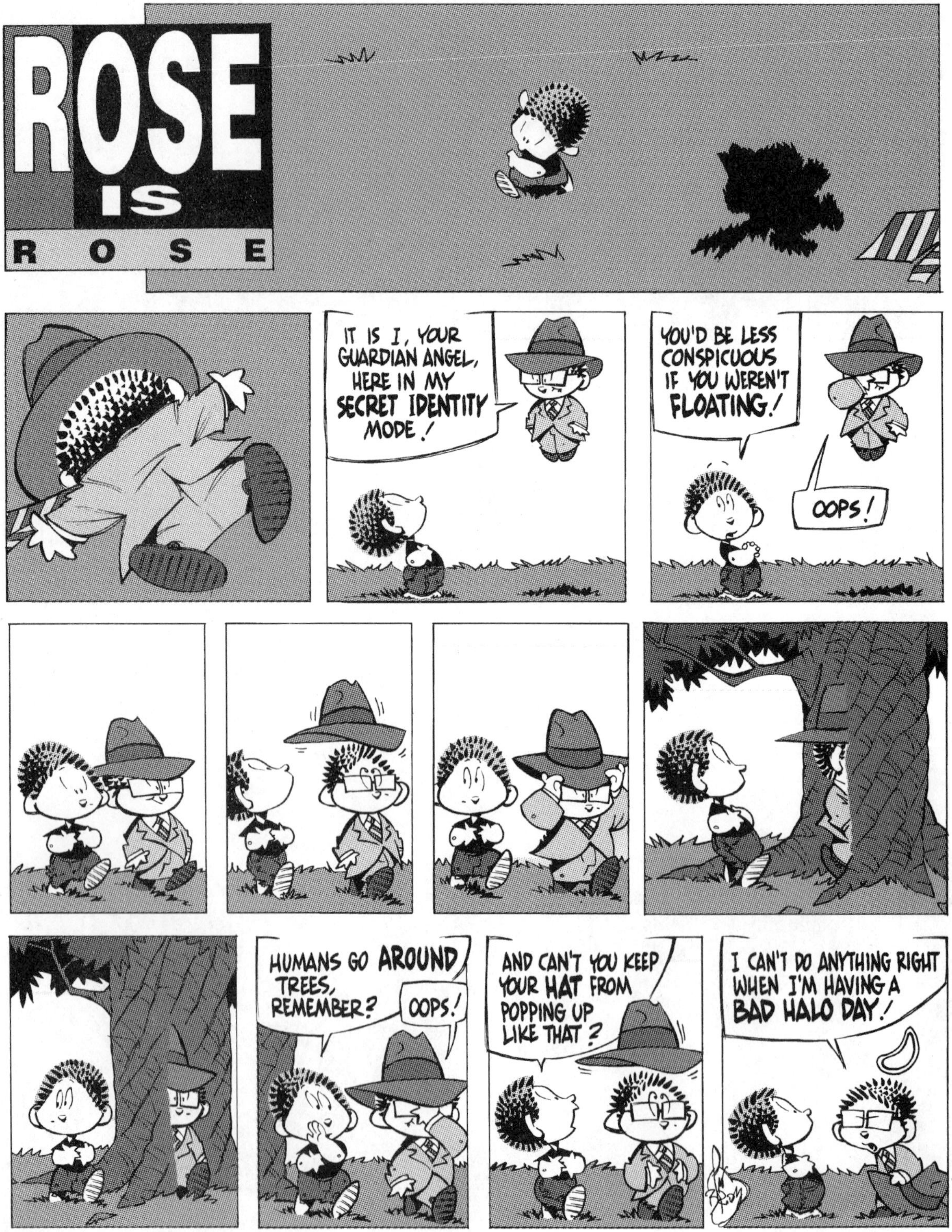
ROSE IS ROSE
IT IS I, YOUR GUARDIAN ANGEL, HERE IN MY SECRET IDENTITY MODE!
YOU'D BE LESS CONSPICUOUS IF YOU WEREN'T FLOATING!
OOPS!
HUMANS GO AROUND TREES, REMEMBER?
OOPS!
AND CAN'T YOU KEEP YOUR HAT FROM POPPING UP LIKE THAT?
I CAN'T DO ANYTHING RIGHT WHEN I'M HAVING A BAD HALO DAY!

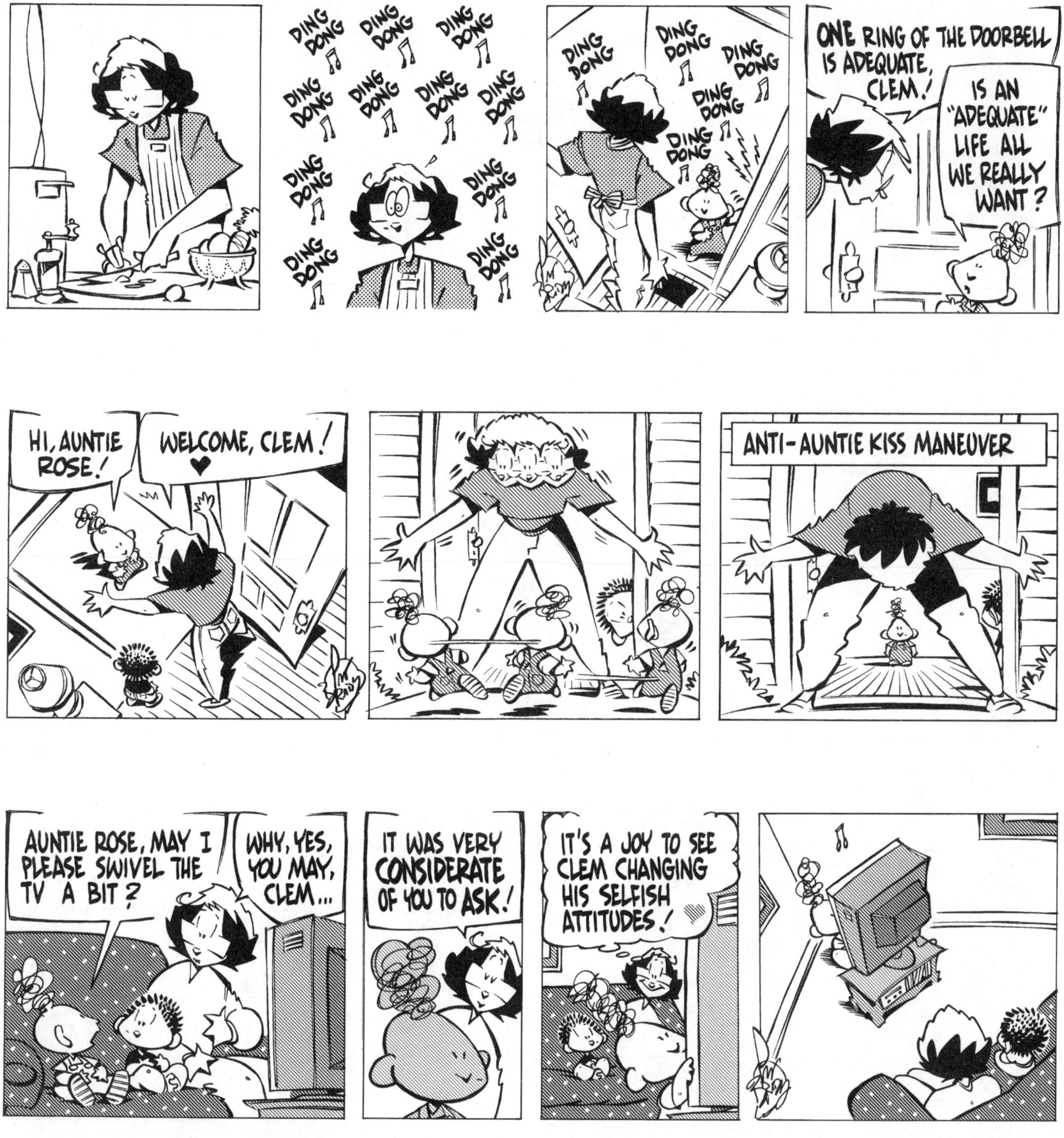
DING DONG
DING DONG
DING DONG
DING DONG
DING DONG
DING DONG
DING DONG
DING DONG
DING DONG
DING DONG
DING DONG
DING DONG
DING DONG
DING DONG
DING DONG
ONE RING OF THE DOORBELL IS ADEQUATE, CLEM!
IS AN "ADEQUATE" LIFE ALL WE REALLY WANT?
HI, AUNTIE ROSE!
WELCOME, CLEM!
ANTI-AUNTIE KISS MANEUVER
AUNTIE ROSE, MAY I PLEASE SWIVEL THE TV A BIT?
WHY, YES, YOU MAY, CLEM...
IT WAS VERY CONSIDERATE OF YOU TO ASK!
IT'S A JOY TO SEE CLEM CHANGING HIS SELFISH ATTITUDES!

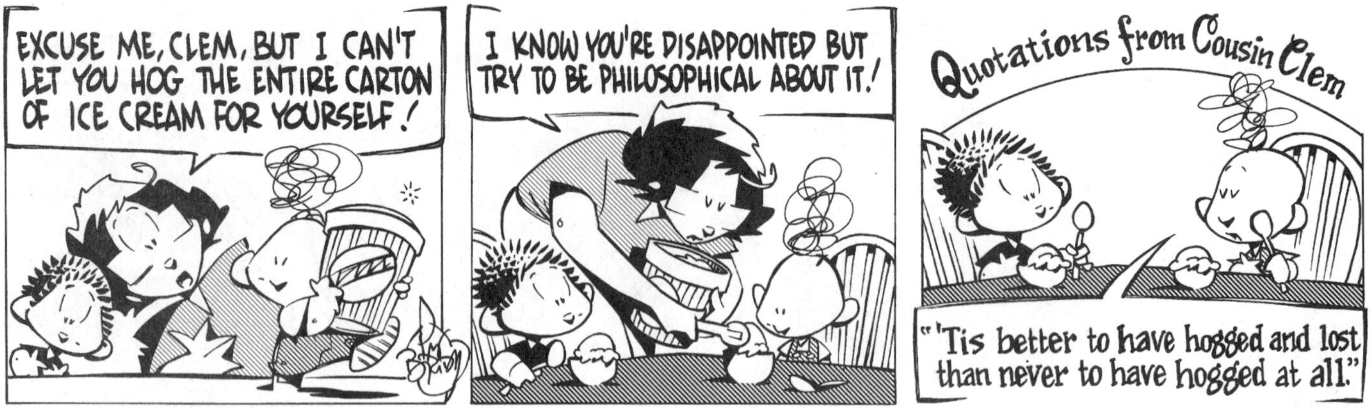
EXCUSE ME, CLEM, BUT I CAN'T LET YOU HOG THE ENTIRE CARTON OF ICE CREAM FOR YOURSELF!
I KNOW YOU'RE DISAPPOINTED BUT TRY TO BE PHILOSOPHICAL ABOUT IT!
Quotations from Cousin Clem
"'Tis better to have hogged and lost than never to have hogged at all."

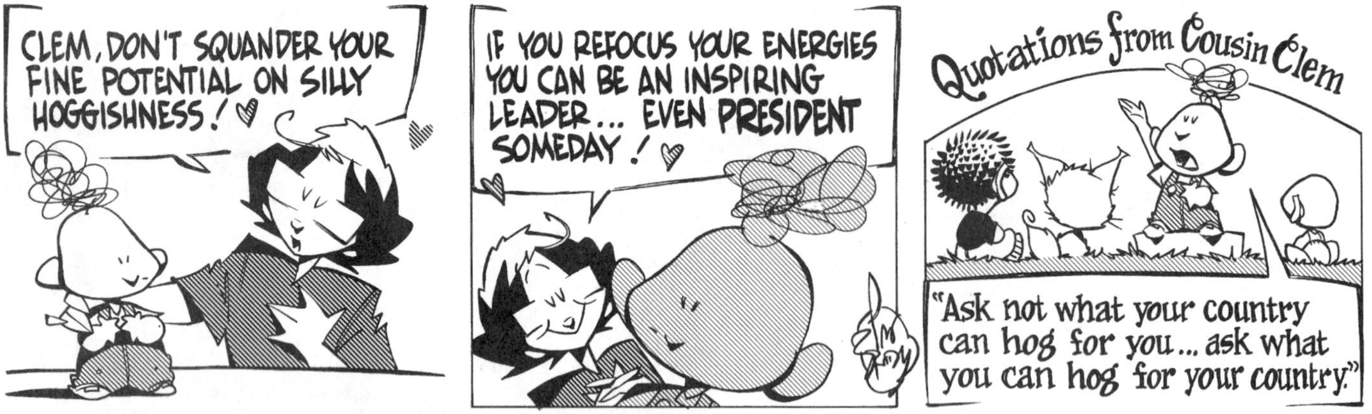
CLEM, DON'T SQUANDER YOUR FINE POTENTIAL ON SILLY HOGGISHNESS!
IF YOU REFOCUS YOUR ENERGIES YOU CAN BE AN INSPIRING LEADER... EVEN PRESIDENT SOMEDAY!
Quotations from Cousin Clem
"Ask not what your country can hog for you... ask what you can hog for your country."

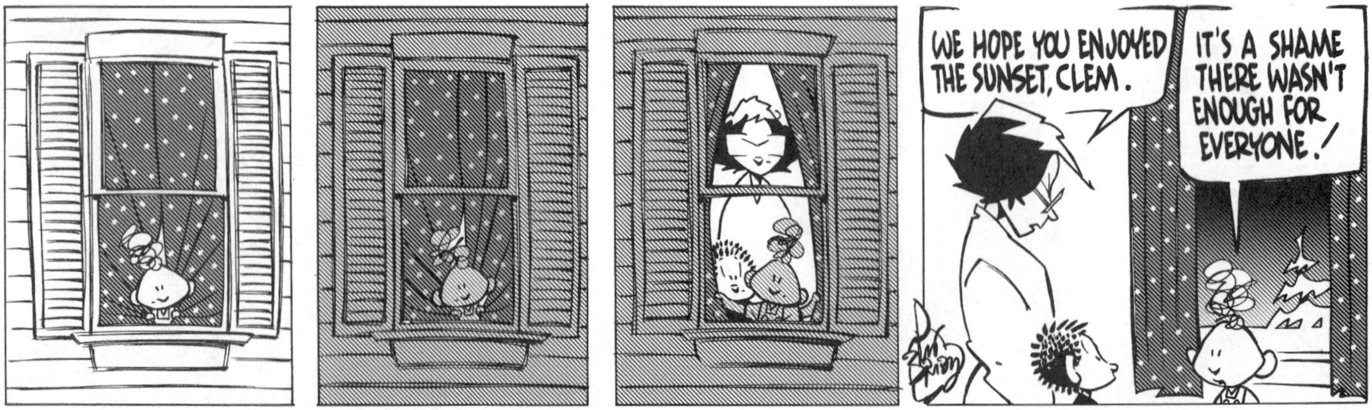
WE HOPE YOU ENJOYED THE SUNSET, CLEM.
IT'S A SHAME THERE WASN'T ENOUGH FOR EVERYONE!

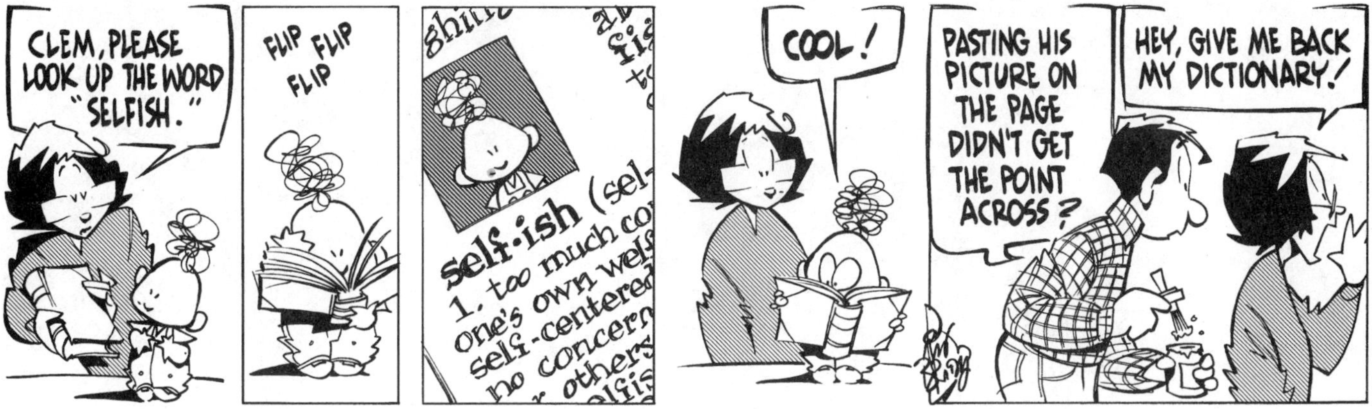

CLEM, PLEASE LOOK UP THE WORD "SELFISH."
FLIP FLIP FLIP
self·ish
COOL!
PASTING HIS PICTURE ON THE PAGE DIDN'T GET THE POINT ACROSS?
HEY, GIVE ME BACK MY DICTIONARY!

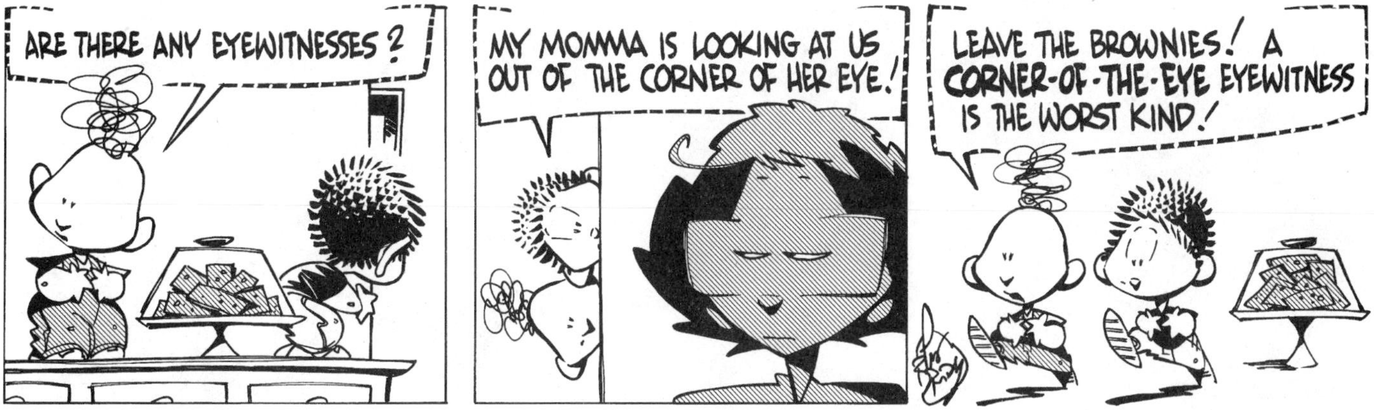

ARE THERE ANY EYEWITNESSES?
MY MOMMA IS LOOKING AT US OUT OF THE CORNER OF HER EYE!
LEAVE THE BROWNIES! A **CORNER-OF-THE-EYE** EYEWITNESS IS THE WORST KIND!

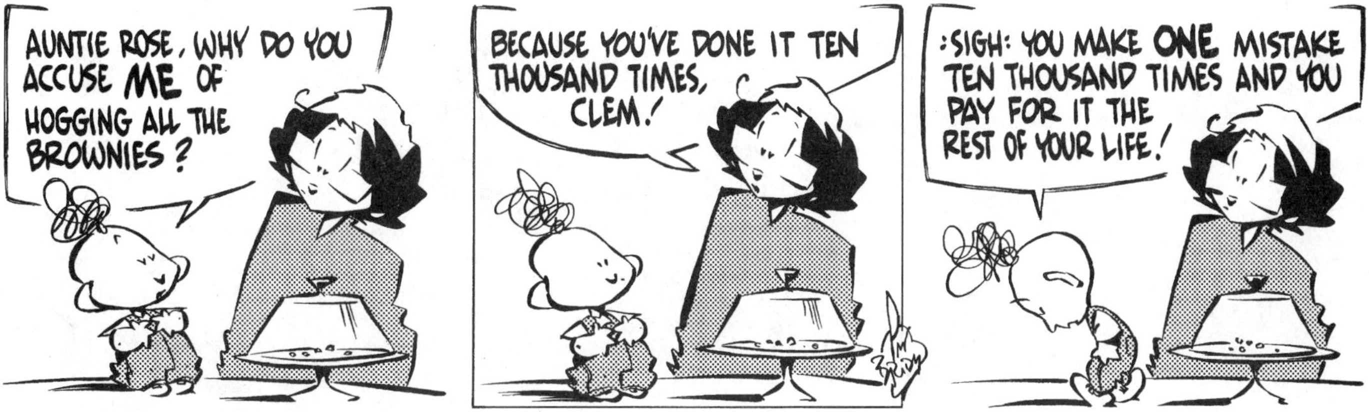

AUNTIE ROSE, WHY DO YOU ACCUSE **ME** OF HOGGING ALL THE BROWNIES?
BECAUSE YOU'VE DONE IT TEN THOUSAND TIMES, CLEM!
:SIGH: YOU MAKE **ONE** MISTAKE TEN THOUSAND TIMES AND YOU PAY FOR IT THE REST OF YOUR LIFE!

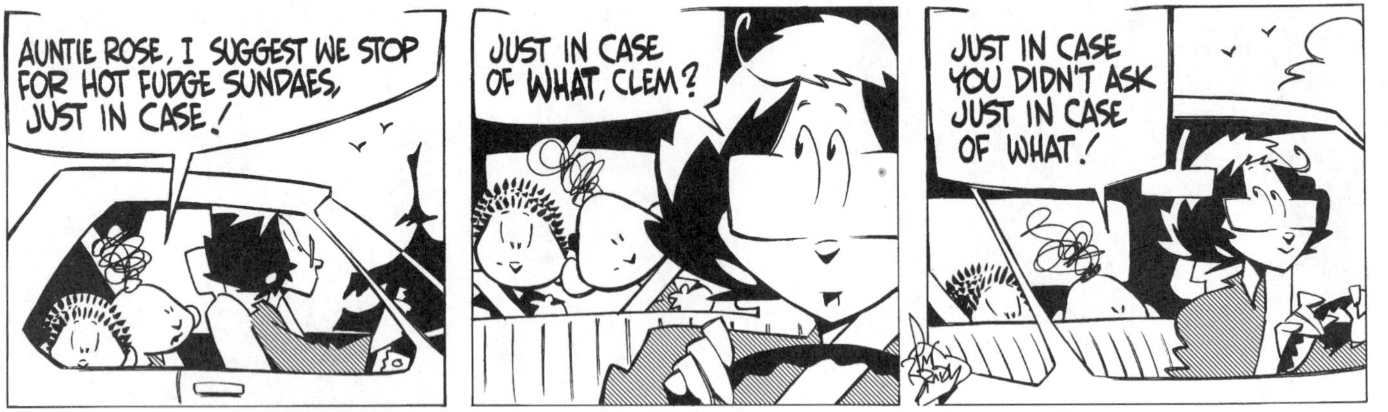
AUNTIE ROSE, I SUGGEST WE STOP FOR HOT FUDGE SUNDAES, JUST IN CASE!
JUST IN CASE OF WHAT, CLEM?
JUST IN CASE YOU DIDN'T ASK JUST IN CASE OF WHAT!

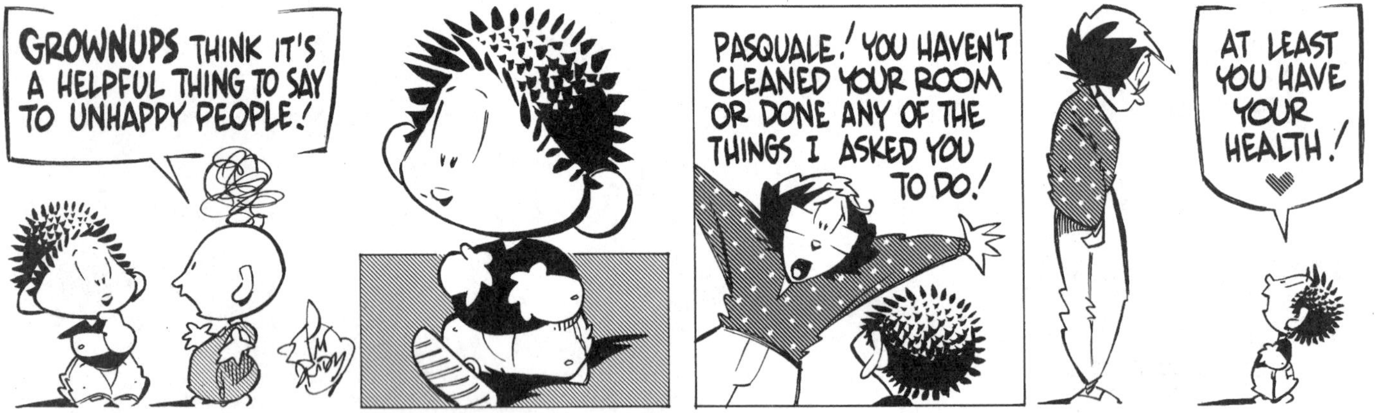
GROWNUPS THINK IT'S A HELPFUL THING TO SAY TO UNHAPPY PEOPLE!
PASQUALE! YOU HAVEN'T CLEANED YOUR ROOM OR DONE ANY OF THE THINGS I ASKED YOU TO DO!
AT LEAST YOU HAVE YOUR HEALTH!

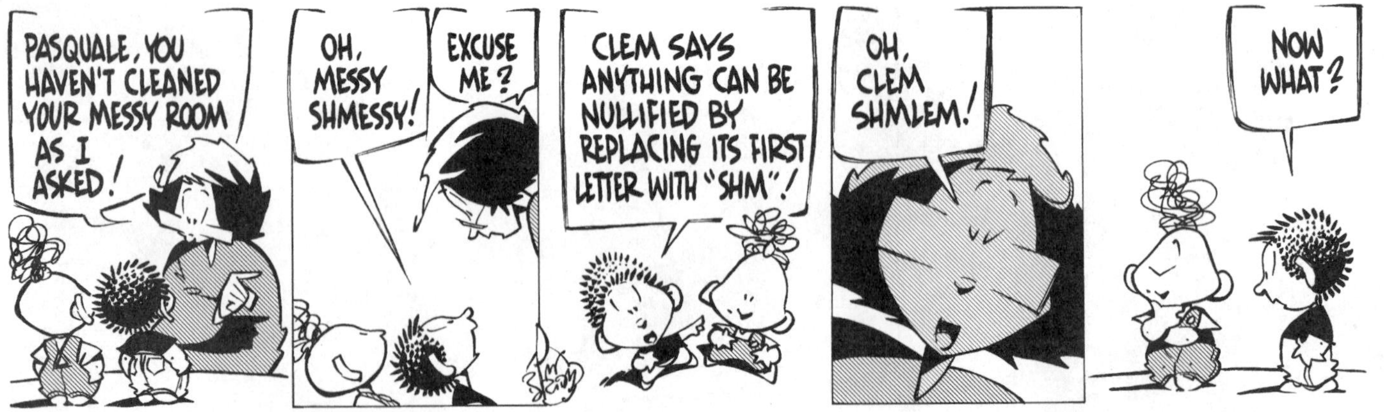
PASQUALE, YOU HAVEN'T CLEANED YOUR MESSY ROOM AS I ASKED!
OH, MESSY SHMESSY!
EXCUSE ME?
CLEM SAYS ANYTHING CAN BE NULLIFIED BY REPLACING ITS FIRST LETTER WITH "SHM"!
OH, CLEM SHMLEM!
NOW WHAT?

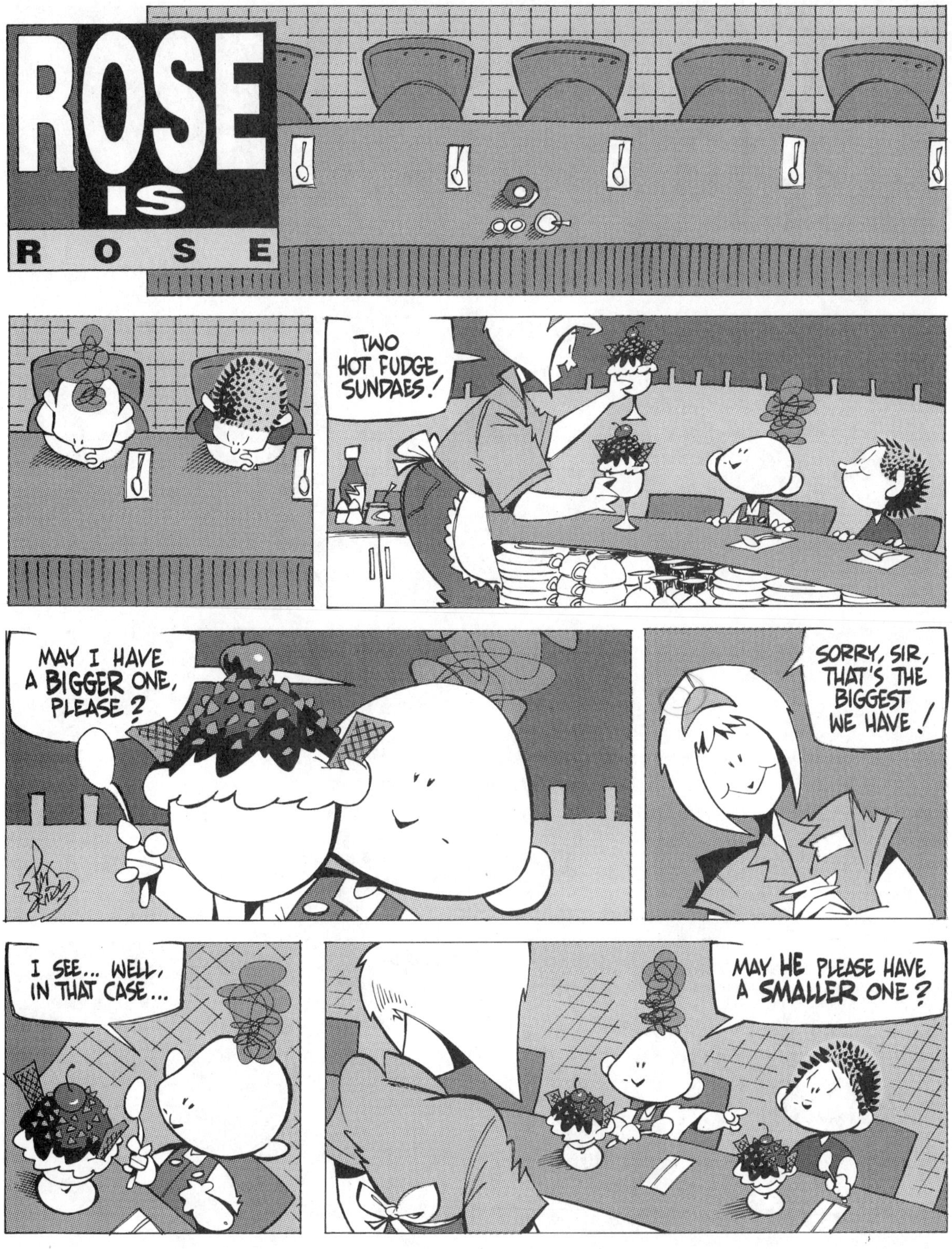
ROSE IS ROSE
TWO HOT FUDGE SUNDAES!
MAY I HAVE A BIGGER ONE, PLEASE?
SORRY, SIR, THAT'S THE BIGGEST WE HAVE!
I SEE... WELL, IN THAT CASE...
MAY HE PLEASE HAVE A SMALLER ONE?

ROSE IS ROSE
PURRRRRRR
I ♥
NOT ONLY DOES PEEKABOO LOVE SOLAR HEATING, BUT SHE'S AN EFFICIENCY EXPERT AS WELL!

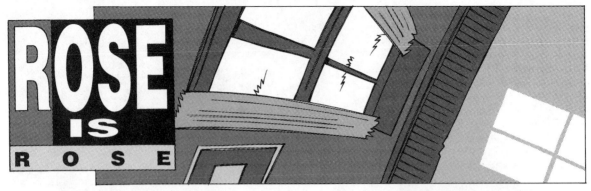

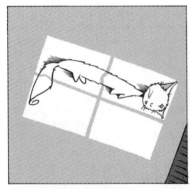

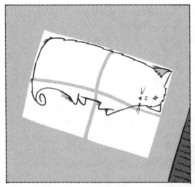

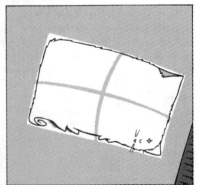

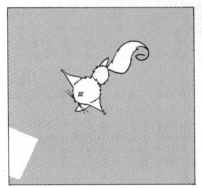

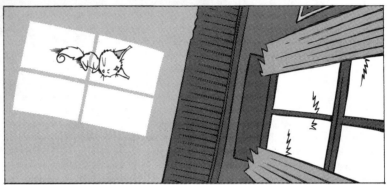

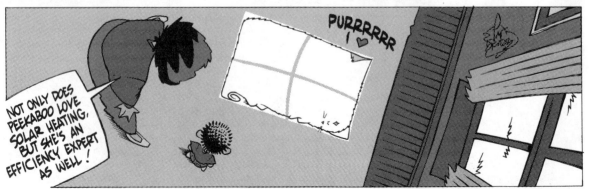

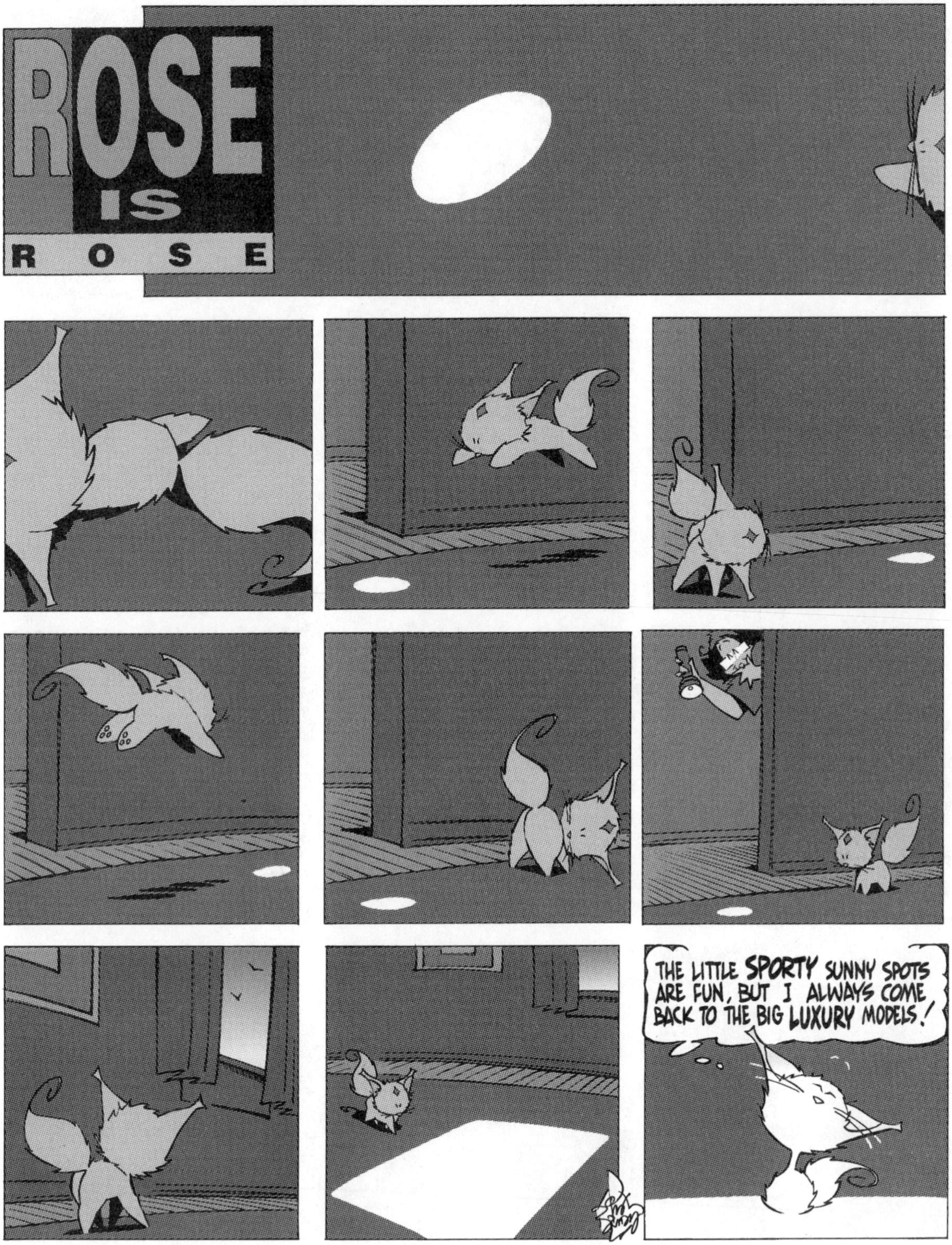
ROSE IS ROSE
THE LITTLE SPORTY SUNNY SPOTS ARE FUN, BUT I ALWAYS COME BACK TO THE BIG LUXURY MODELS!

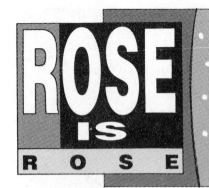

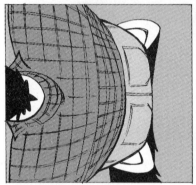

THE CHALLENGER FAILS
TO UNSEAT PEEKABOO
IN THE CHAIR COMPETITION.

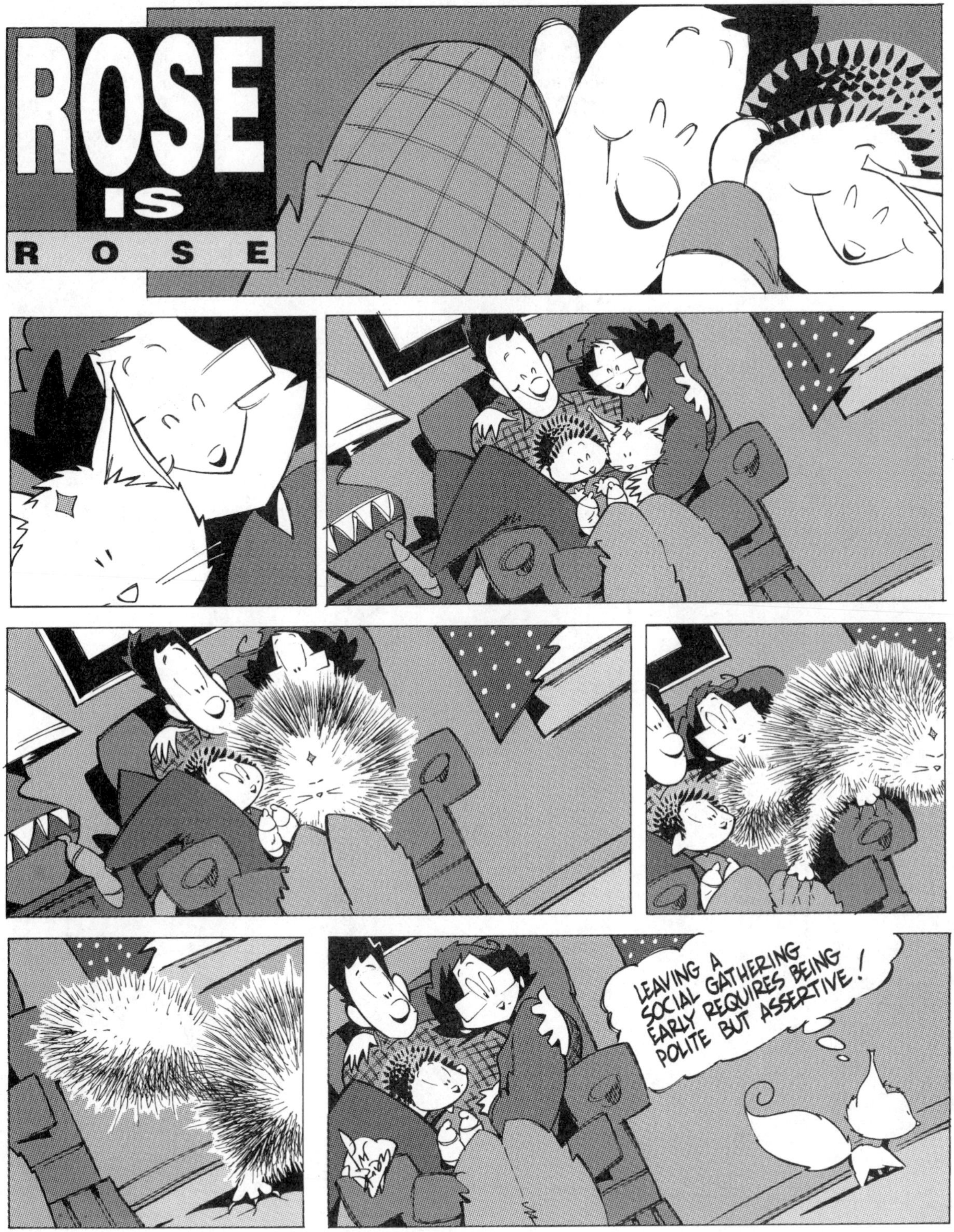
ROSE IS ROSE
LEAVING A SOCIAL GATHERING EARLY REQUIRES BEING POLITE BUT ASSERTIVE!

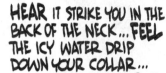

CLOSE YOUR EYES AND VISUALIZE A BIG, WHITE, GLISTENING SNOWBALL FLYING TOWARD YOU...

HEAR IT STRIKE YOU IN THE BACK OF THE NECK... FEEL THE ICY WATER DRIP DOWN YOUR COLLAR...

AAUUGGHH

ANY SIGN OF SNOW?

A HIGH PRIEST OF THE SNOWBALL ARTS DOESN'T NEED SNOW!

BRUSH BRUSH

I NEVER WATCHED A HIGH PRIEST OF THE SNOWBALL ARTS MEDITATE BEFORE!

I FIND IT GRACEFUL BUT NERVE-RACKING!

THANK YOU! SOME DAYS I JUST...

NEED A LITTLE MORE...

SECURITY THAN OTHER DAYS!

STAY AS LONG AS YOU LIKE!

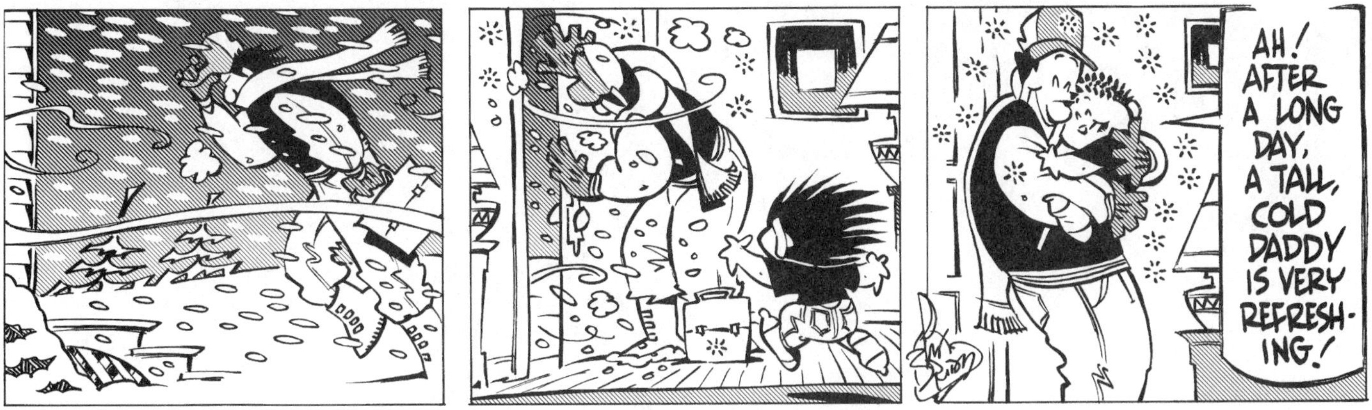
AH! AFTER A LONG DAY, A TALL, COLD DADDY IS VERY REFRESHING!

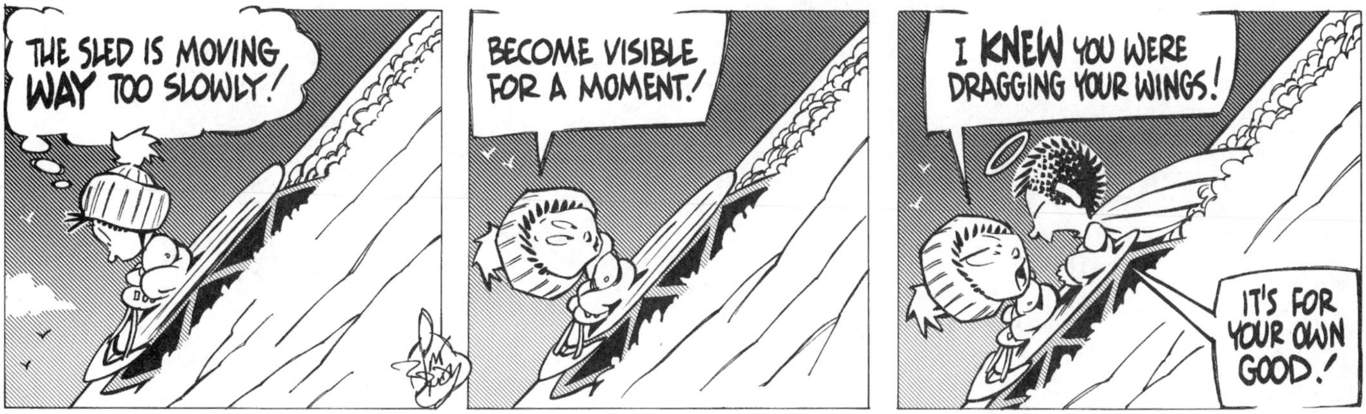
THE SLED IS MOVING WAY TOO SLOWLY!
BECOME VISIBLE FOR A MOMENT!
I KNEW YOU WERE DRAGGING YOUR WINGS!
IT'S FOR YOUR OWN GOOD!

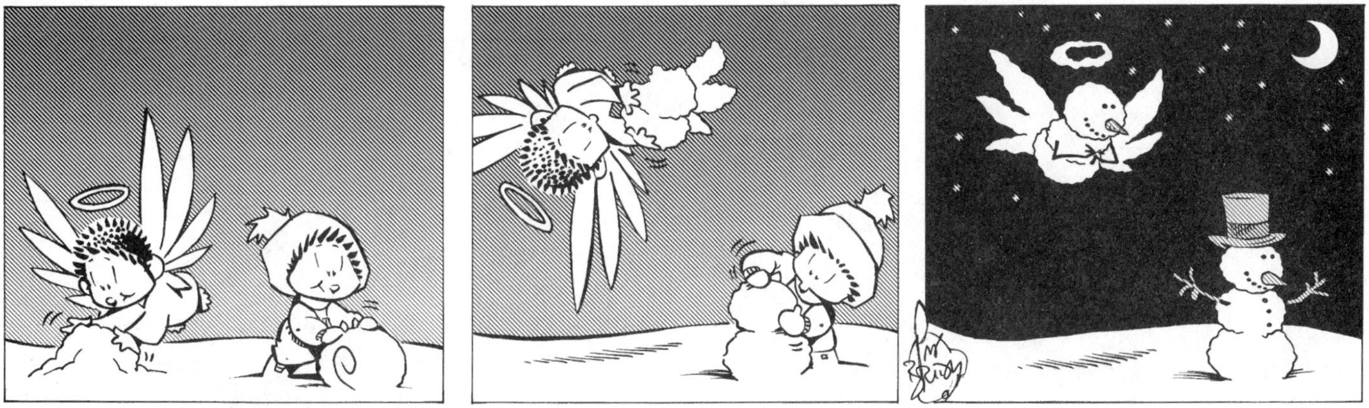

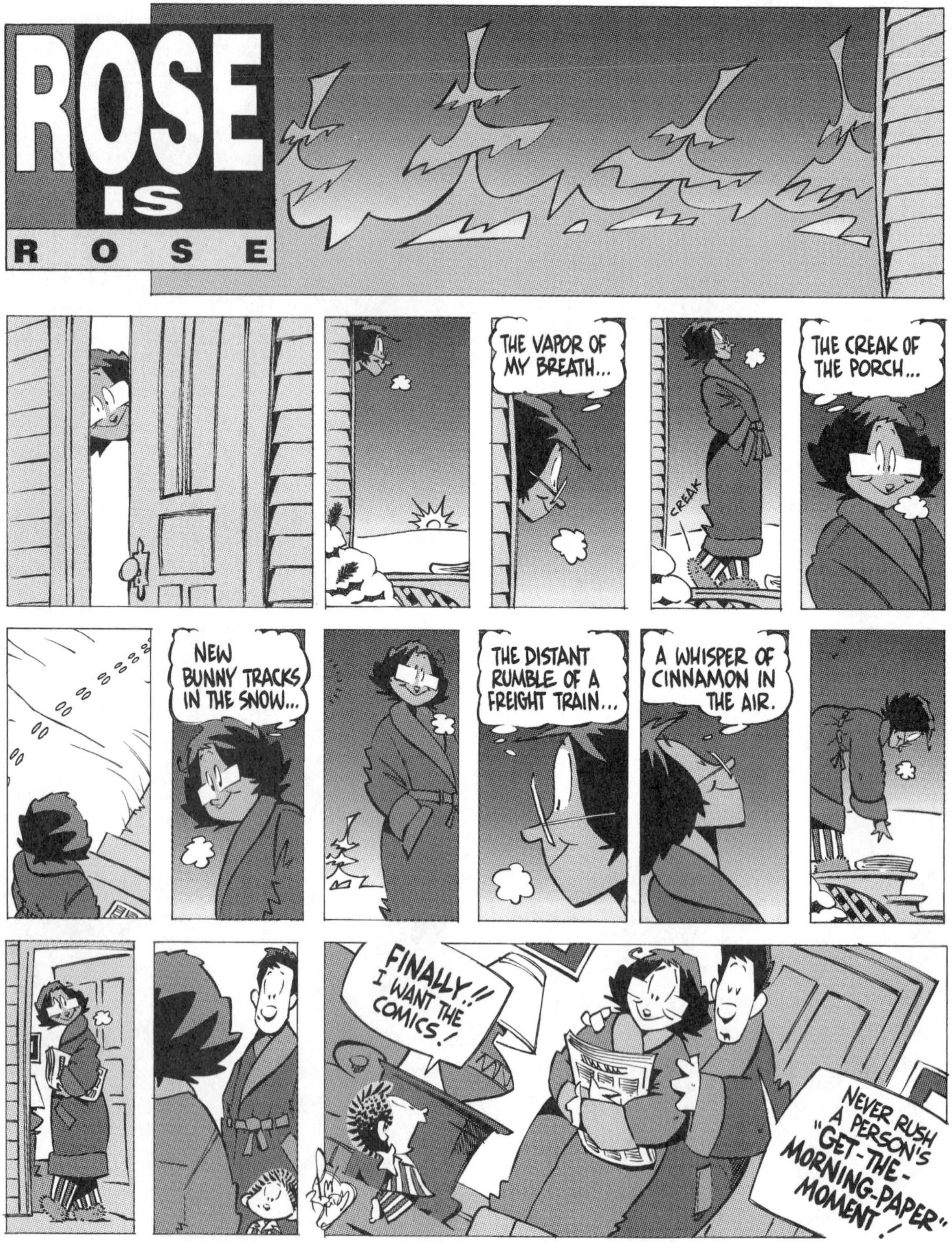
ROSE IS ROSE
THE VAPOR OF MY BREATH...
CREAK
THE CREAK OF THE PORCH...
NEW BUNNY TRACKS IN THE SNOW...
THE DISTANT RUMBLE OF A FREIGHT TRAIN...
A WHISPER OF CINNAMON IN THE AIR.
FINALLY!! I WANT THE COMICS!
NEVER RUSH A PERSON'S "GET-THE-MORNING-PAPER" MOMENT!

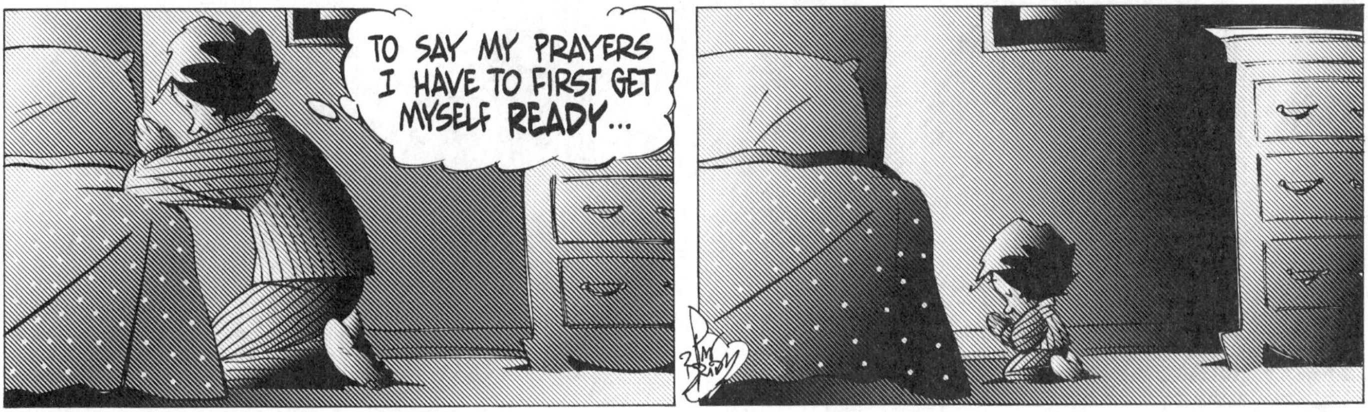
TO SAY MY PRAYERS I HAVE TO FIRST GET MYSELF READY...

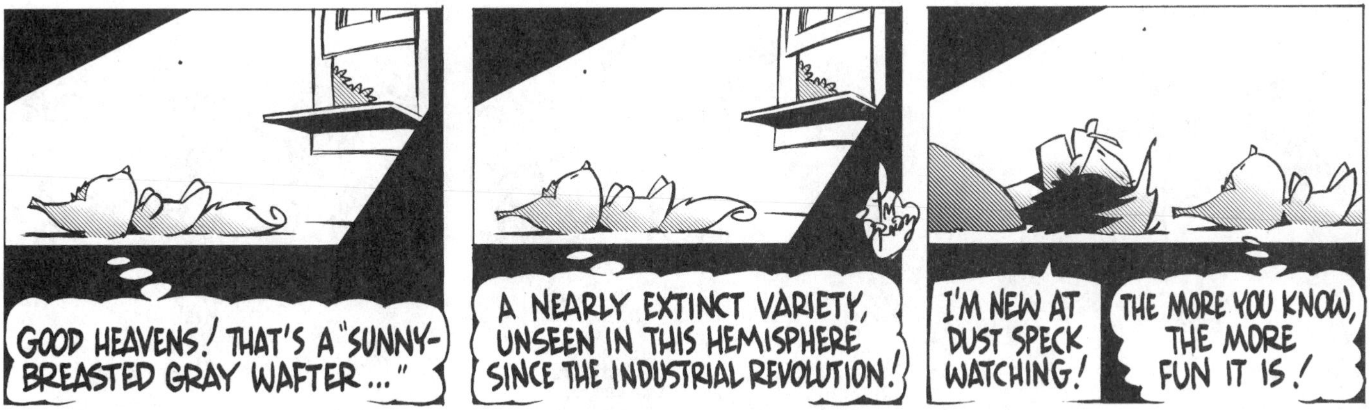
GOOD HEAVENS! THAT'S A "SUNNY-BREASTED GRAY WAFTER ..."
A NEARLY EXTINCT VARIETY, UNSEEN IN THIS HEMISPHERE SINCE THE INDUSTRIAL REVOLUTION!
I'M NEW AT DUST SPECK WATCHING!
THE MORE YOU KNOW, THE MORE FUN IT IS!

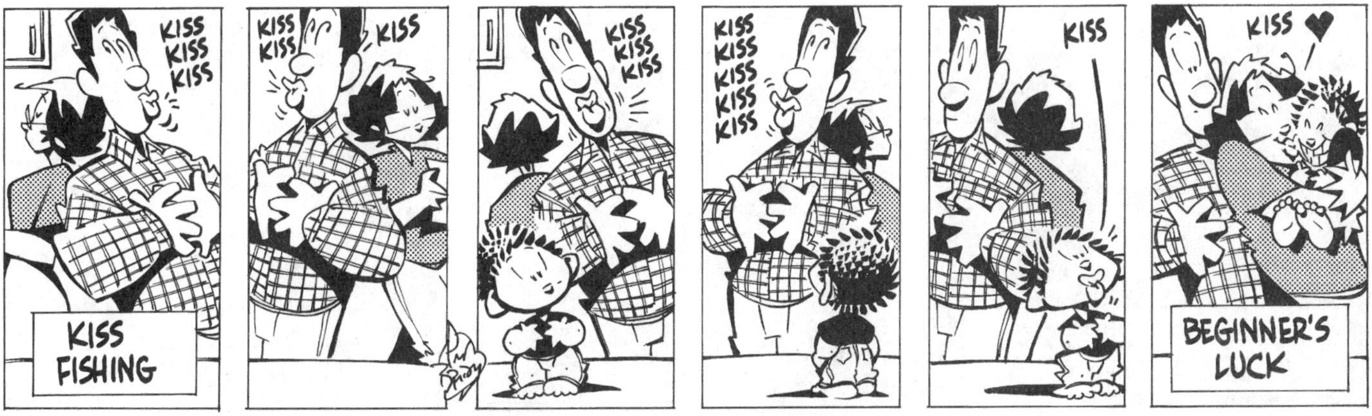
KISS KISS KISS
KISS FISHING
KISS KISS
KISS
KISS KISS KISS
KISS KISS KISS KISS KISS
KISS
KISS
BEGINNER'S LUCK

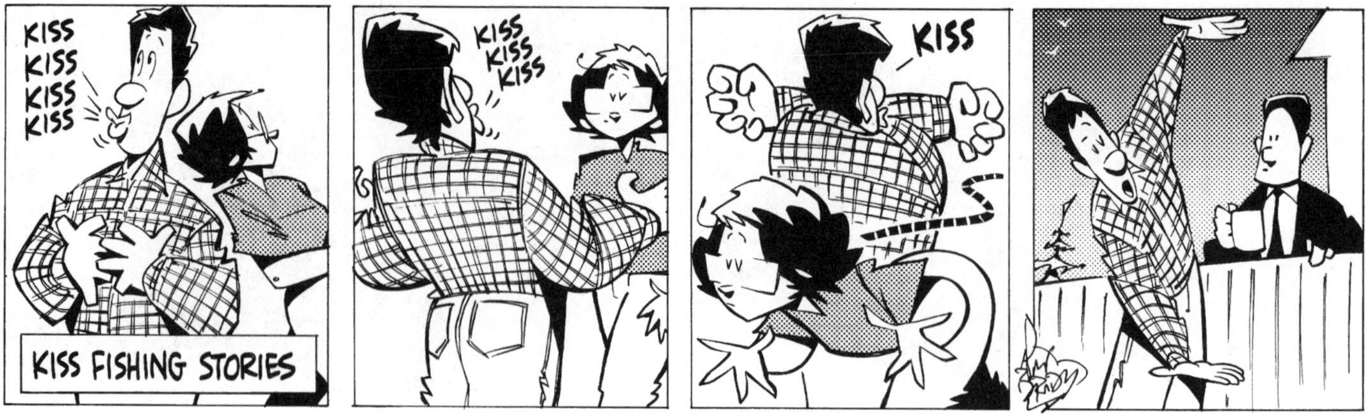
KISS FISHING STORIES
KISS KISS KISS KISS
KISS KISS KISS
KISS

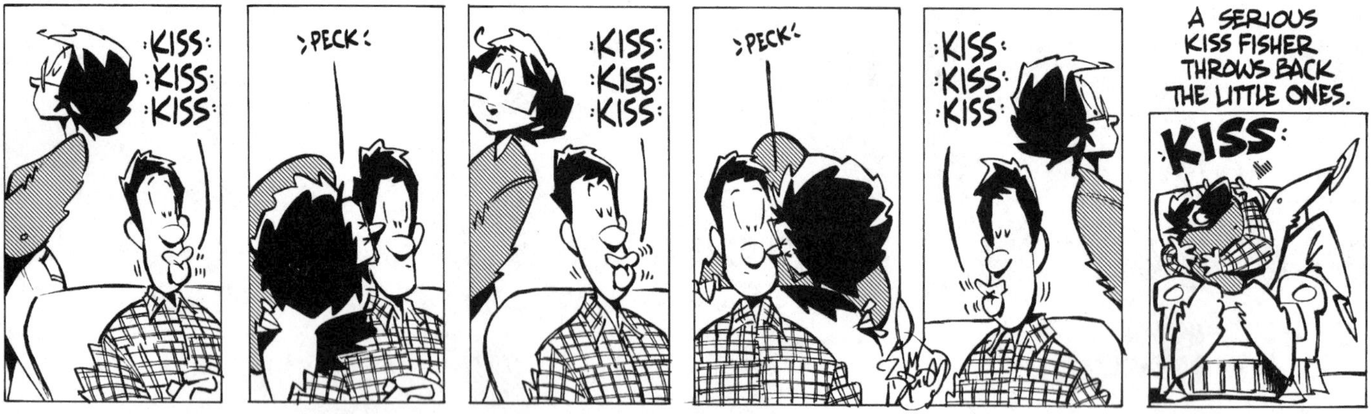
KISS KISS KISS
PECK
KISS KISS KISS
PECK
KISS KISS KISS
A SERIOUS KISS FISHER THROWS BACK THE LITTLE ONES.
KISS

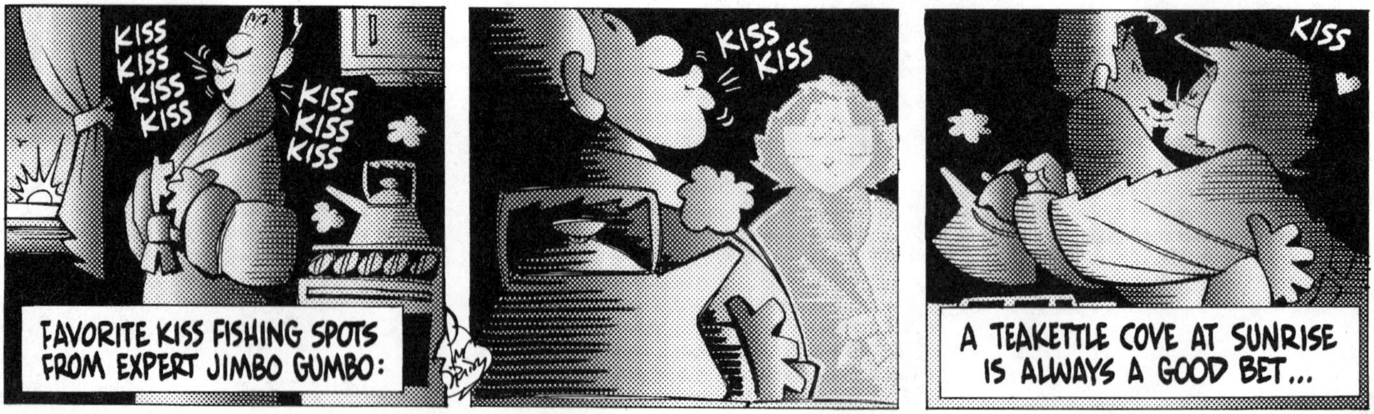
FAVORITE KISS FISHING SPOTS FROM EXPERT JIMBO GUMBO:
KISS KISS KISS KISS
KISS KISS KISS
KISS KISS
A TEAKETTLE COVE AT SUNRISE IS ALWAYS A GOOD BET...
KISS

HEADPHONES ARE THE LEADING CAUSE OF KISS FISHER EXHAUSTION.

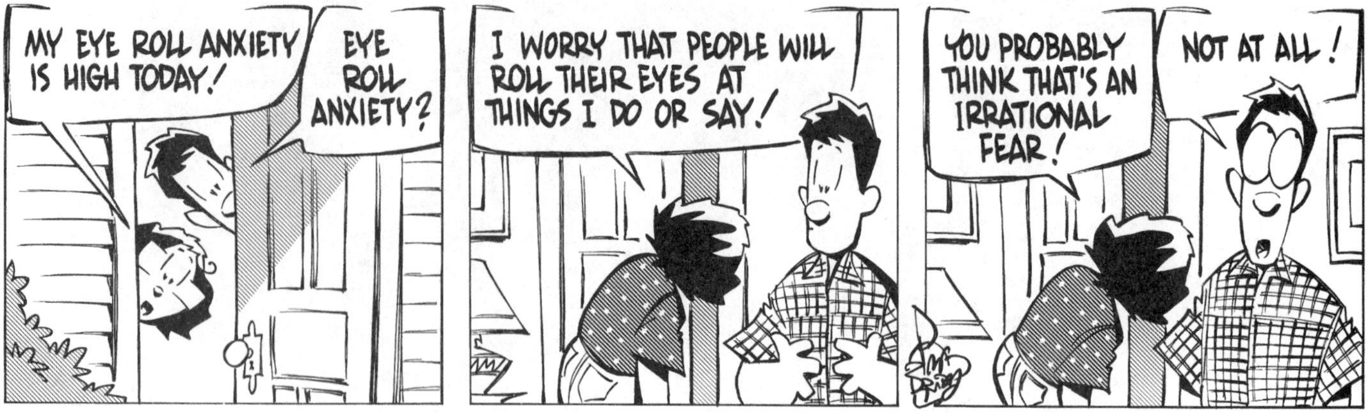
MY EYE ROLL ANXIETY IS HIGH TODAY!
EYE ROLL ANXIETY?
I WORRY THAT PEOPLE WILL ROLL THEIR EYES AT THINGS I DO OR SAY!
YOU PROBABLY THINK THAT'S AN IRRATIONAL FEAR!
NOT AT ALL!

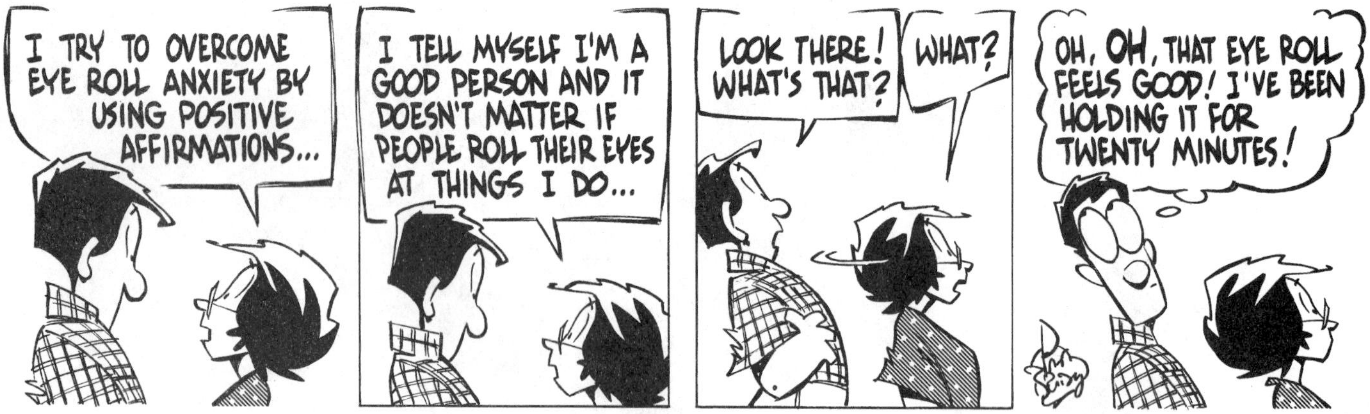
I TRY TO OVERCOME EYE ROLL ANXIETY BY USING POSITIVE AFFIRMATIONS...
I TELL MYSELF I'M A GOOD PERSON AND IT DOESN'T MATTER IF PEOPLE ROLL THEIR EYES AT THINGS I DO...
LOOK THERE! WHAT'S THAT?
WHAT?
OH, **OH**, THAT EYE ROLL FEELS GOOD! I'VE BEEN HOLDING IT FOR TWENTY MINUTES!

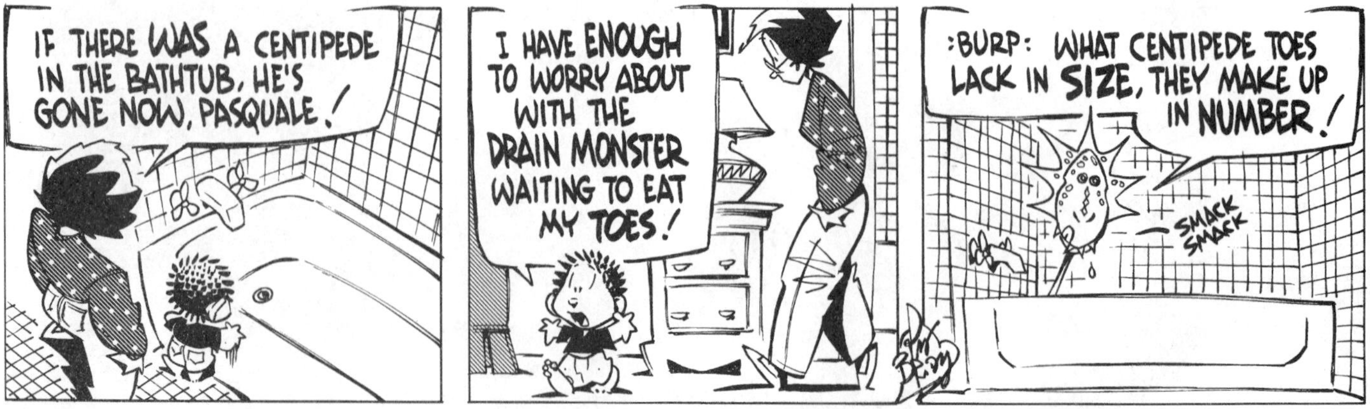
IF THERE **WAS** A CENTIPEDE IN THE BATHTUB, HE'S GONE NOW, PASQUALE!
I HAVE **ENOUGH** TO WORRY ABOUT WITH THE **DRAIN MONSTER** WAITING TO EAT MY **TOES**!
:BURP: WHAT CENTIPEDE TOES LACK IN **SIZE**, THEY MAKE UP IN **NUMBER**!
SMACK SMACK

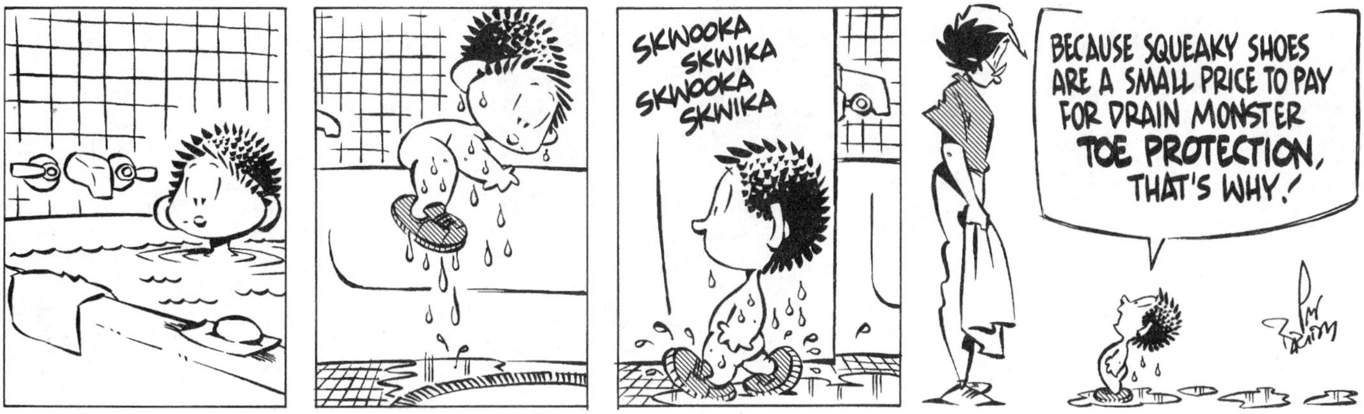
SKWOOKA
SKWIKA
SKWOOKA
SKWIKA
BECAUSE SQUEAKY SHOES ARE A SMALL PRICE TO PAY FOR DRAIN MONSTER TOE PROTECTION, THAT'S WHY!

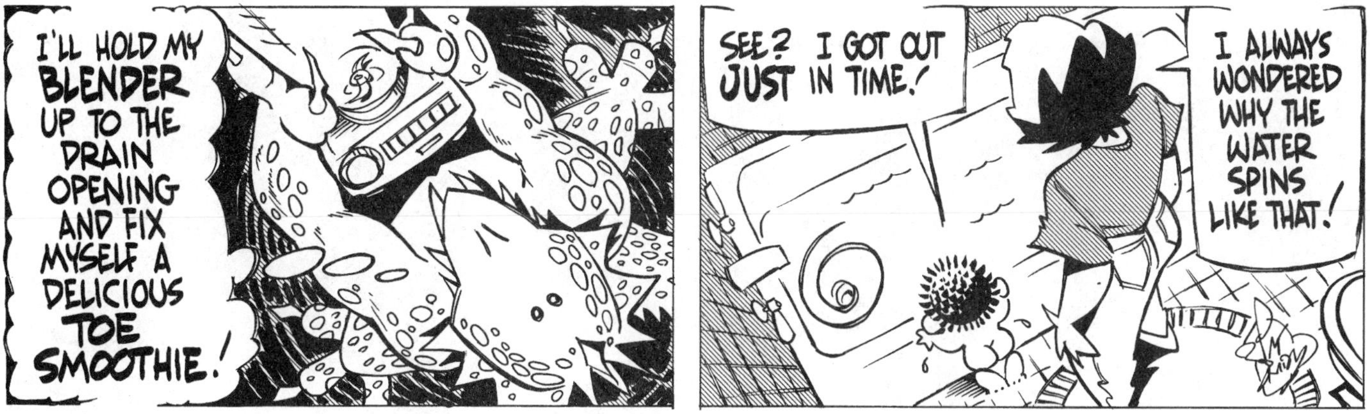
I'LL HOLD MY BLENDER UP TO THE DRAIN OPENING AND FIX MYSELF A DELICIOUS TOE SMOOTHIE!
SEE? I GOT OUT JUST IN TIME!
I ALWAYS WONDERED WHY THE WATER SPINS LIKE THAT!

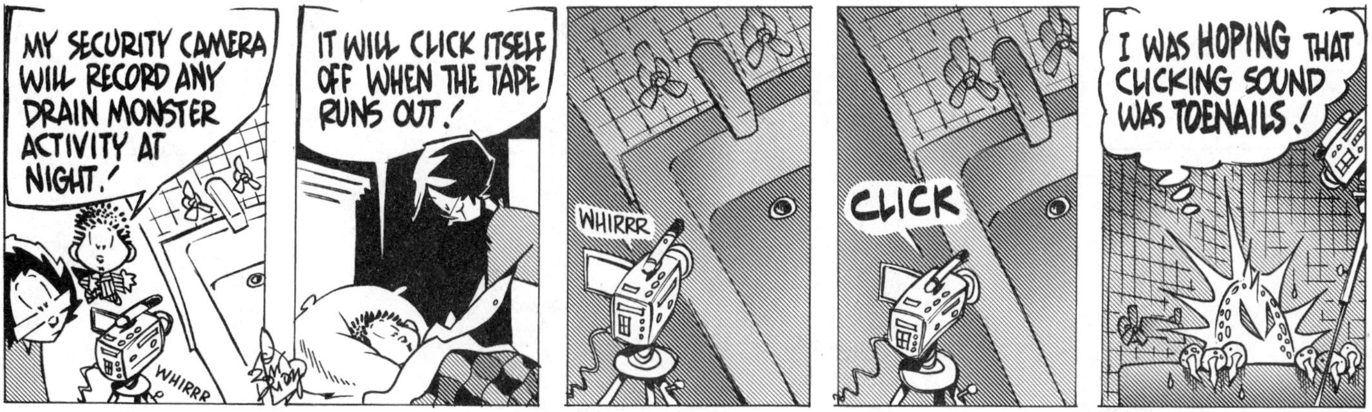
MY SECURITY CAMERA WILL RECORD ANY DRAIN MONSTER ACTIVITY AT NIGHT!
WHIRRR
IT WILL CLICK ITSELF OFF WHEN THE TAPE RUNS OUT!
WHIRRR
CLICK
I WAS HOPING THAT CLICKING SOUND WAS TOENAILS!

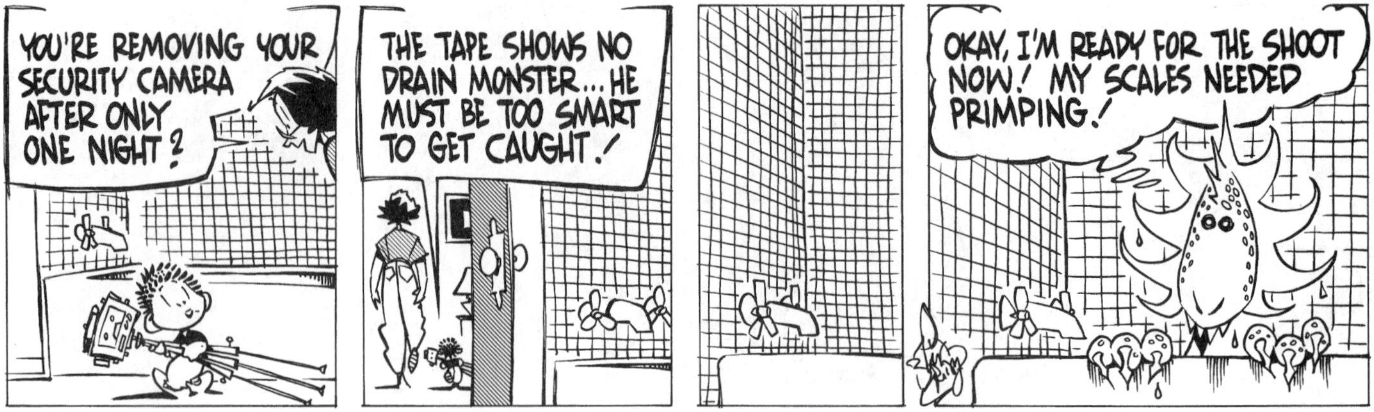
YOU'RE REMOVING YOUR SECURITY CAMERA AFTER ONLY ONE NIGHT?
THE TAPE SHOWS NO DRAIN MONSTER... HE MUST BE TOO SMART TO GET CAUGHT!
OKAY, I'M READY FOR THE SHOOT NOW! MY SCALES NEEDED PRIMPING!

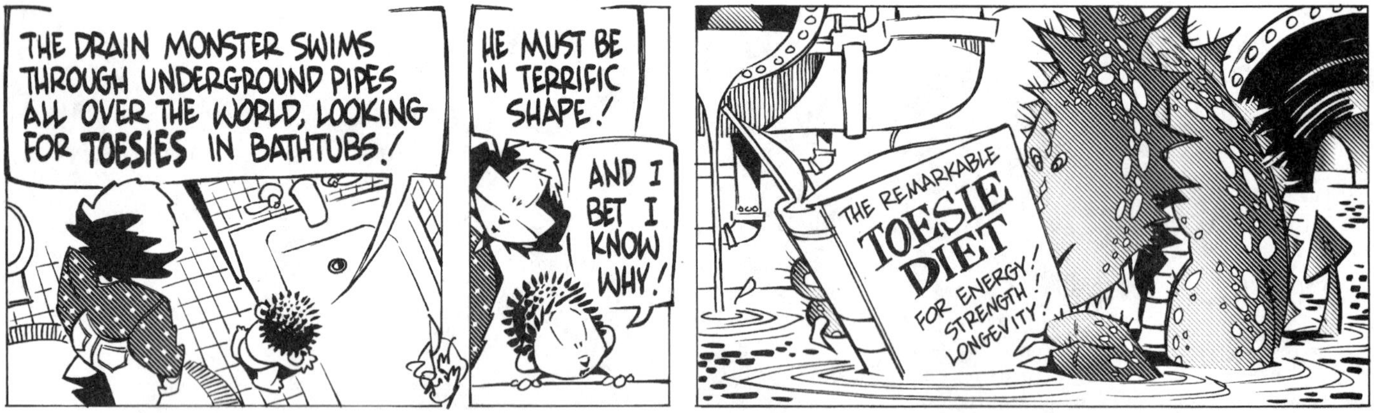
THE DRAIN MONSTER SWIMS THROUGH UNDERGROUND PIPES ALL OVER THE WORLD, LOOKING FOR TOESIES IN BATHTUBS!
HE MUST BE IN TERRIFIC SHAPE!
AND I BET I KNOW WHY!
THE REMARKABLE TOESIE DIET
FOR ENERGY! STRENGTH! LONGEVITY!

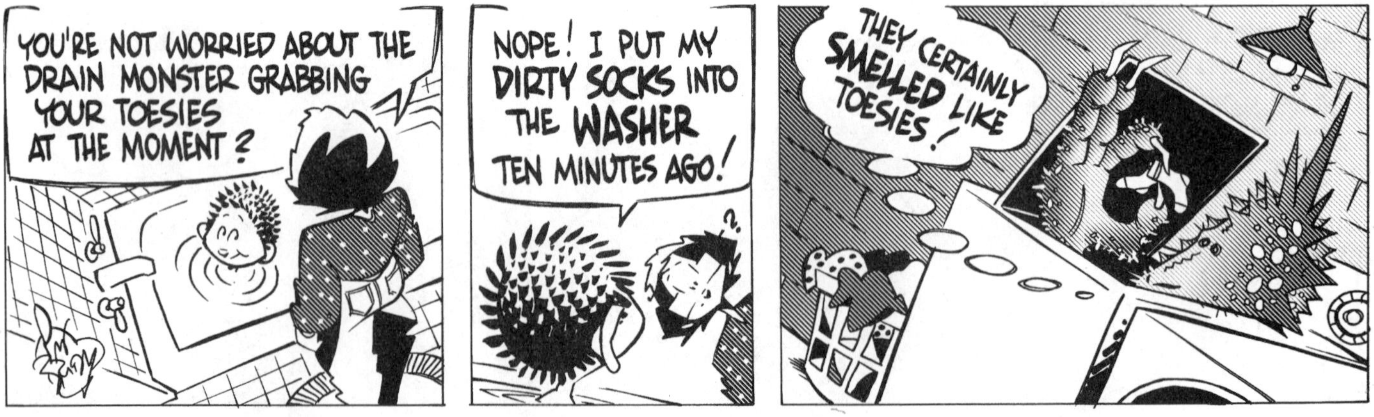
YOU'RE NOT WORRIED ABOUT THE DRAIN MONSTER GRABBING YOUR TOESIES AT THE MOMENT?
NOPE! I PUT MY DIRTY SOCKS INTO THE WASHER TEN MINUTES AGO!
THEY CERTAINLY SMELLED LIKE TOESIES!

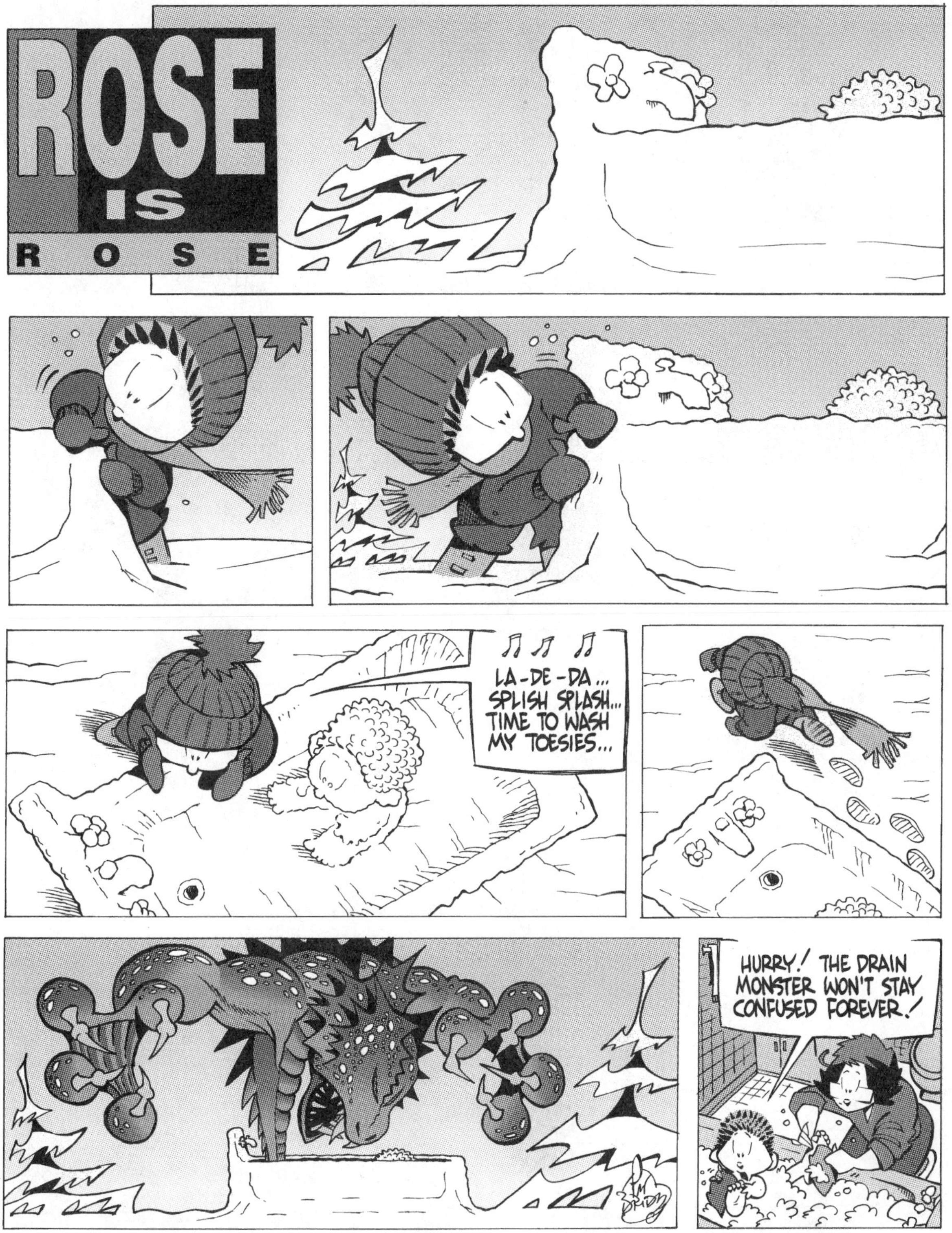
ROSE IS ROSE
♫ ♫ ♫
LA-DE-DA... SPLISH SPLASH... TIME TO WASH MY TOESIES...
HURRY! THE DRAIN MONSTER WON'T STAY CONFUSED FOREVER!

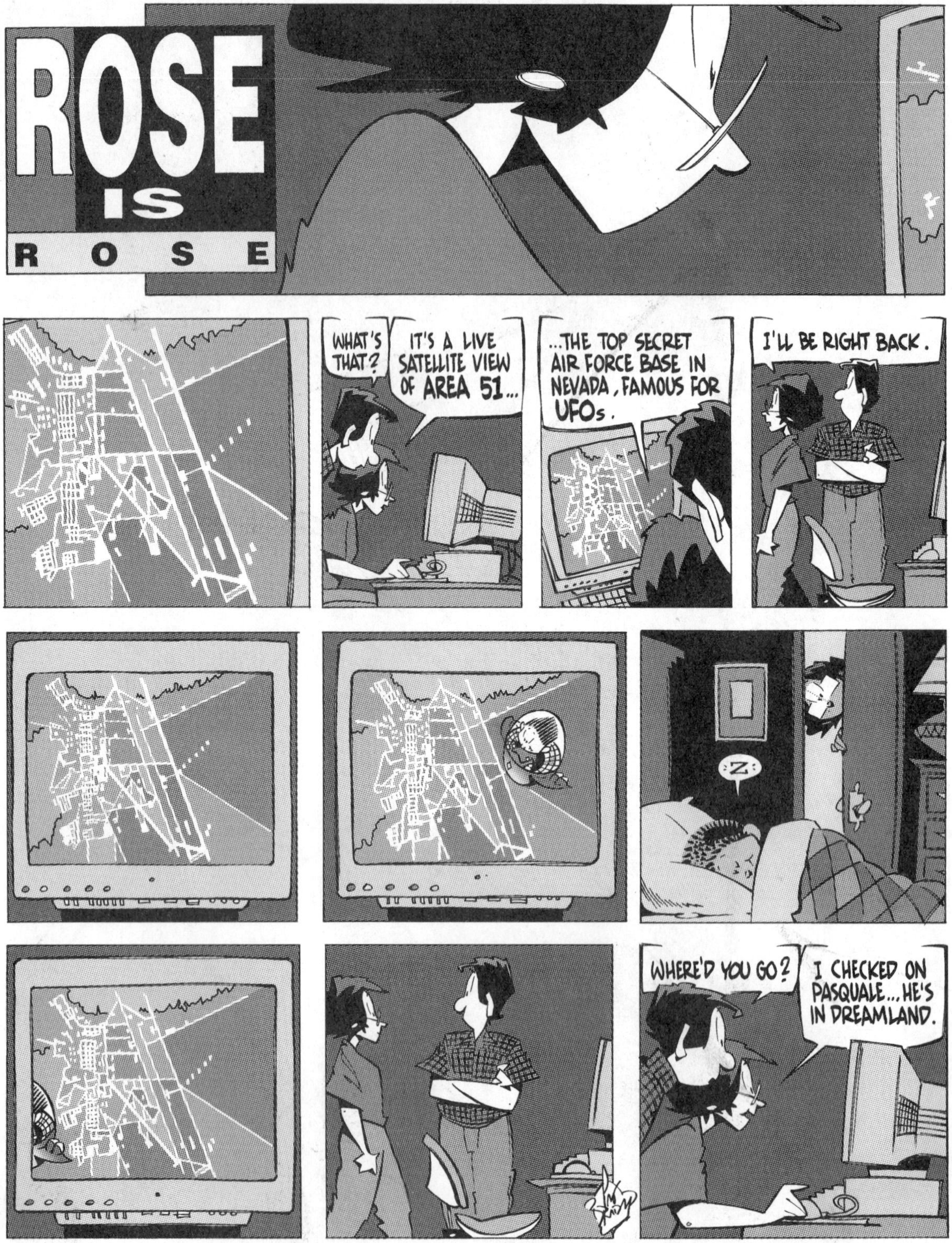
ROSE IS ROSE
WHAT'S THAT?
IT'S A LIVE SATELLITE VIEW OF AREA 51...
...THE TOP SECRET AIR FORCE BASE IN NEVADA, FAMOUS FOR UFOs.
I'LL BE RIGHT BACK.
Z
WHERE'D YOU GO?
I CHECKED ON PASQUALE... HE'S IN DREAMLAND.

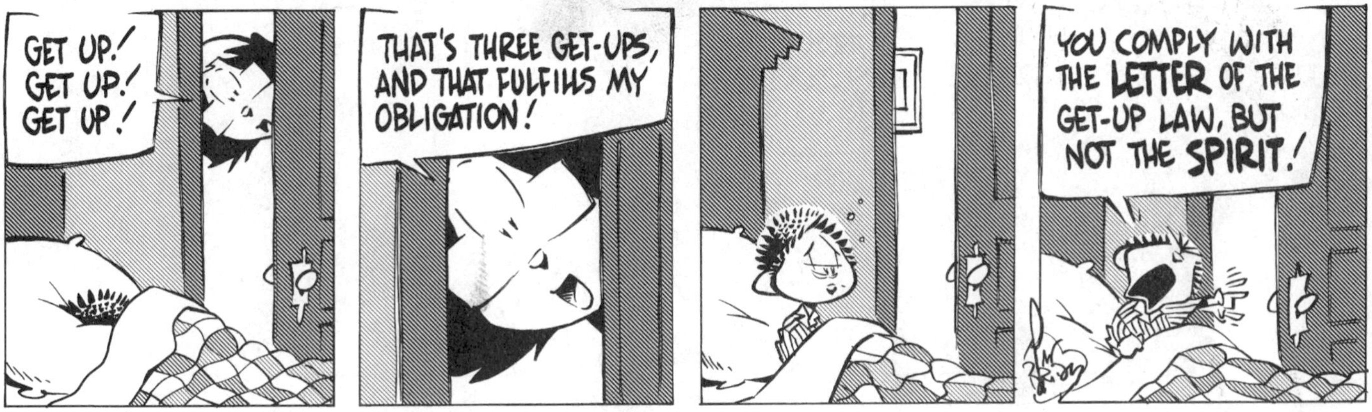
GET UP! GET UP! GET UP!
THAT'S THREE GET-UPS, AND THAT FULFILLS MY OBLIGATION!
YOU COMPLY WITH THE LETTER OF THE GET-UP LAW, BUT NOT THE SPIRIT!

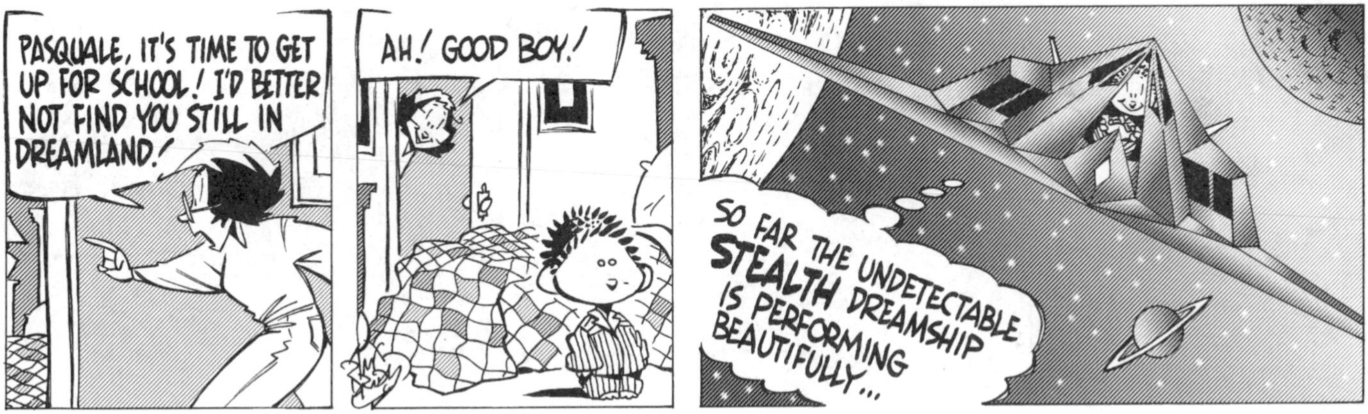
PASQUALE, IT'S TIME TO GET UP FOR SCHOOL! I'D BETTER NOT FIND YOU STILL IN DREAMLAND!
AH! GOOD BOY!
SO FAR THE UNDETECTABLE STEALTH DREAMSHIP IS PERFORMING BEAUTIFULLY...

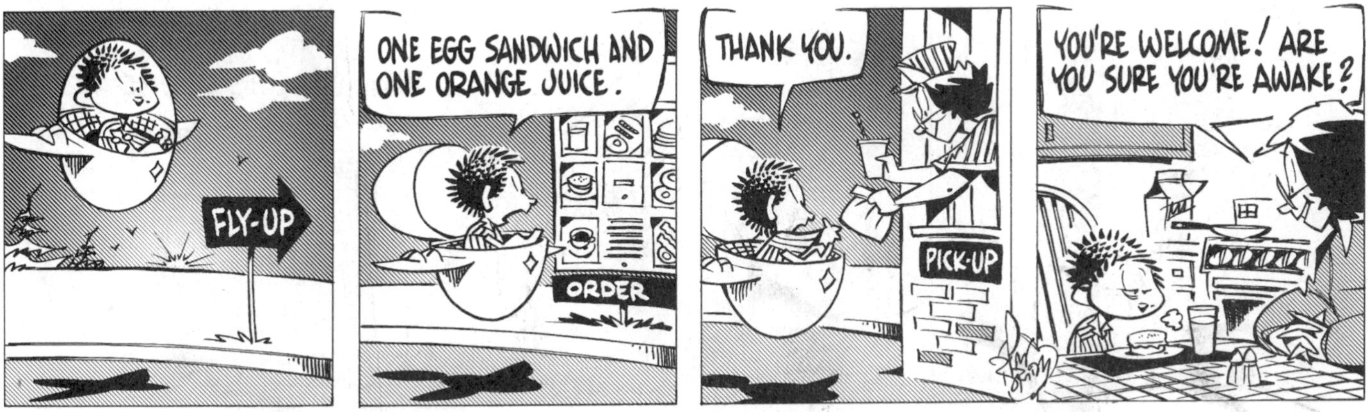
FLY-UP
ONE EGG SANDWICH AND ONE ORANGE JUICE.
ORDER
THANK YOU.
PICK-UP
YOU'RE WELCOME! ARE YOU SURE YOU'RE AWAKE?

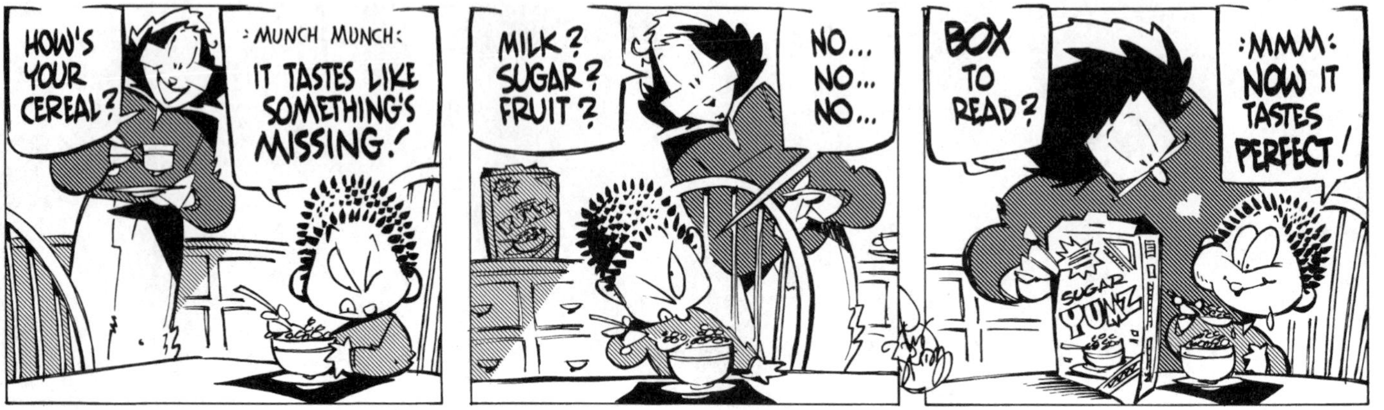
HOW'S YOUR CEREAL?
:MUNCH MUNCH:
IT TASTES LIKE SOMETHING'S MISSING!
MILK? SUGAR? FRUIT?
NO... NO... NO...
BOX TO READ?
:MMM: NOW IT TASTES PERFECT!
SUGAR YUMZ

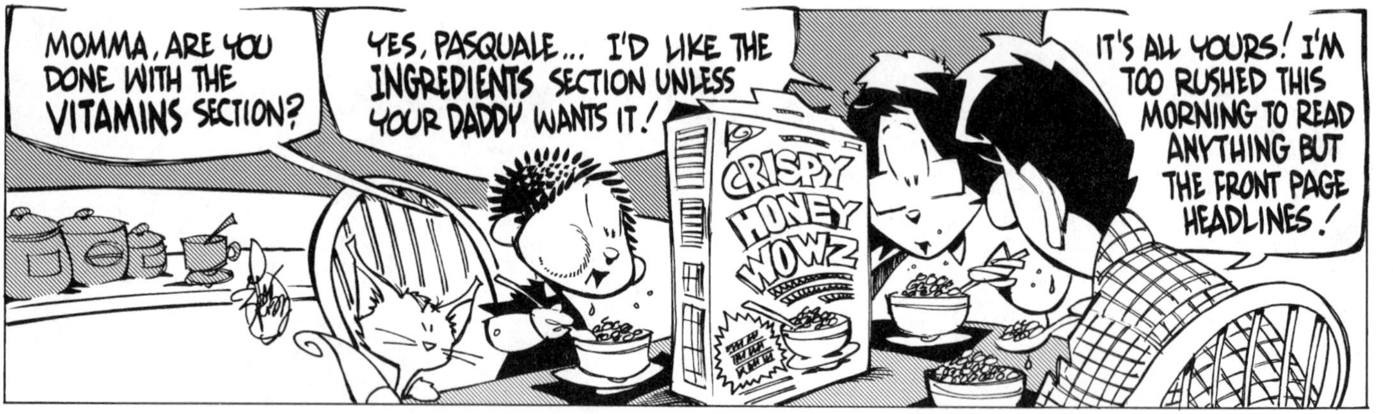
MOMMA, ARE YOU DONE WITH THE VITAMINS SECTION?
YES, PASQUALE... I'D LIKE THE INGREDIENTS SECTION UNLESS YOUR DADDY WANTS IT!
IT'S ALL YOURS! I'M TOO RUSHED THIS MORNING TO READ ANYTHING BUT THE FRONT PAGE HEADLINES!
CRISPY HONEY WOWZ

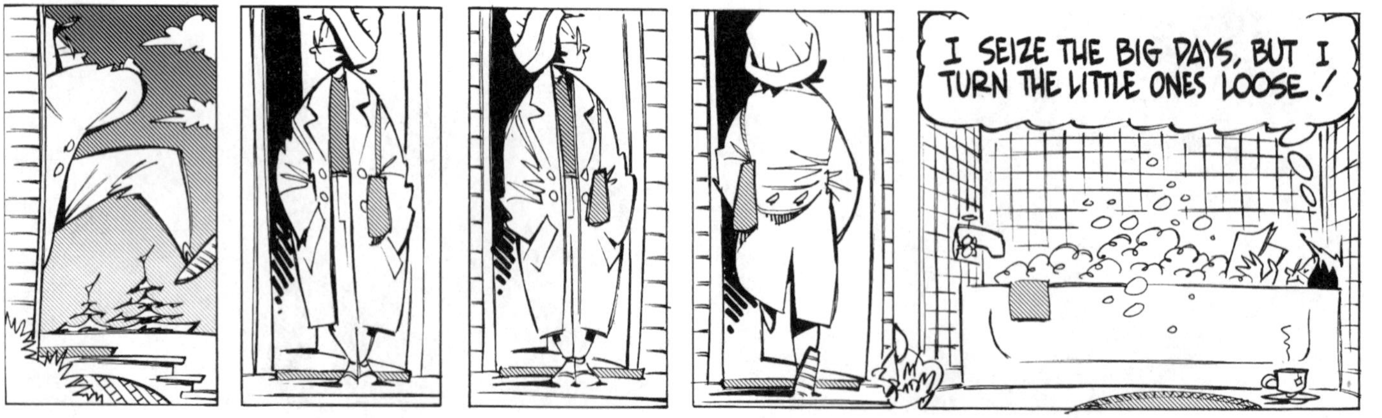
I SEIZE THE BIG DAYS, BUT I TURN THE LITTLE ONES LOOSE!

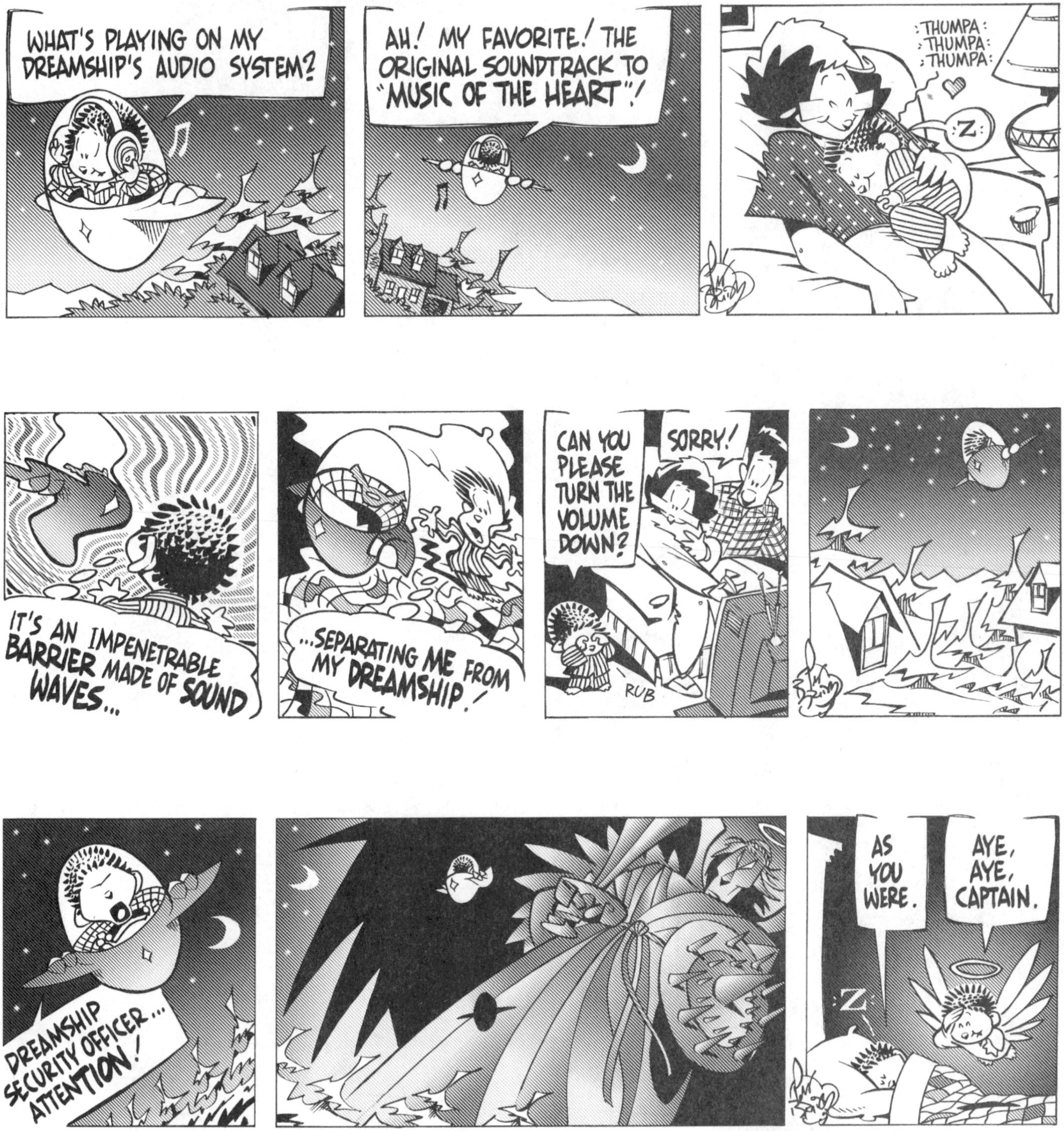
WHAT'S PLAYING ON MY DREAMSHIP'S AUDIO SYSTEM?
AH! MY FAVORITE! THE ORIGINAL SOUNDTRACK TO "MUSIC OF THE HEART"!
THUMPA THUMPA THUMPA
Z
IT'S AN IMPENETRABLE BARRIER MADE OF SOUND WAVES...
...SEPARATING ME FROM MY DREAMSHIP!
CAN YOU PLEASE TURN THE VOLUME DOWN?
SORRY!
RUB
DREAMSHIP SECURITY OFFICER... ATTENTION!
Z
AS YOU WERE.
AYE, AYE, CAPTAIN.

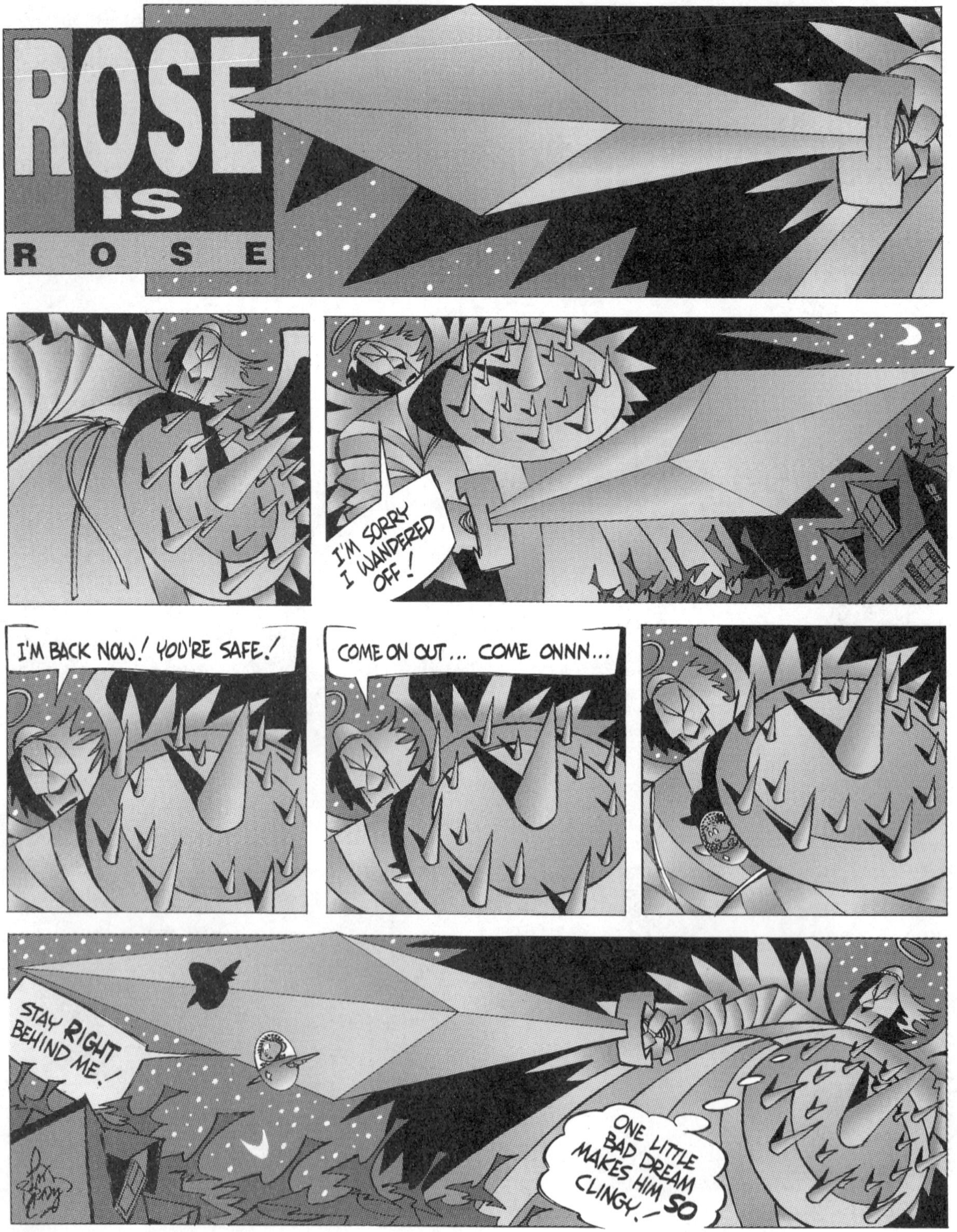
ROSE IS ROSE
I'M SORRY I WANDERED OFF!
I'M BACK NOW! YOU'RE SAFE!
COME ON OUT... COME ONNN...
STAY RIGHT BEHIND ME!
ONE LITTLE BAD DREAM MAKES HIM SO CLINGY!

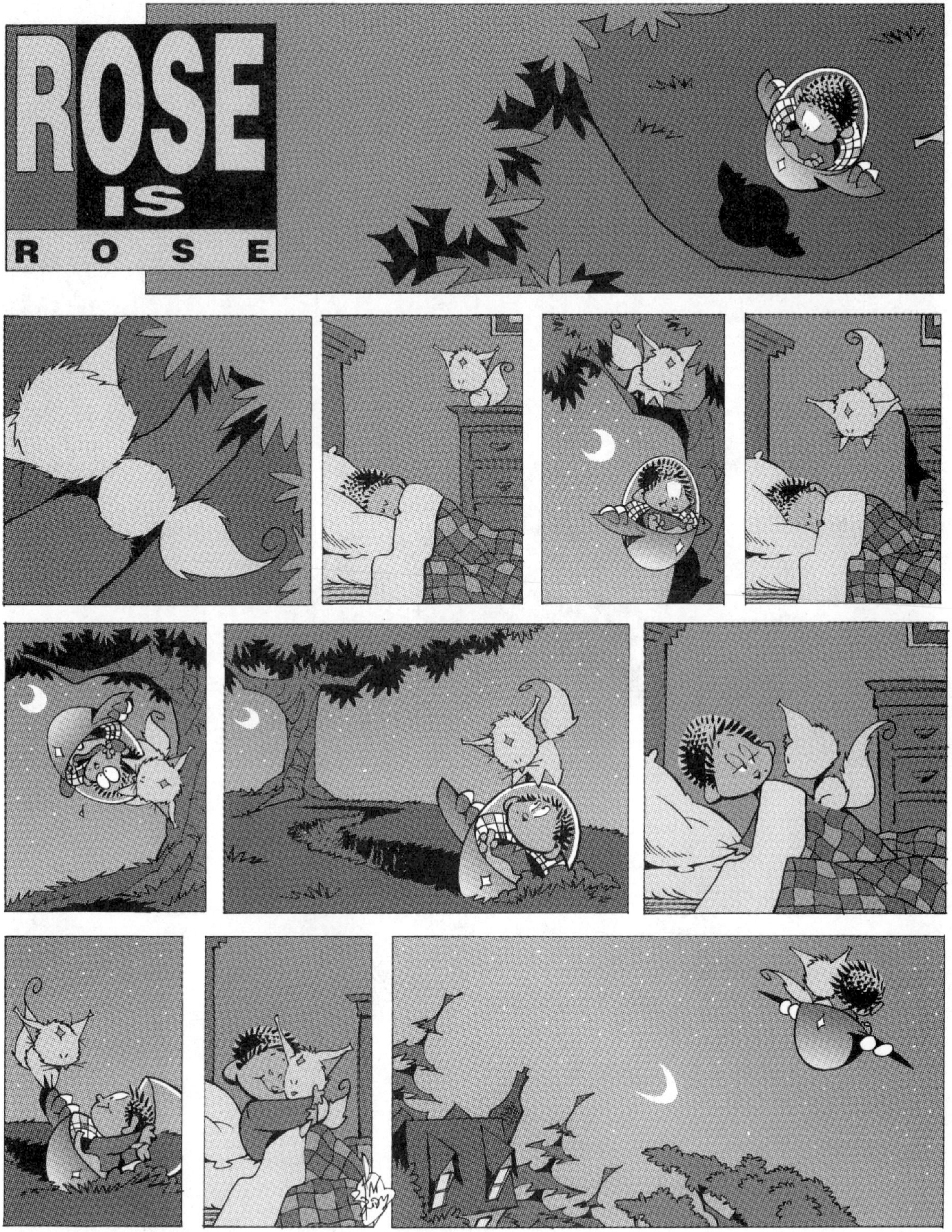
ROSE
IS
ROSE

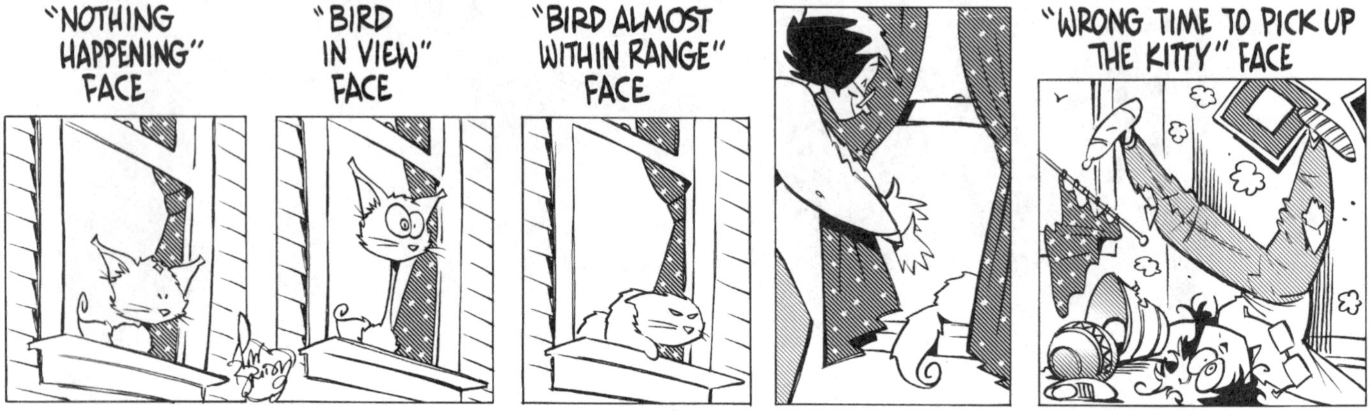
"NOTHING HAPPENING" FACE
"BIRD IN VIEW" FACE
"BIRD ALMOST WITHIN RANGE" FACE
"WRONG TIME TO PICK UP THE KITTY" FACE

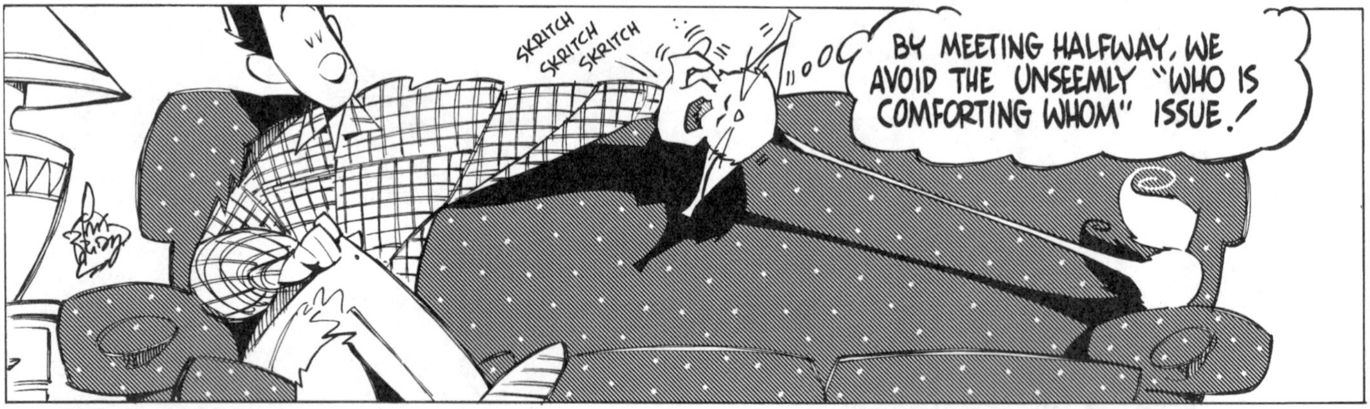
SKRITCH SKRITCH SKRITCH
BY MEETING HALFWAY, WE AVOID THE UNSEEMLY "WHO IS COMFORTING WHOM" ISSUE!

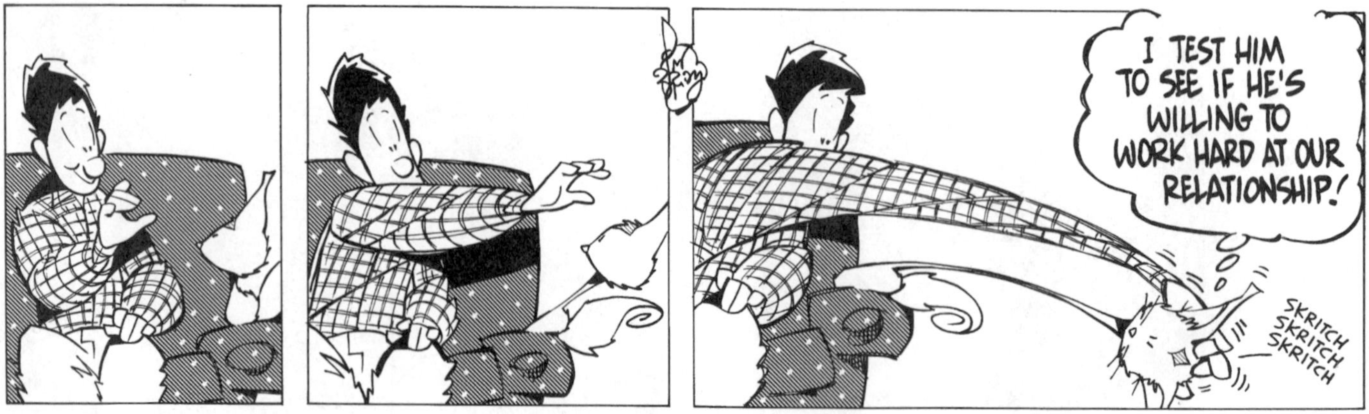
I TEST HIM TO SEE IF HE'S WILLING TO WORK HARD AT OUR RELATIONSHIP!
SKRITCH SKRITCH SKRITCH

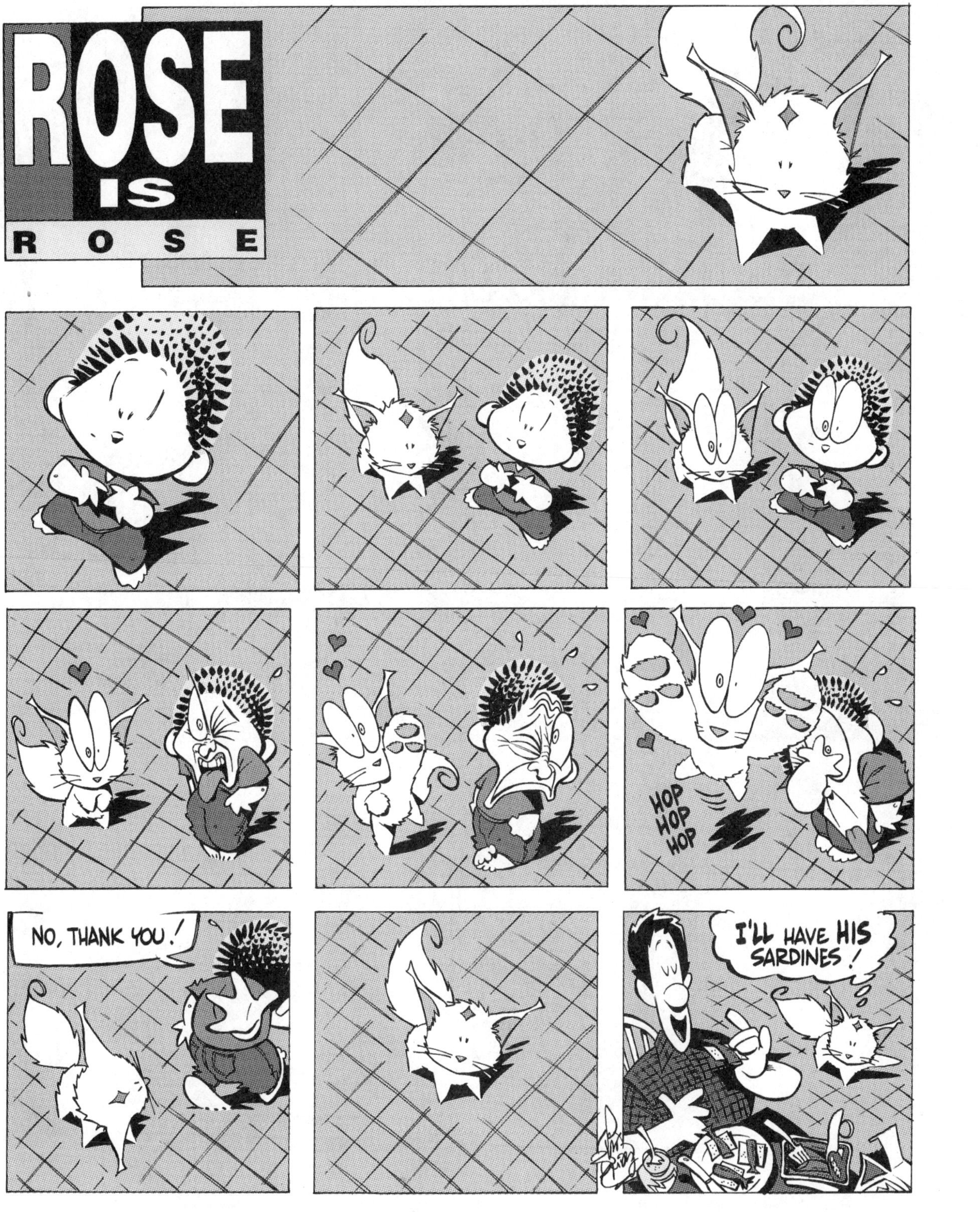
ROSE IS ROSE
HOP HOP HOP
NO, THANK YOU!
I'LL HAVE HIS SARDINES!

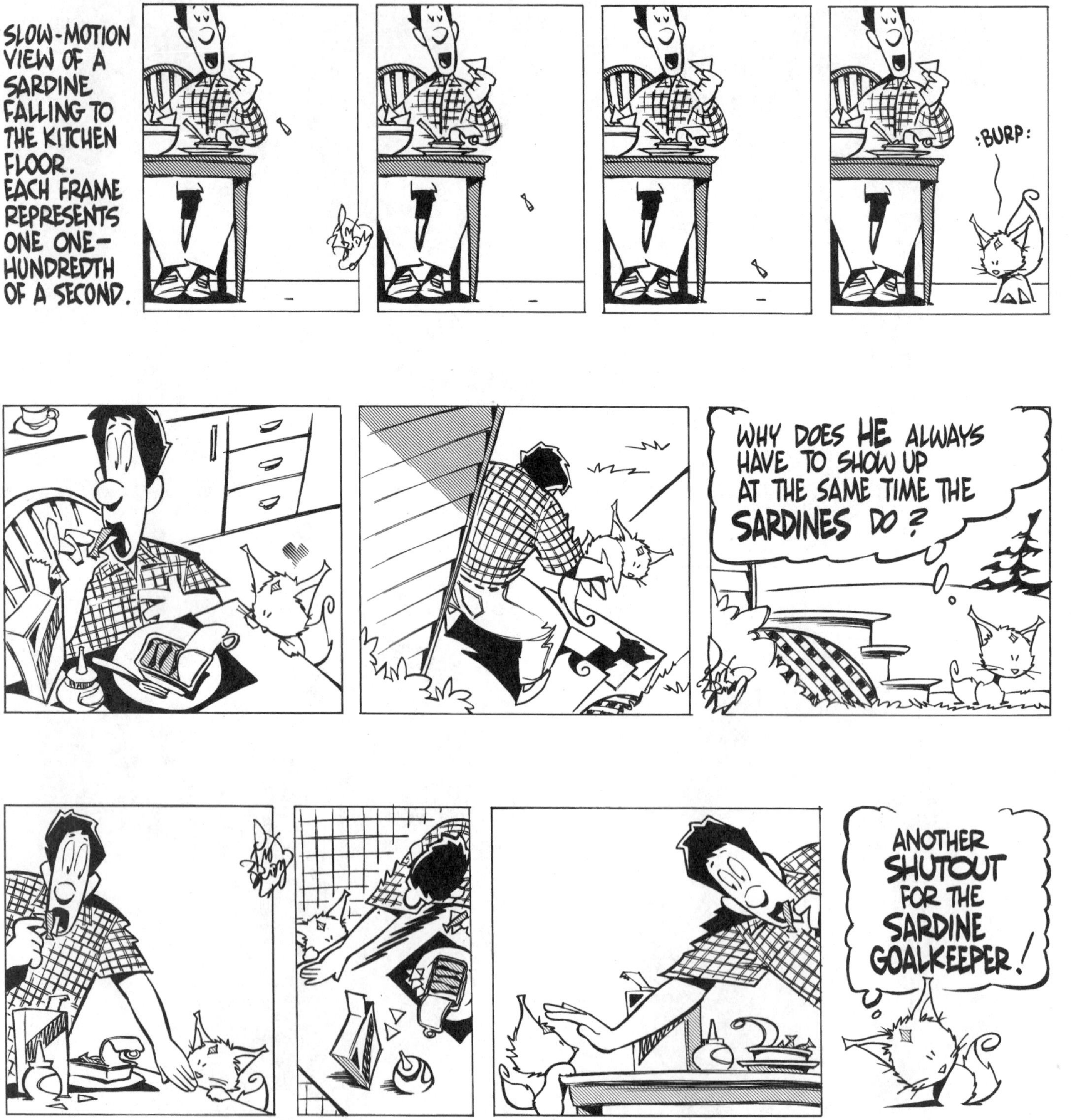
SLOW-MOTION VIEW OF A SARDINE FALLING TO THE KITCHEN FLOOR. EACH FRAME REPRESENTS ONE ONE-HUNDREDTH OF A SECOND.
:BURP:
WHY DOES HE ALWAYS HAVE TO SHOW UP AT THE SAME TIME THE SARDINES DO?
ANOTHER SHUTOUT FOR THE SARDINE GOALKEEPER!

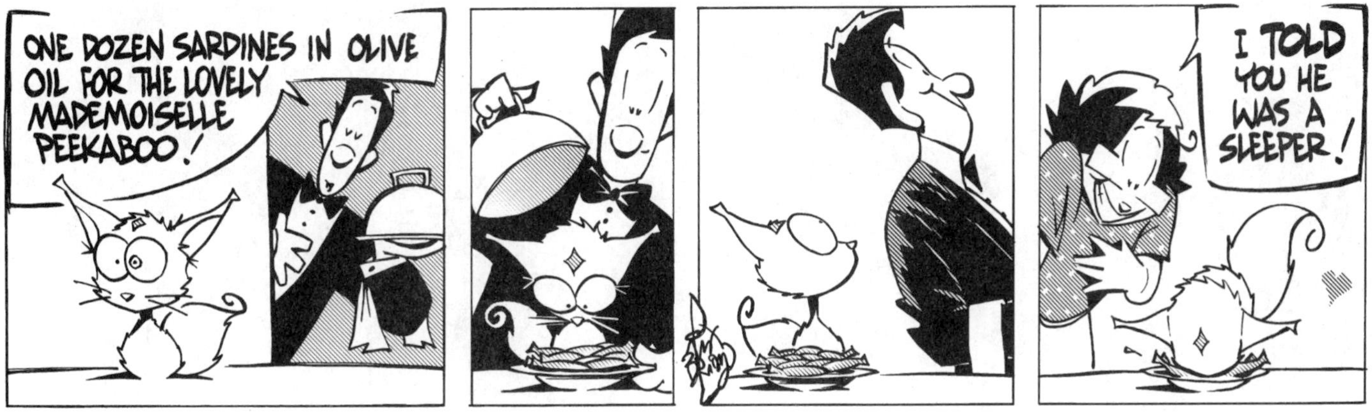
ONE DOZEN SARDINES IN OLIVE OIL FOR THE LOVELY MADEMOISELLE PEEKABOO!
I TOLD YOU HE WAS A SLEEPER!

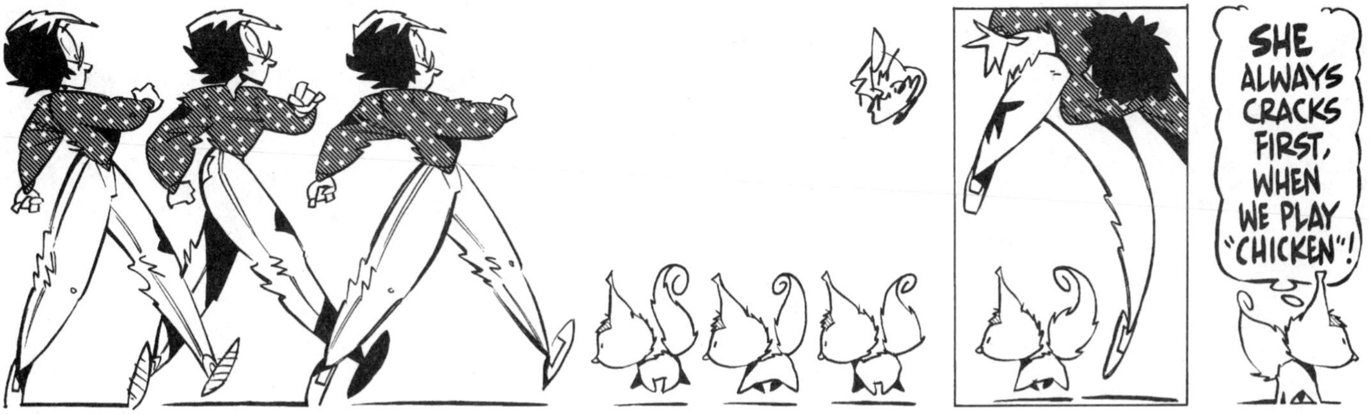
SHE ALWAYS CRACKS FIRST, WHEN WE PLAY "CHICKEN"!

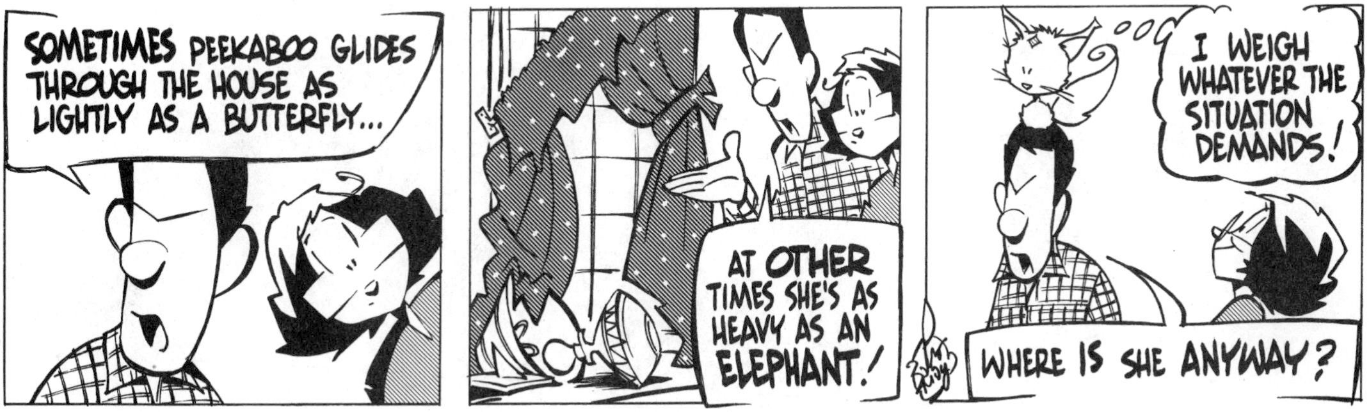
SOMETIMES PEEKABOO GLIDES THROUGH THE HOUSE AS LIGHTLY AS A BUTTERFLY...
AT OTHER TIMES SHE'S AS HEAVY AS AN ELEPHANT!
I WEIGH WHATEVER THE SITUATION DEMANDS!
WHERE IS SHE ANYWAY?

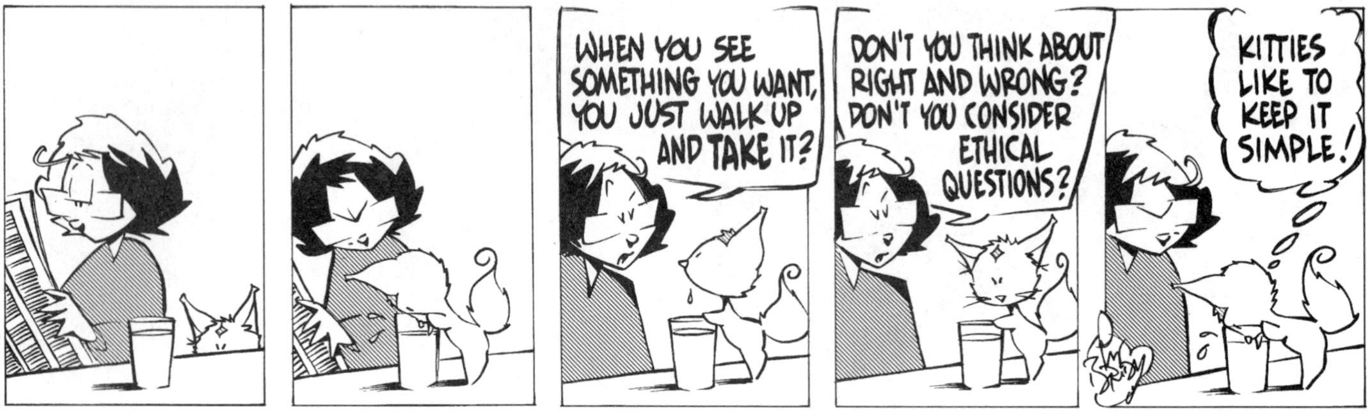
WHEN YOU SEE SOMETHING YOU WANT, YOU JUST WALK UP AND TAKE IT?
DON'T YOU THINK ABOUT RIGHT AND WRONG? DON'T YOU CONSIDER ETHICAL QUESTIONS?
KITTIES LIKE TO KEEP IT SIMPLE!

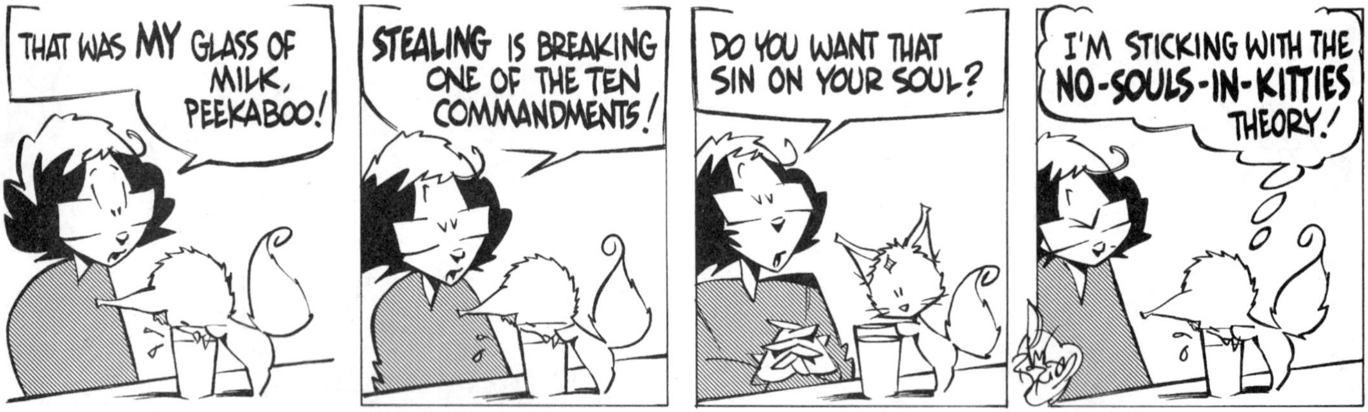
THAT WAS MY GLASS OF MILK, PEEKABOO!
STEALING IS BREAKING ONE OF THE TEN COMMANDMENTS!
DO YOU WANT THAT SIN ON YOUR SOUL?
I'M STICKING WITH THE NO-SOULS-IN-KITTIES THEORY!

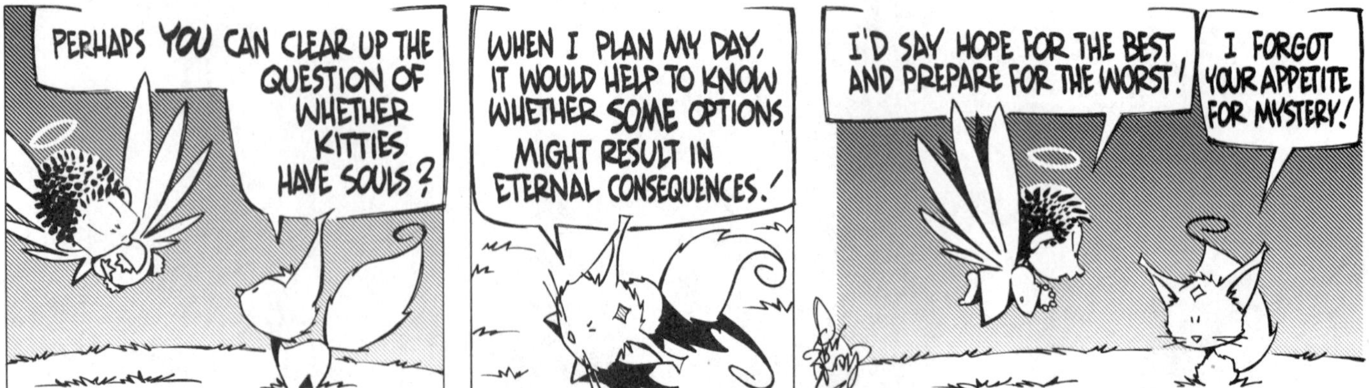
PERHAPS YOU CAN CLEAR UP THE QUESTION OF WHETHER KITTIES HAVE SOULS?
WHEN I PLAN MY DAY, IT WOULD HELP TO KNOW WHETHER SOME OPTIONS MIGHT RESULT IN ETERNAL CONSEQUENCES!
I'D SAY HOPE FOR THE BEST AND PREPARE FOR THE WORST!
I FORGOT YOUR APPETITE FOR MYSTERY!

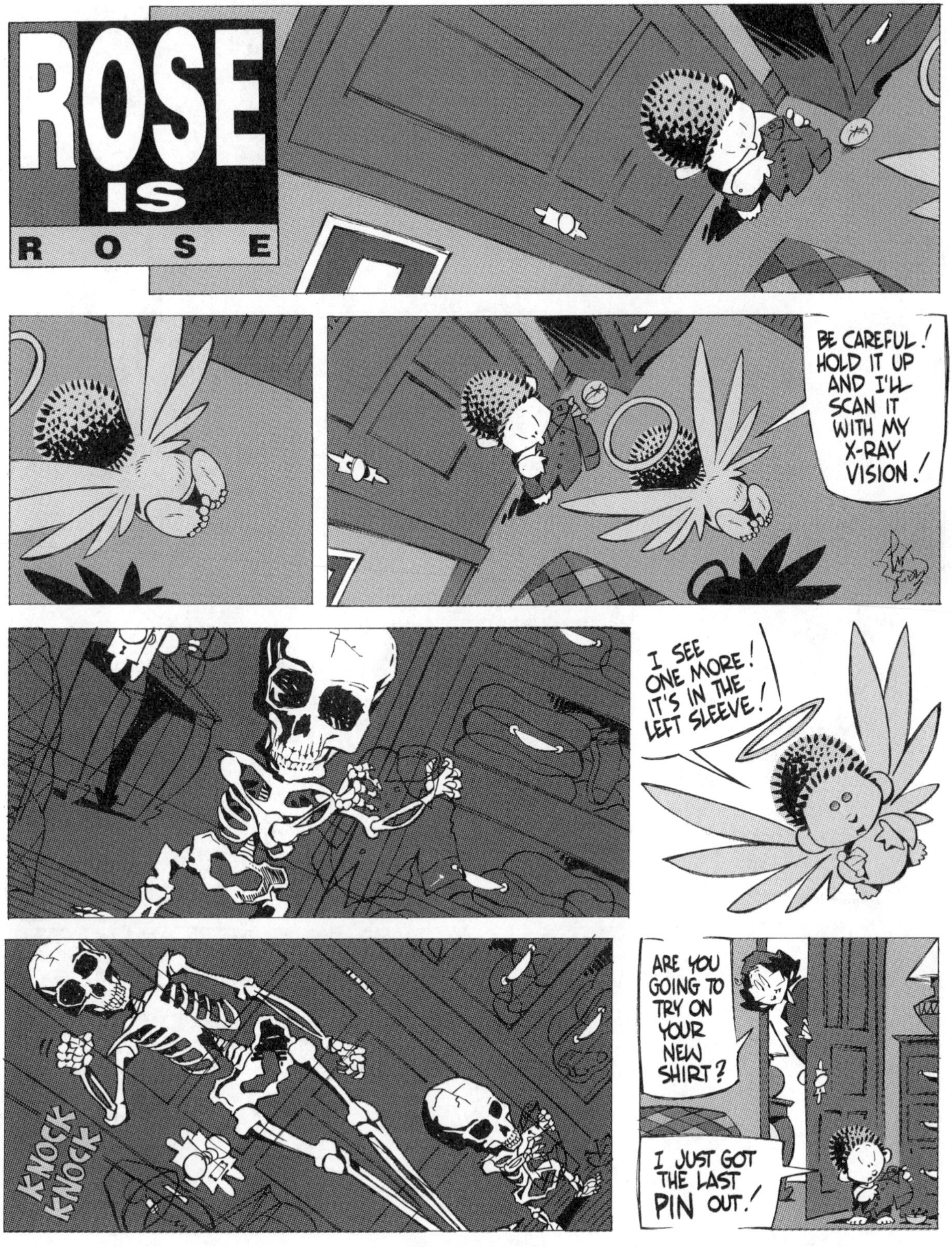

ROSE IS ROSE
BE CAREFUL! HOLD IT UP AND I'LL SCAN IT WITH MY X-RAY VISION!
I SEE ONE MORE! IT'S IN THE LEFT SLEEVE!
KNOCK KNOCK
ARE YOU GOING TO TRY ON YOUR NEW SHIRT?
I JUST GOT THE LAST PIN OUT!

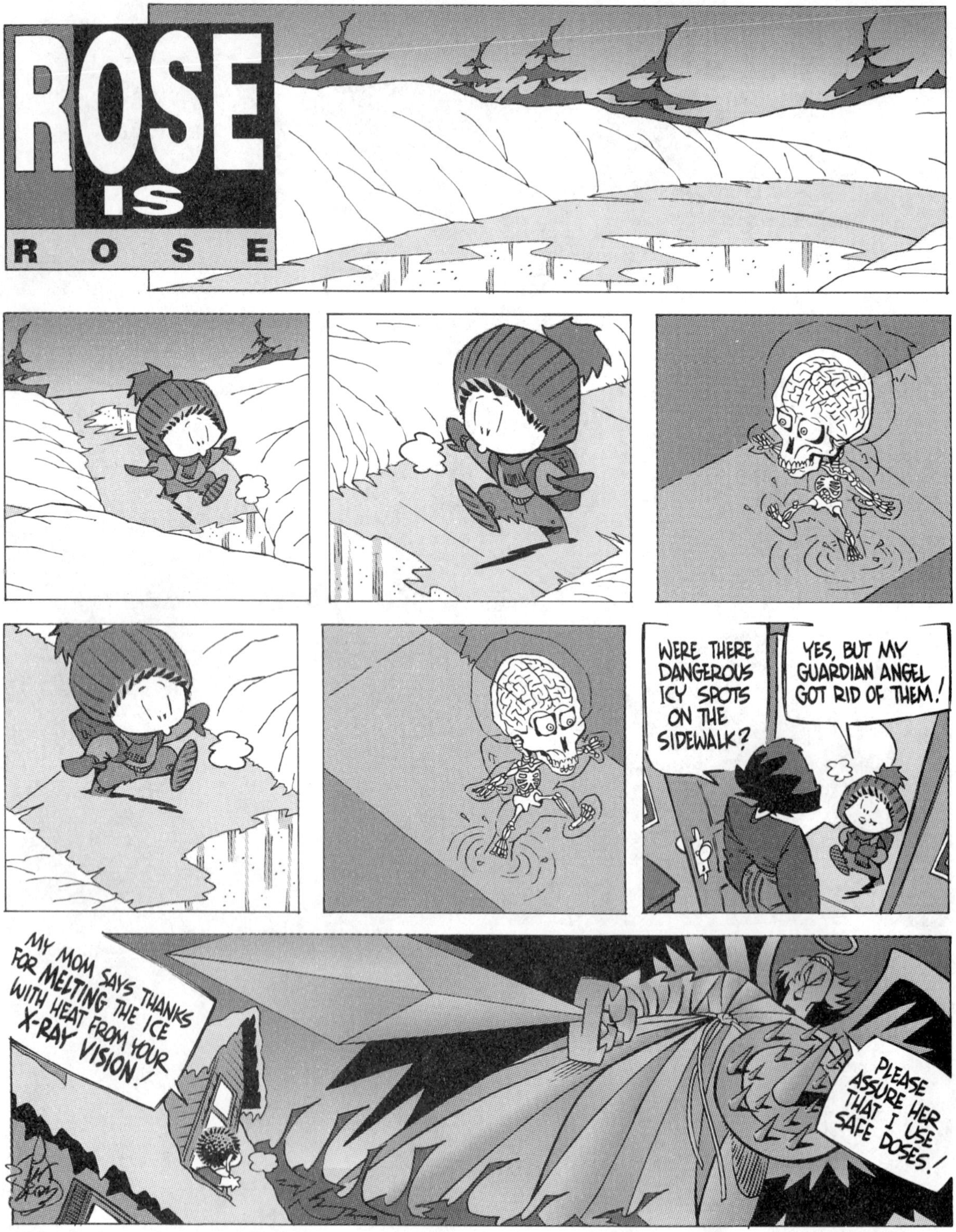
ROSE IS ROSE
WERE THERE DANGEROUS ICY SPOTS ON THE SIDEWALK?
YES, BUT MY GUARDIAN ANGEL GOT RID OF THEM!
MY MOM SAYS THANKS FOR MELTING THE ICE WITH HEAT FROM YOUR X-RAY VISION!
PLEASE ASSURE HER THAT I USE SAFE DOSES!

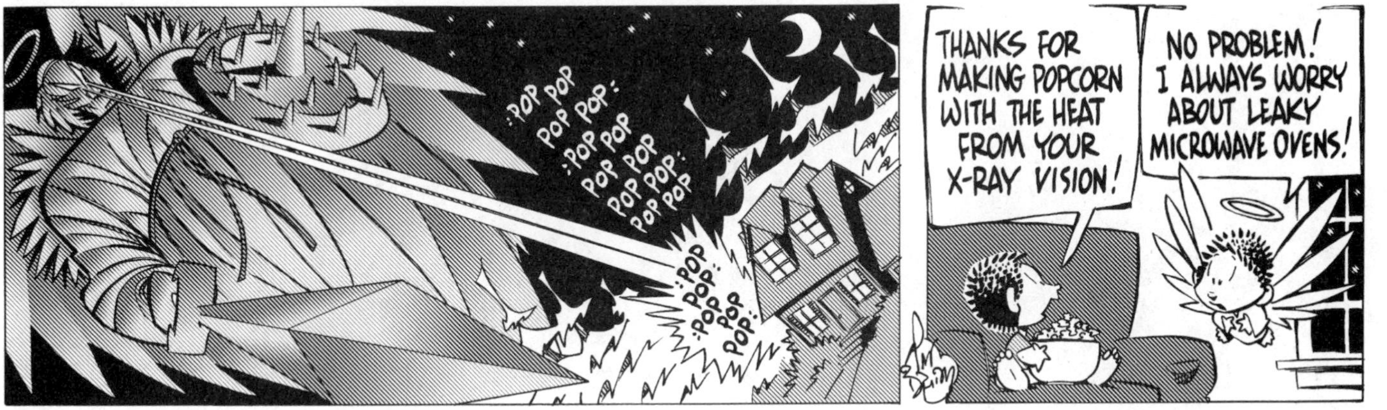
POP POP POP POP POP POP POP POP POP POP POP POP POP
POP POP POP POP POP POP
THANKS FOR MAKING POPCORN WITH THE HEAT FROM YOUR X-RAY VISION!
NO PROBLEM! I ALWAYS WORRY ABOUT LEAKY MICROWAVE OVENS!

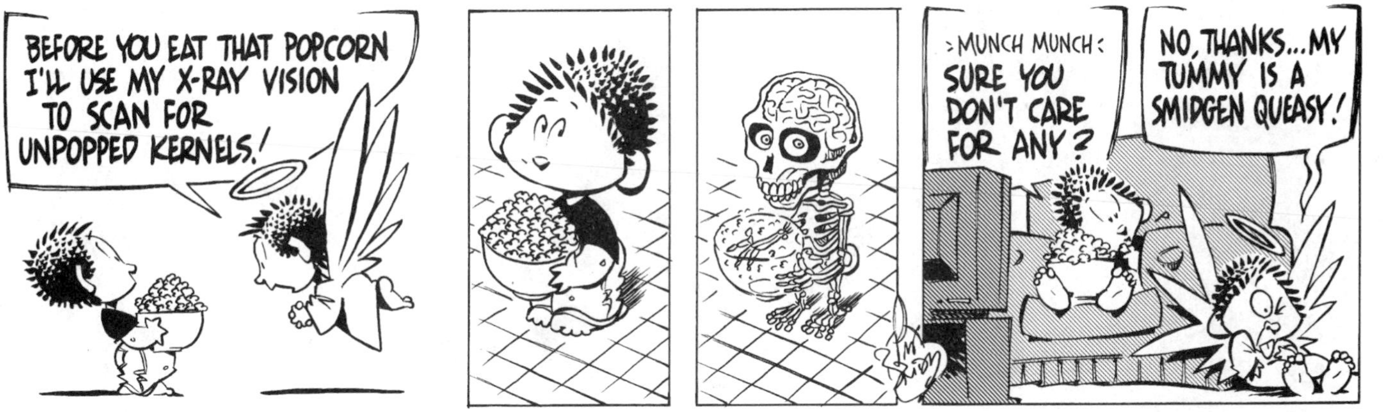
BEFORE YOU EAT THAT POPCORN I'LL USE MY X-RAY VISION TO SCAN FOR UNPOPPED KERNELS!
MUNCH MUNCH
SURE YOU DON'T CARE FOR ANY?
NO, THANKS... MY TUMMY IS A SMIDGEN QUEASY!

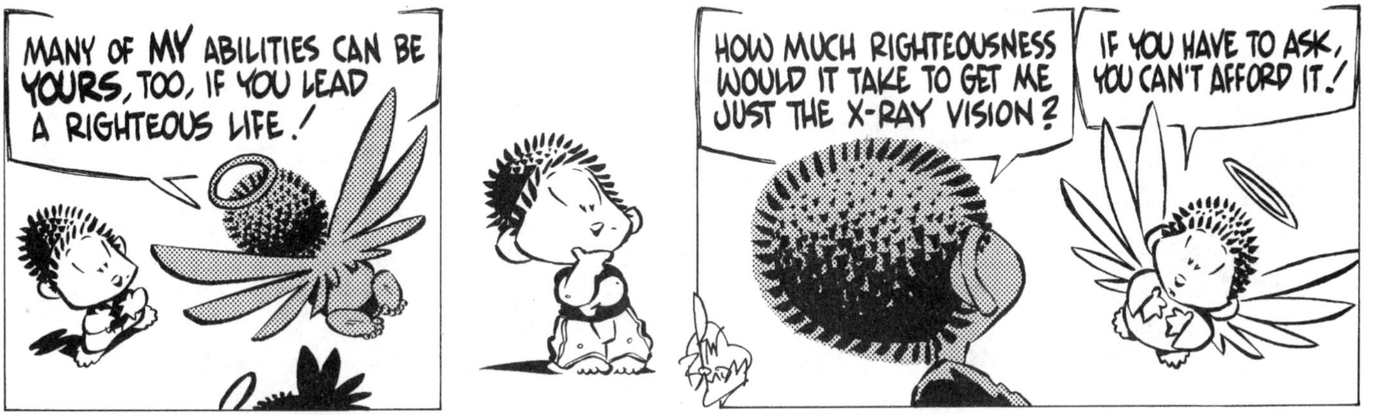
MANY OF MY ABILITIES CAN BE YOURS, TOO, IF YOU LEAD A RIGHTEOUS LIFE!
HOW MUCH RIGHTEOUSNESS WOULD IT TAKE TO GET ME JUST THE X-RAY VISION?
IF YOU HAVE TO ASK, YOU CAN'T AFFORD IT!

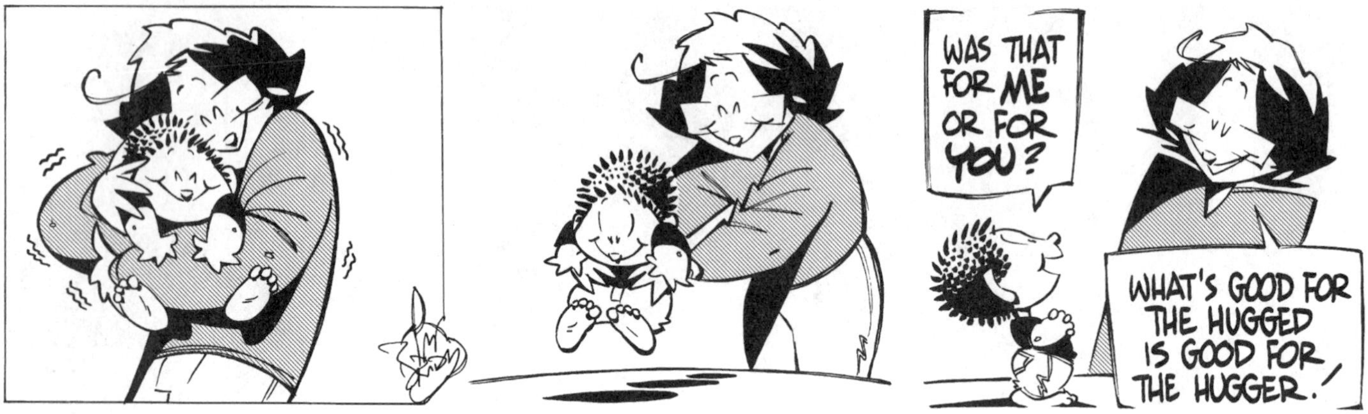
WAS THAT FOR ME OR FOR YOU?
WHAT'S GOOD FOR THE HUGGED IS GOOD FOR THE HUGGER!

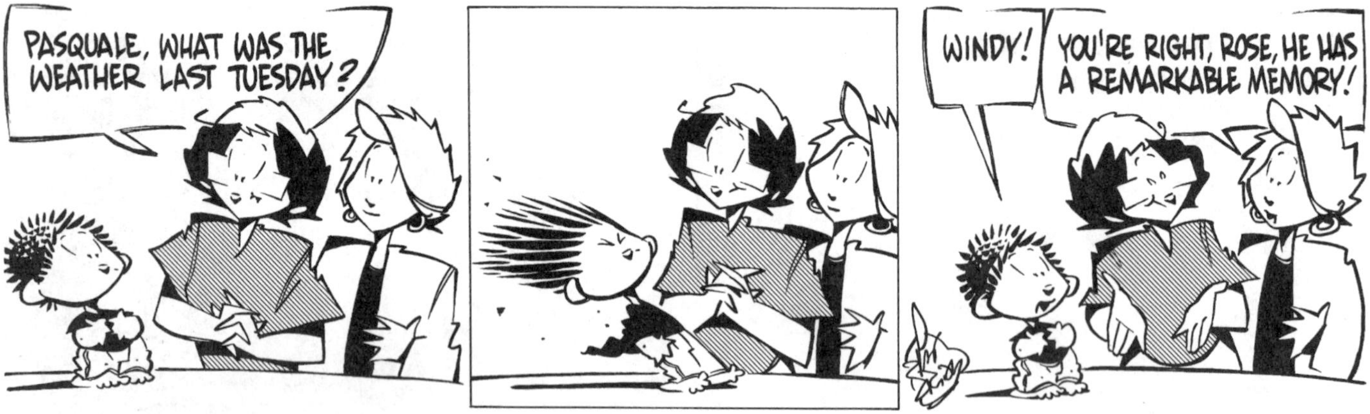
PASQUALE, WHAT WAS THE WEATHER LAST TUESDAY?
WINDY!
YOU'RE RIGHT, ROSE, HE HAS A REMARKABLE MEMORY!

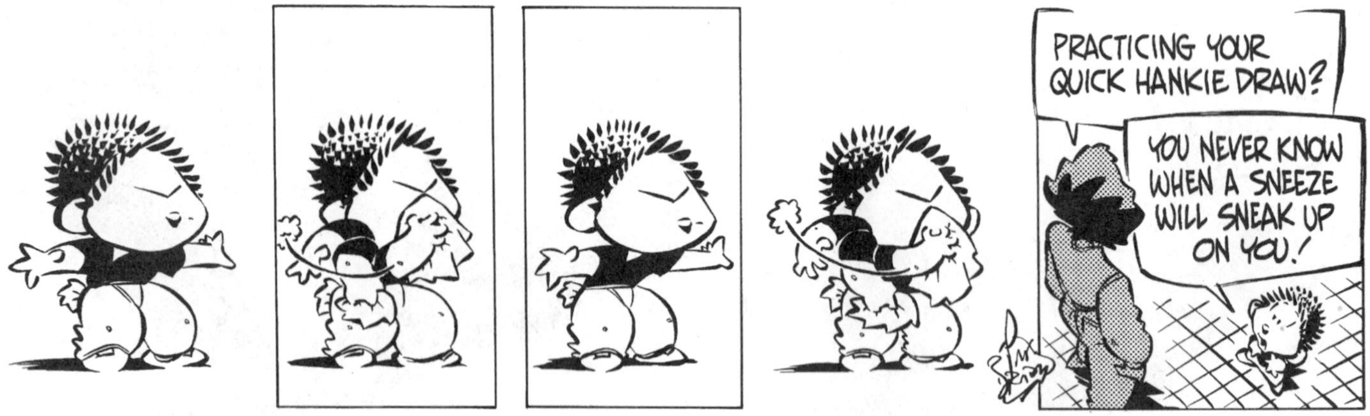
PRACTICING YOUR QUICK HANKIE DRAW?
YOU NEVER KNOW WHEN A SNEEZE WILL SNEAK UP ON YOU!

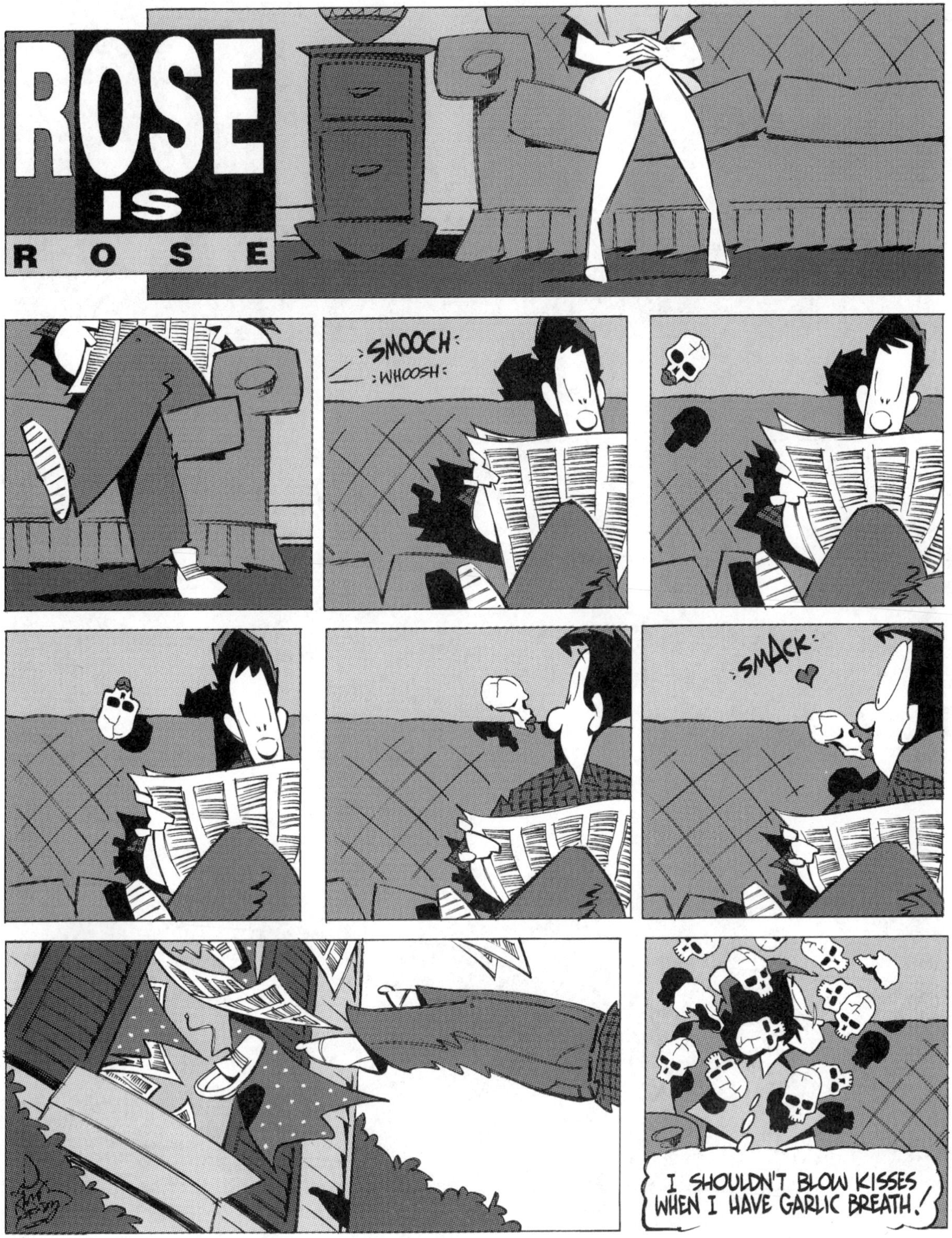
ROSE IS ROSE
SMOOCH
WHOOSH
SMACK
I SHOULDN'T BLOW KISSES WHEN I HAVE GARLIC BREATH!

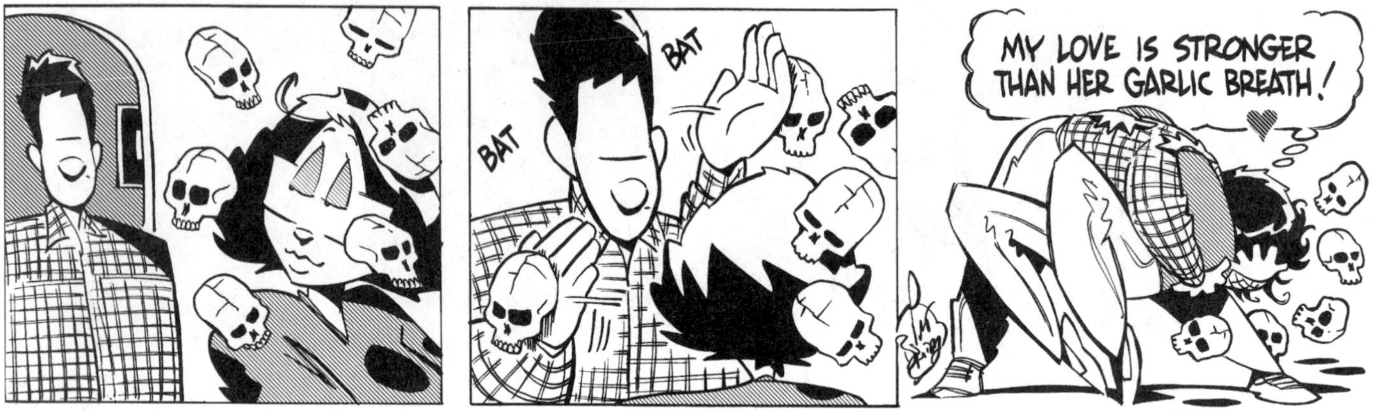
BAT
BAT
MY LOVE IS STRONGER THAN HER GARLIC BREATH!

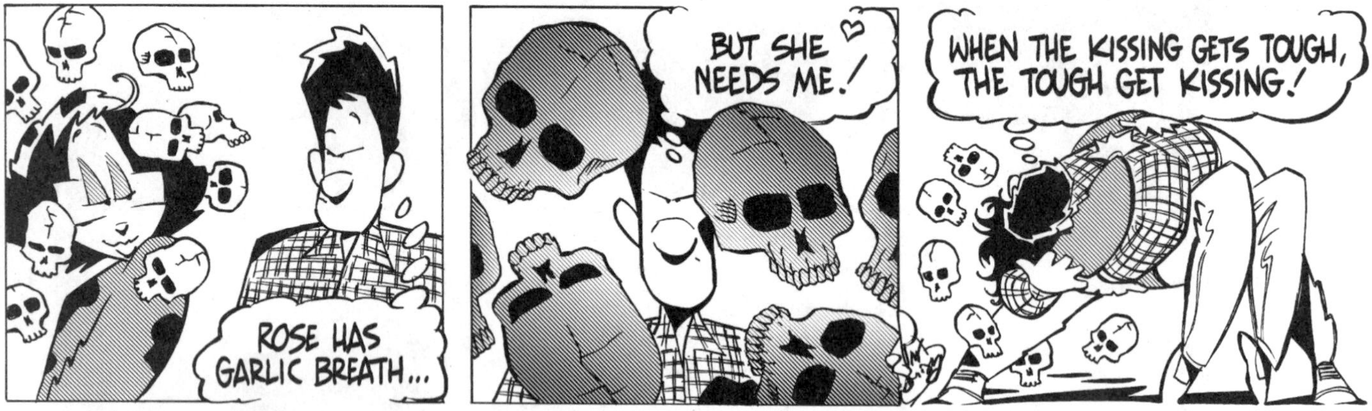
ROSE HAS GARLIC BREATH...
BUT SHE NEEDS ME!
WHEN THE KISSING GETS TOUGH, THE TOUGH GET KISSING!

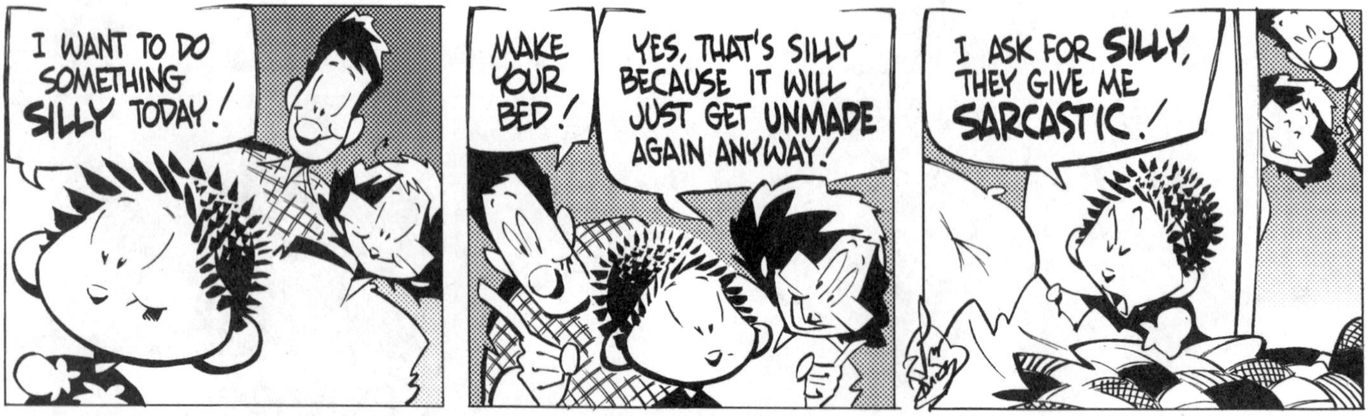
I WANT TO DO SOMETHING **SILLY** TODAY!
MAKE YOUR BED!
YES, THAT'S SILLY BECAUSE IT WILL JUST GET **UNMADE** AGAIN ANYWAY!
I ASK FOR **SILLY**, THEY GIVE ME **SARCASTIC**!

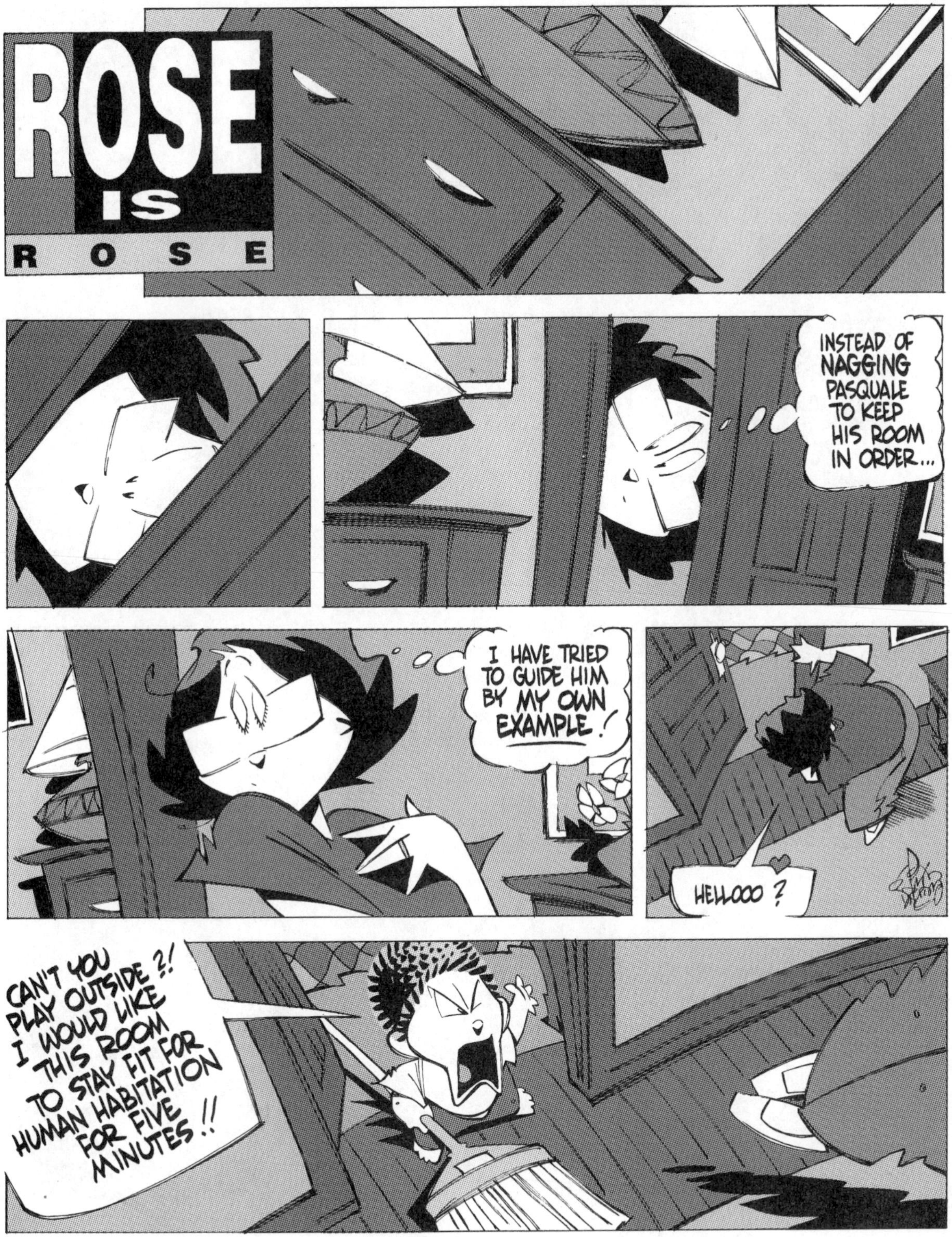
ROSE IS ROSE
INSTEAD OF NAGGING PASQUALE TO KEEP HIS ROOM IN ORDER...
I HAVE TRIED TO GUIDE HIM BY MY OWN EXAMPLE!
HELLOOO?
CAN'T YOU PLAY OUTSIDE?! I WOULD LIKE THIS ROOM TO STAY FIT FOR HUMAN HABITATION FOR FIVE MINUTES!!

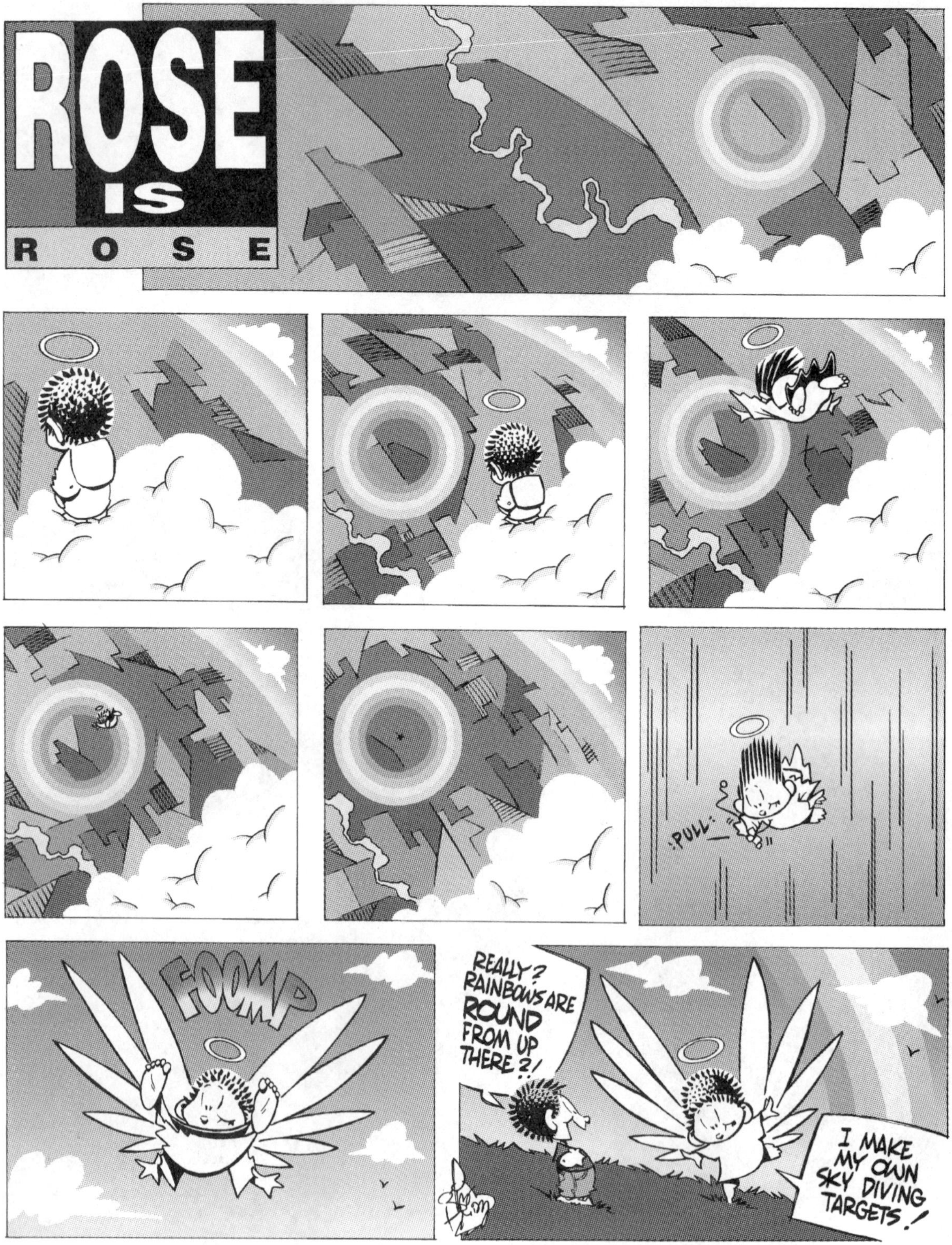
ROSE IS ROSE
:PULL:
FOOMP
REALLY? RAINBOWS ARE ROUND FROM UP THERE?!
I MAKE MY OWN SKY DIVING TARGETS!

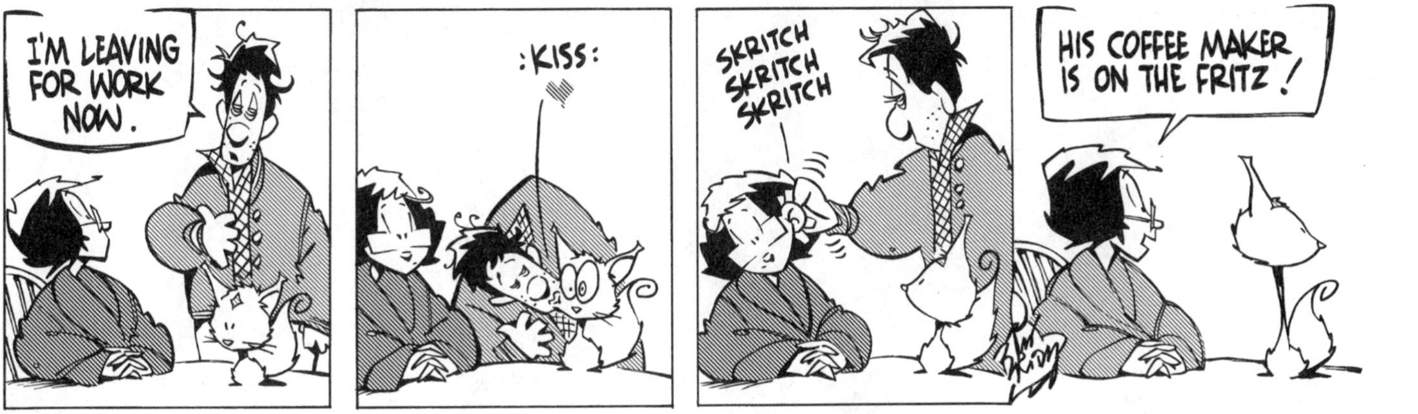
I'M LEAVING FOR WORK NOW.
:KISS:
SKRITCH SKRITCH SKRITCH
HIS COFFEE MAKER IS ON THE FRITZ!

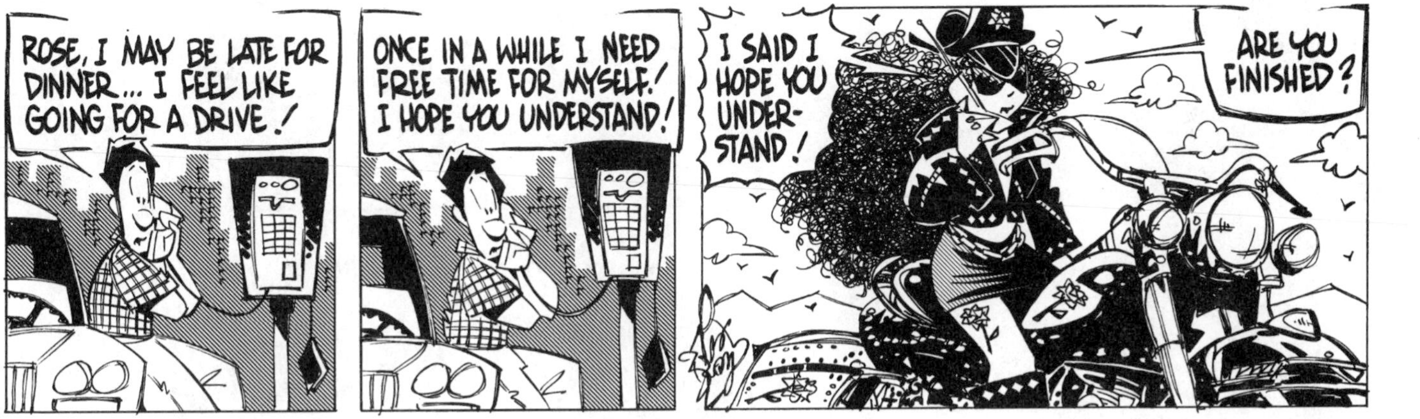
ROSE, I MAY BE LATE FOR DINNER... I FEEL LIKE GOING FOR A DRIVE!
ONCE IN A WHILE I NEED FREE TIME FOR MYSELF! I HOPE YOU UNDERSTAND!
I SAID I HOPE YOU UNDER-STAND!
ARE YOU FINISHED?

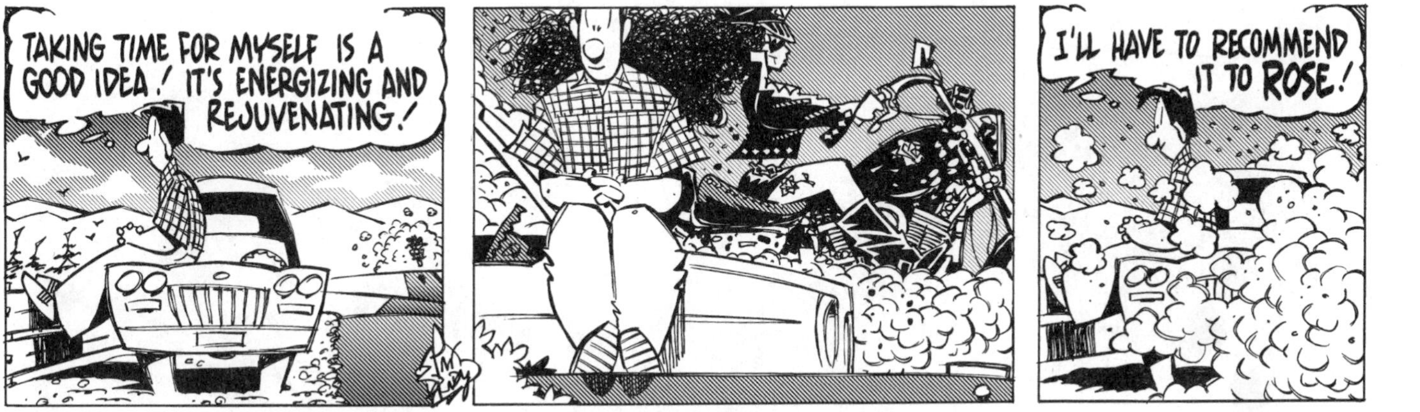
TAKING TIME FOR MYSELF IS A GOOD IDEA! IT'S ENERGIZING AND REJUVENATING!
I'LL HAVE TO RECOMMEND IT TO ROSE!

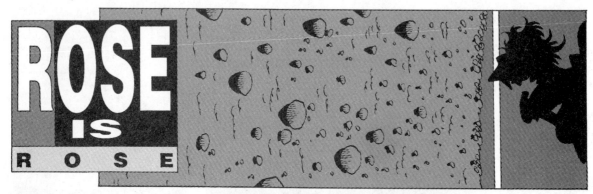

I DON'T NEED A MENU! I KNOW EXACTLY WHAT I WANT!

I'LL HAVE GREEN TEA AND A SMALL GARDEN SALAD SPRINKLED WITH LEMON JUICE!

A DECISION TO TAKE GOOD CARE OF YOURSELF DEMANDS GRIT!

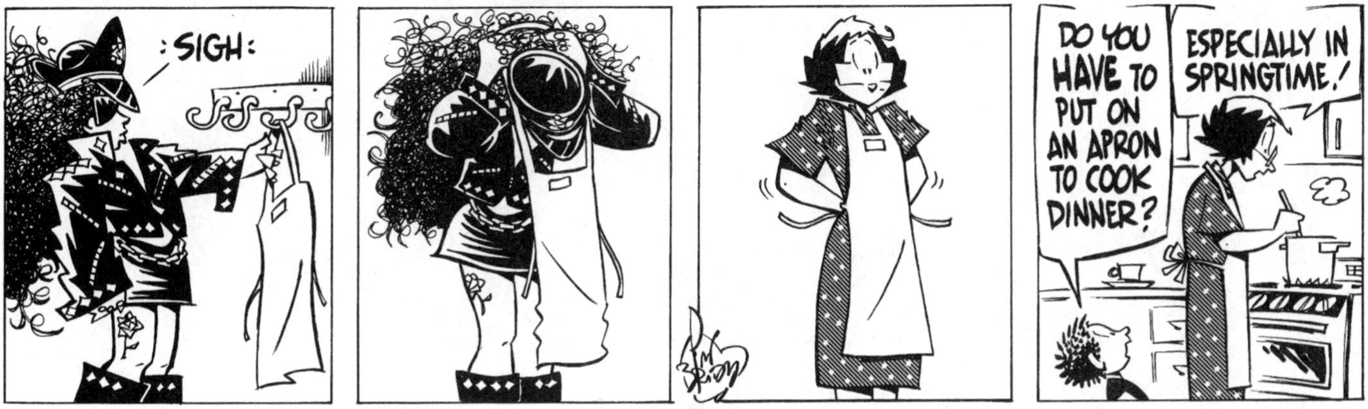
:SIGH:
DO YOU HAVE TO PUT ON AN APRON TO COOK DINNER?
ESPECIALLY IN SPRINGTIME!

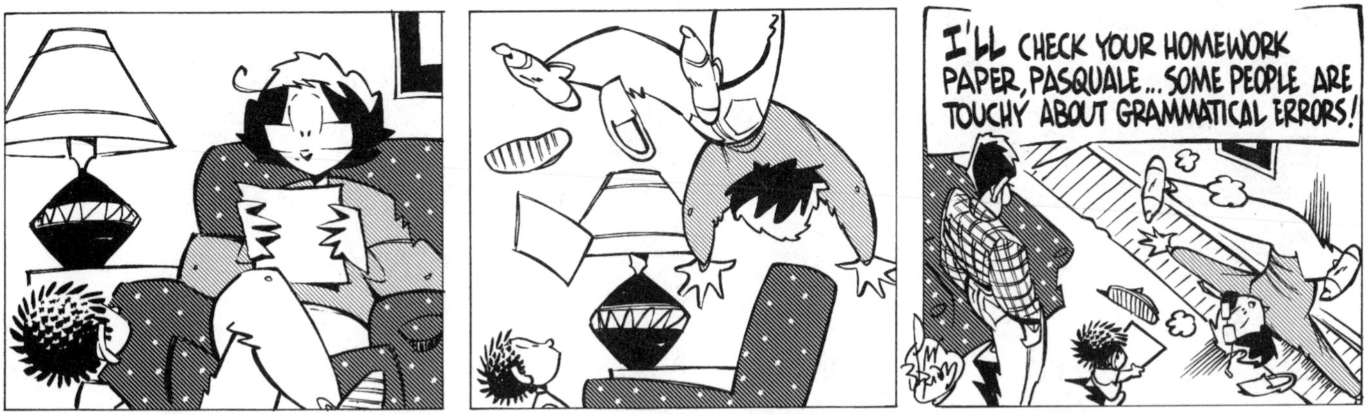
I'LL CHECK YOUR HOMEWORK PAPER, PASQUALE... SOME PEOPLE ARE TOUCHY ABOUT GRAMMATICAL ERRORS!

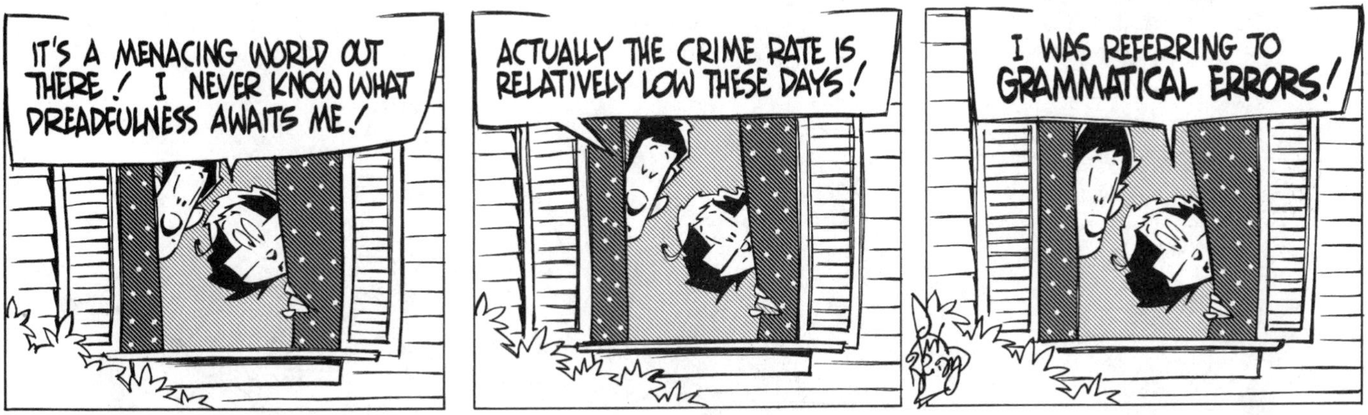
IT'S A MENACING WORLD OUT THERE! I NEVER KNOW WHAT DREADFULNESS AWAITS ME!
ACTUALLY THE CRIME RATE IS RELATIVELY LOW THESE DAYS!
I WAS REFERRING TO GRAMMATICAL ERRORS!

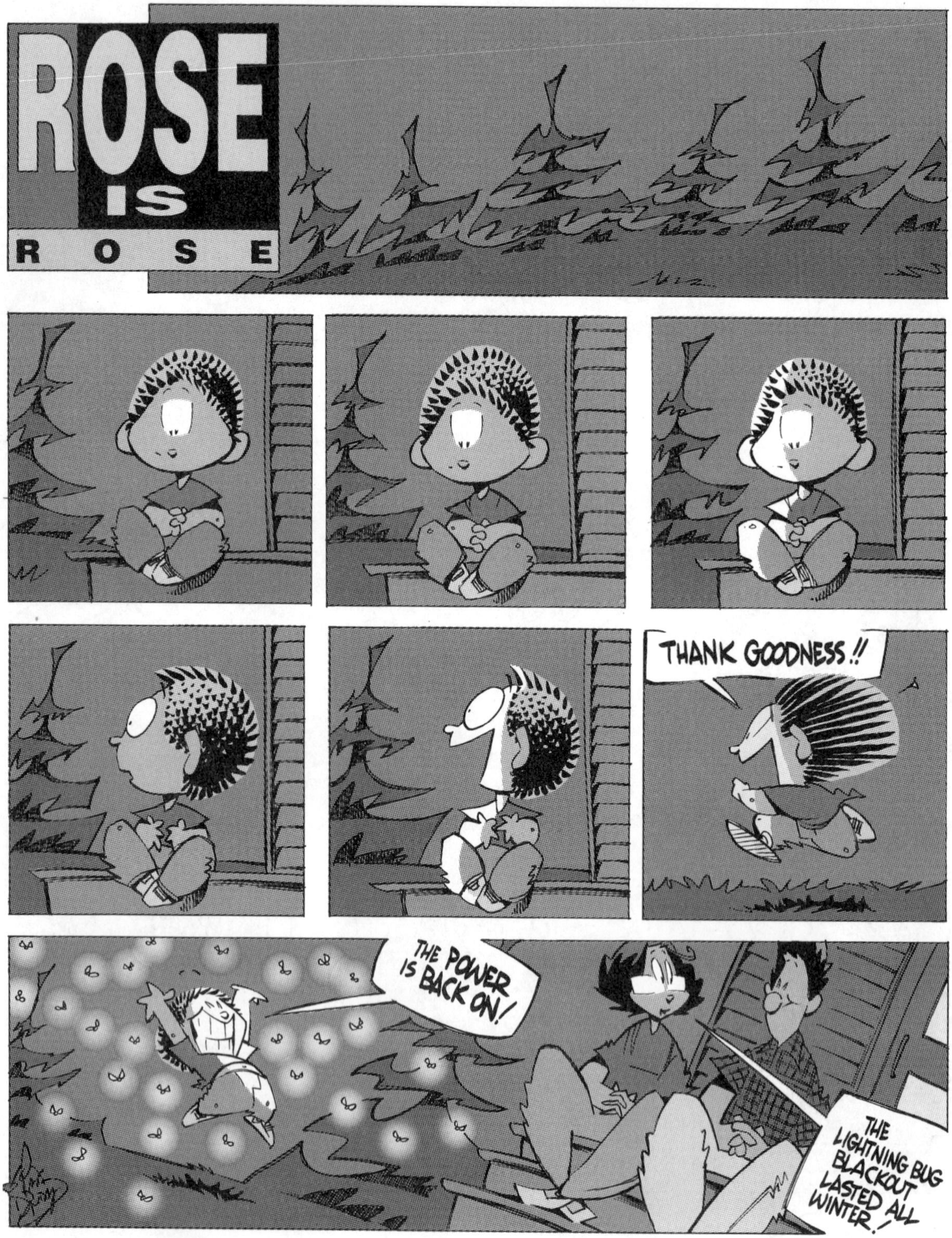
ROSE IS ROSE
THANK GOODNESS!!
THE POWER IS BACK ON!
THE LIGHTNING BUG BLACKOUT LASTED ALL WINTER!

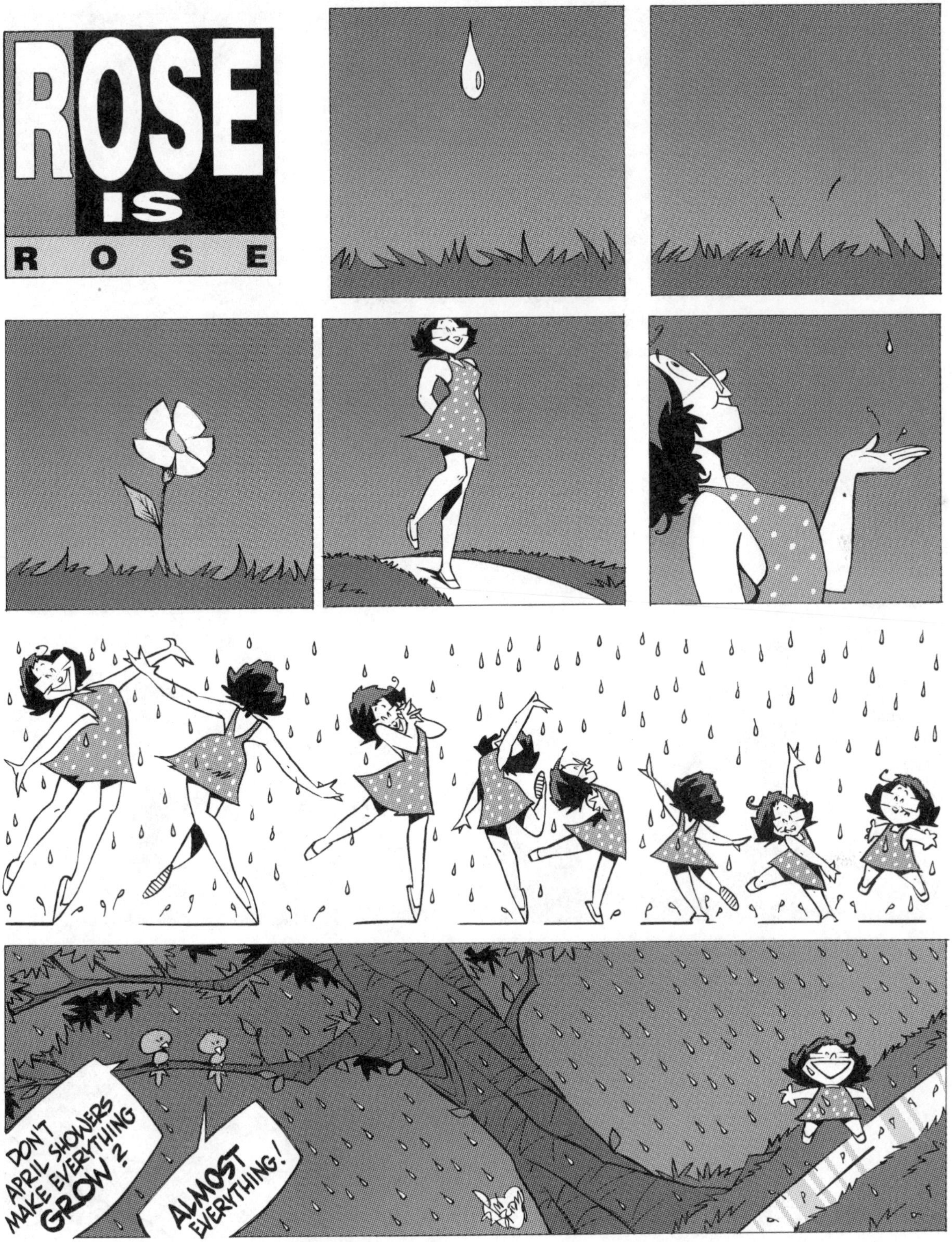
ROSE IS ROSE
DON'T APRIL SHOWERS MAKE EVERYTHING GROW?
ALMOST EVERYTHING!

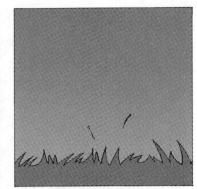

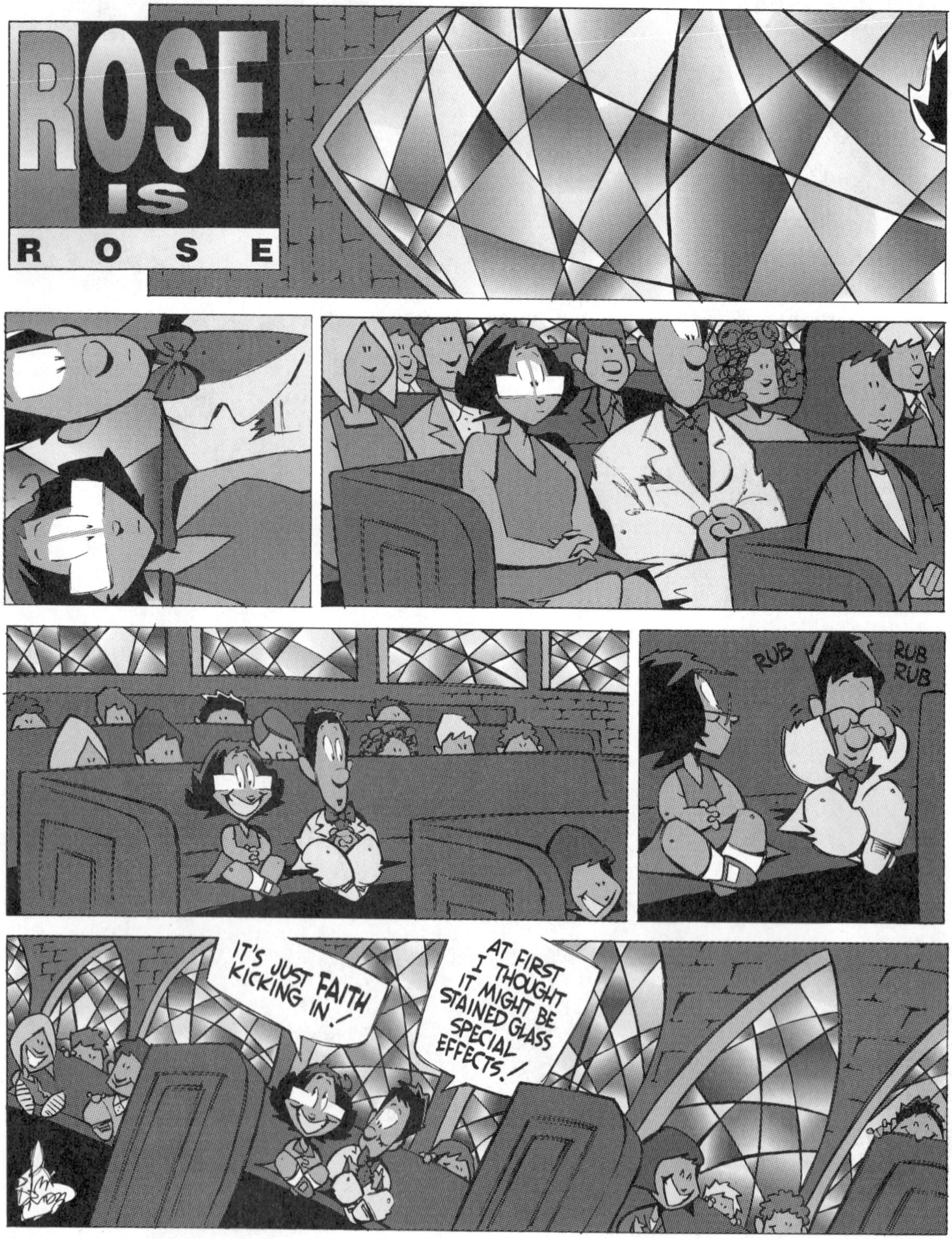
ROSE IS ROSE
RUB
RUB RUB
IT'S JUST FAITH KICKING IN!
AT FIRST I THOUGHT IT MIGHT BE STAINED GLASS SPECIAL EFFECTS!

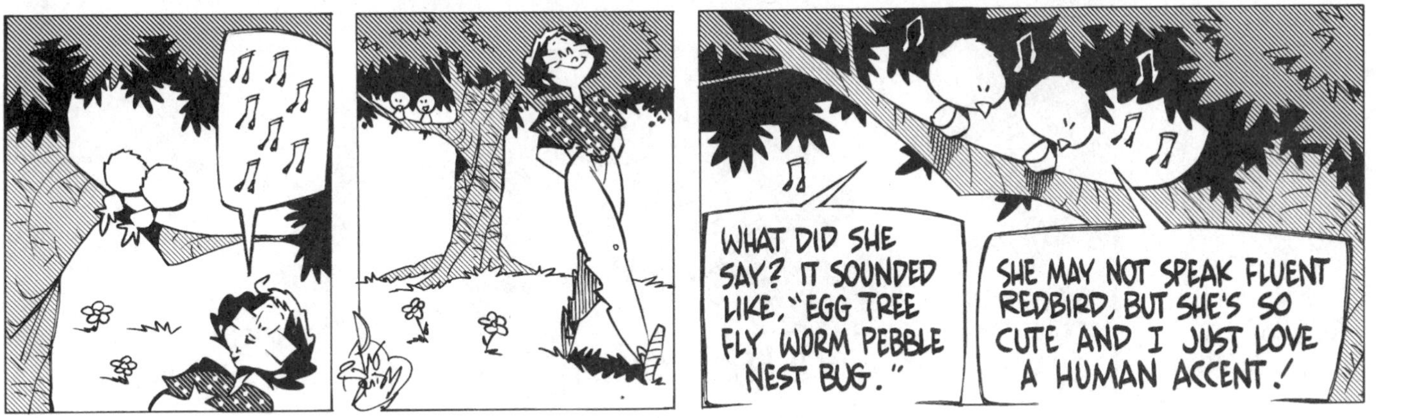
WHAT DID SHE SAY? IT SOUNDED LIKE, "EGG TREE FLY WORM PEBBLE NEST BUG."
SHE MAY NOT SPEAK FLUENT REDBIRD, BUT SHE'S SO CUTE AND I JUST LOVE A HUMAN ACCENT!

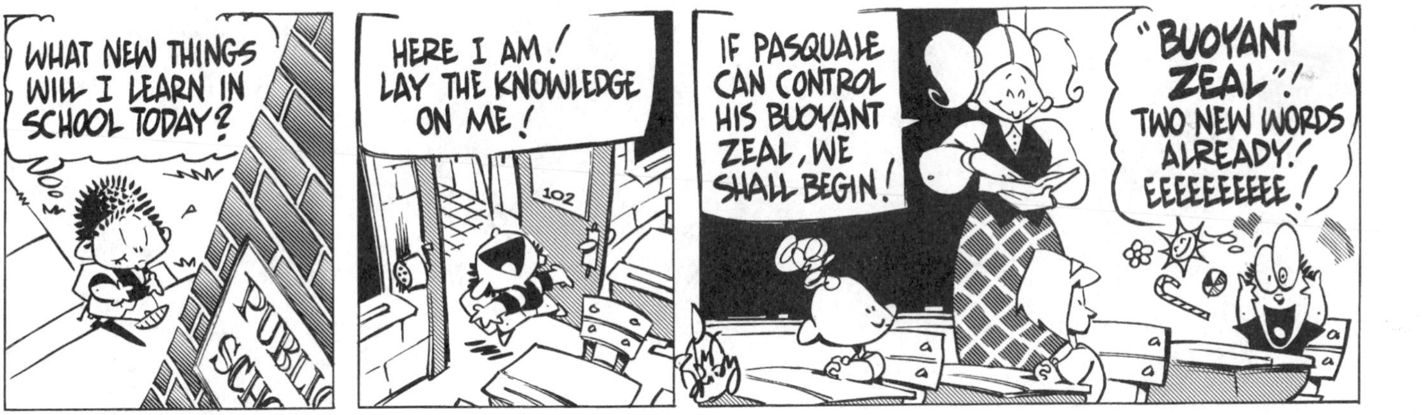
WHAT NEW THINGS WILL I LEARN IN SCHOOL TODAY?
PUBLIC SCH
HERE I AM! LAY THE KNOWLEDGE ON ME!
102
IF PASQUALE CAN CONTROL HIS BUOYANT ZEAL, WE SHALL BEGIN!
"BUOYANT ZEAL"! TWO NEW WORDS ALREADY! EEEEEEEEEE!

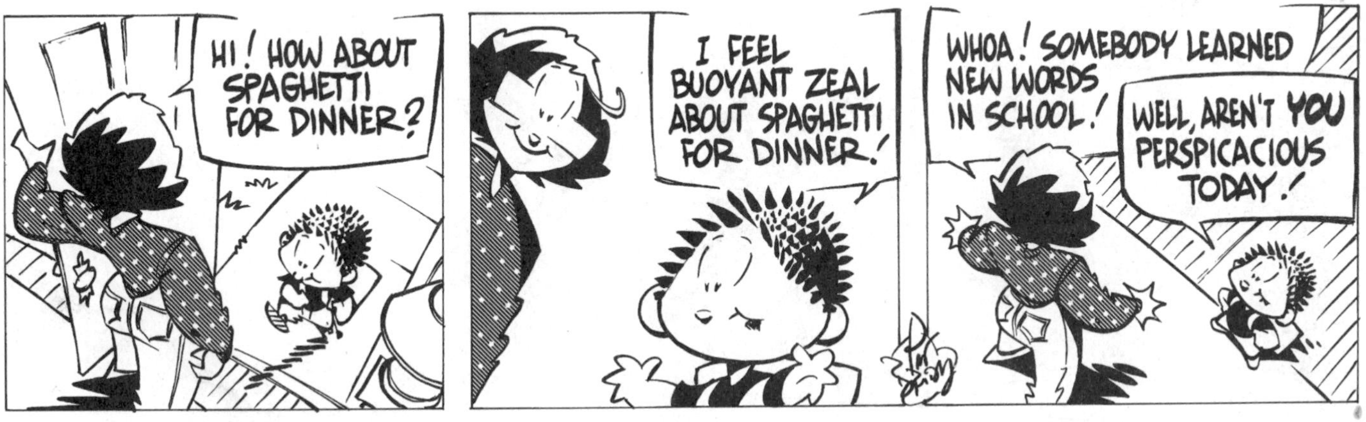
HI! HOW ABOUT SPAGHETTI FOR DINNER?
I FEEL BUOYANT ZEAL ABOUT SPAGHETTI FOR DINNER!
WHOA! SOMEBODY LEARNED NEW WORDS IN SCHOOL!
WELL, AREN'T YOU PERSPICACIOUS TODAY!

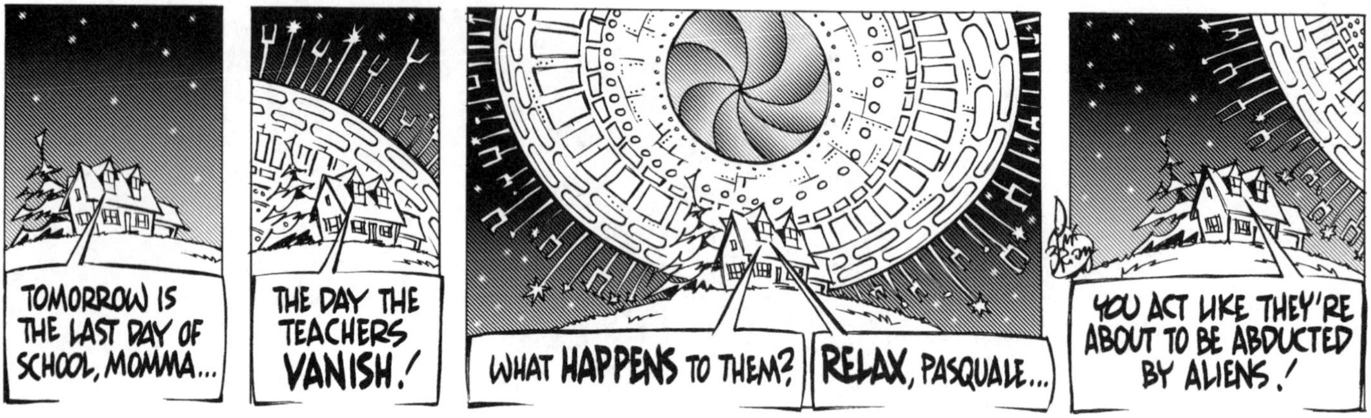
TOMORROW IS THE LAST DAY OF SCHOOL, MOMMA...
THE DAY THE TEACHERS VANISH!
WHAT HAPPENS TO THEM?
RELAX, PASQUALE...
YOU ACT LIKE THEY'RE ABOUT TO BE ABDUCTED BY ALIENS!

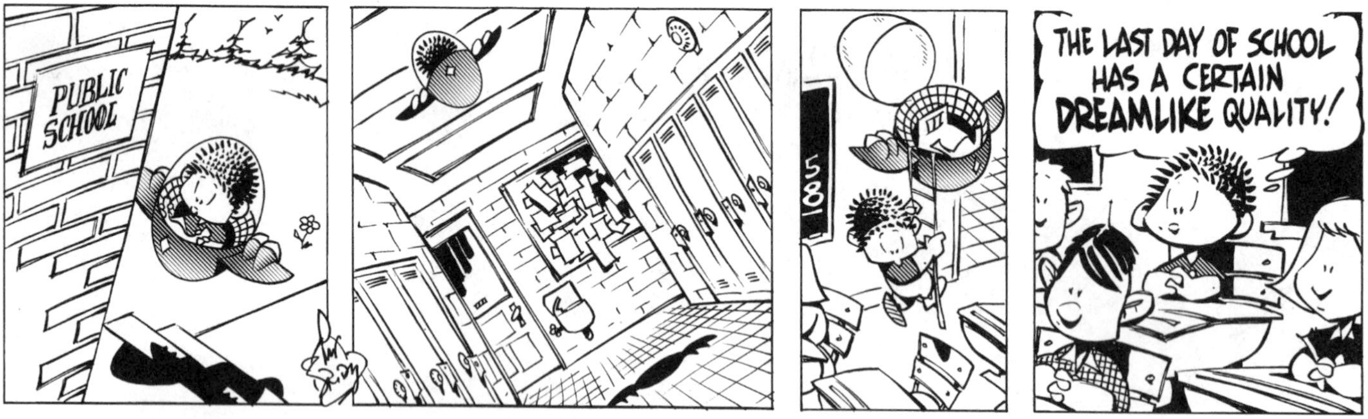
PUBLIC SCHOOL
THE LAST DAY OF SCHOOL HAS A CERTAIN DREAMLIKE QUALITY!

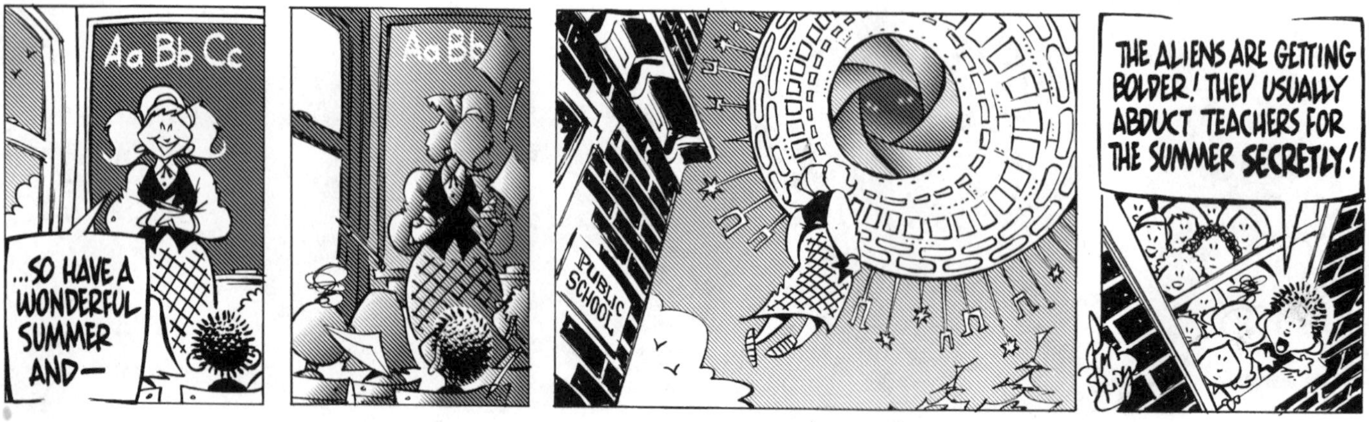
Aa Bb Cc
...SO HAVE A WONDERFUL SUMMER AND—
PUBLIC SCHOOL
THE ALIENS ARE GETTING BOLDER! THEY USUALLY ABDUCT TEACHERS FOR THE SUMMER SECRETLY!

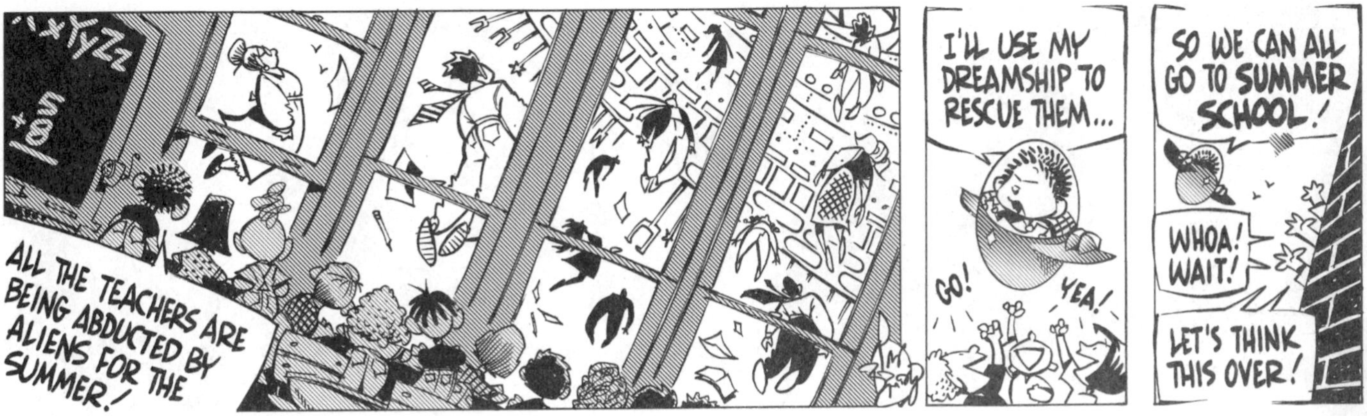
ALL THE TEACHERS ARE BEING ABDUCTED BY ALIENS FOR THE SUMMER!
I'LL USE MY DREAMSHIP TO RESCUE THEM...
GO!
YEA!
SO WE CAN ALL GO TO SUMMER SCHOOL!
WHOA! WAIT!
LET'S THINK THIS OVER!

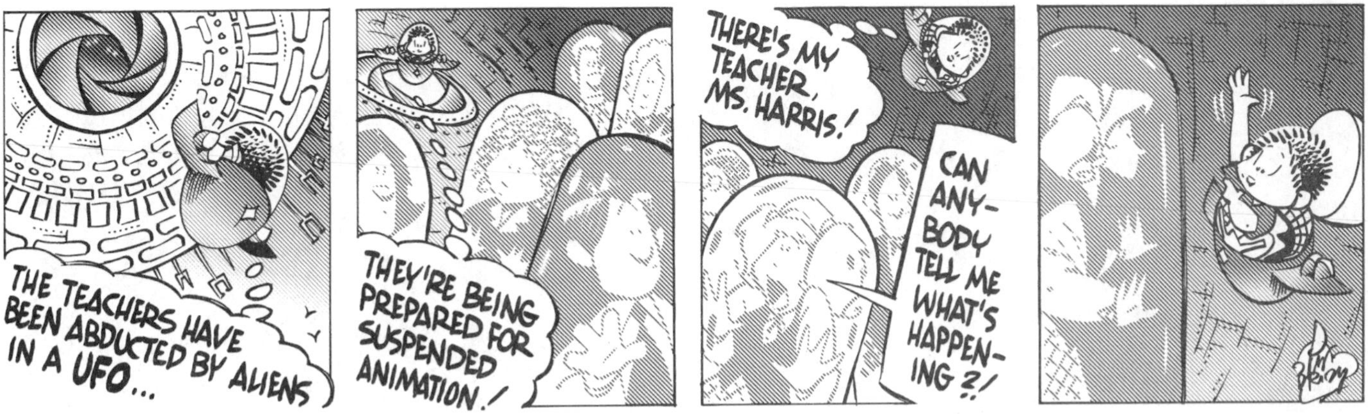
THE TEACHERS HAVE BEEN ABDUCTED BY ALIENS IN A UFO...
THEY'RE BEING PREPARED FOR SUSPENDED ANIMATION!
THERE'S MY TEACHER, MS. HARRIS!
CAN ANY-BODY TELL ME WHAT'S HAPPEN-ING?!

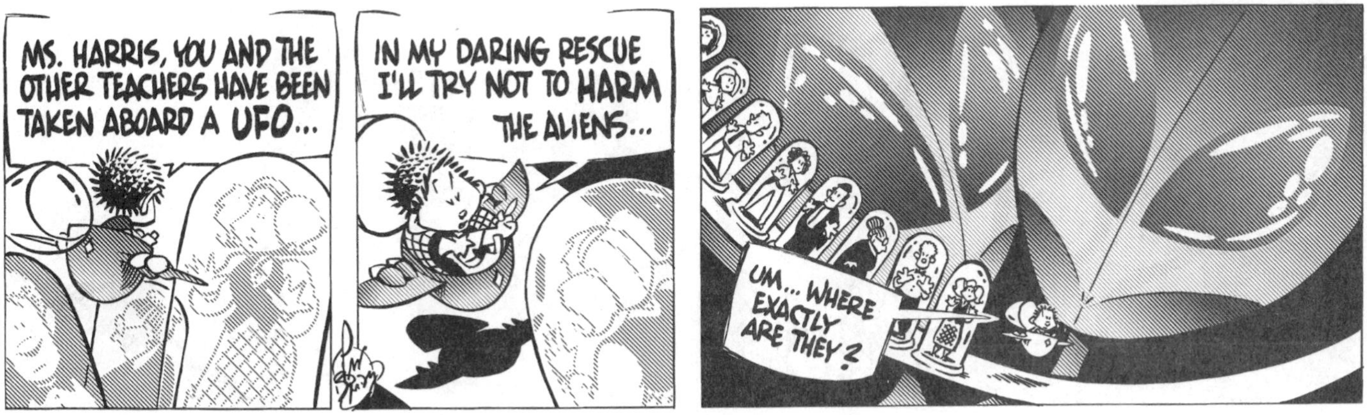
MS. HARRIS, YOU AND THE OTHER TEACHERS HAVE BEEN TAKEN ABOARD A UFO...
IN MY DARING RESCUE I'LL TRY NOT TO HARM THE ALIENS...
UM... WHERE EXACTLY ARE THEY?

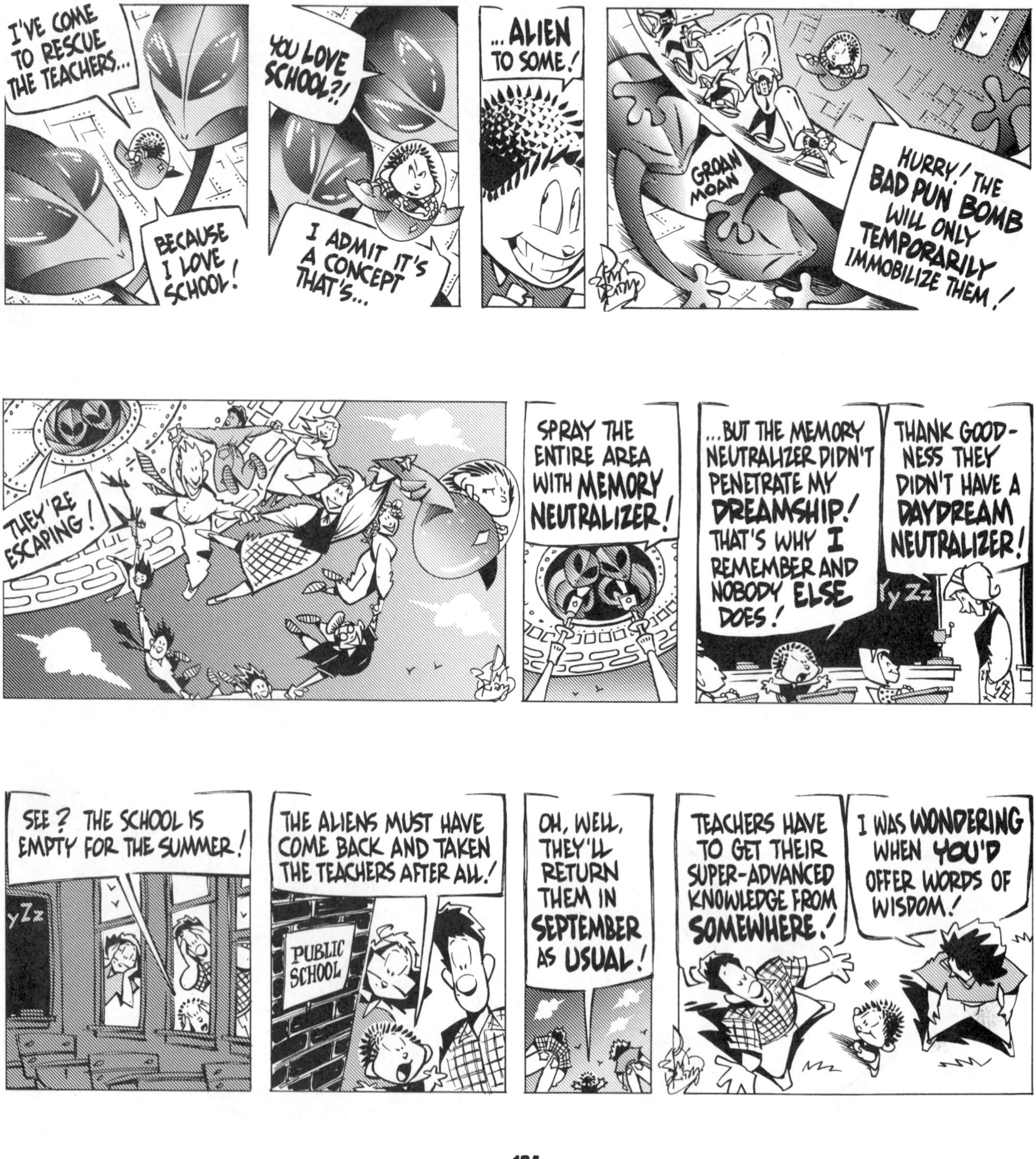
I'VE COME TO RESCUE THE TEACHERS...
YOU LOVE SCHOOL?!
BECAUSE I LOVE SCHOOL!
I ADMIT IT'S A CONCEPT THAT'S...
...ALIEN TO SOME!
GROAN MOAN
HURRY! THE BAD PUN BOMB WILL ONLY TEMPORARILY IMMOBILIZE THEM!
THEY'RE ESCAPING!
SPRAY THE ENTIRE AREA WITH MEMORY NEUTRALIZER!
...BUT THE MEMORY NEUTRALIZER DIDN'T PENETRATE MY DREAMSHIP! THAT'S WHY I REMEMBER AND NOBODY ELSE DOES!
THANK GOODNESS THEY DIDN'T HAVE A DAYDREAM NEUTRALIZER!
SEE? THE SCHOOL IS EMPTY FOR THE SUMMER!
THE ALIENS MUST HAVE COME BACK AND TAKEN THE TEACHERS AFTER ALL!
PUBLIC SCHOOL
OH, WELL, THEY'LL RETURN THEM IN SEPTEMBER AS USUAL!
TEACHERS HAVE TO GET THEIR SUPER-ADVANCED KNOWLEDGE FROM SOMEWHERE!
I WAS WONDERING WHEN YOU'D OFFER WORDS OF WISDOM!

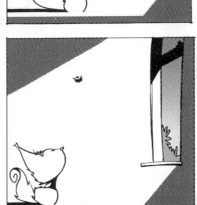

IS IT TRUE THAT KITTENS CAN SEE SPIRITS?

YES, BUT THEY WON'T PLAY WITH ME UNLESS I DO MY DUST SPECK IMPERSONATION!

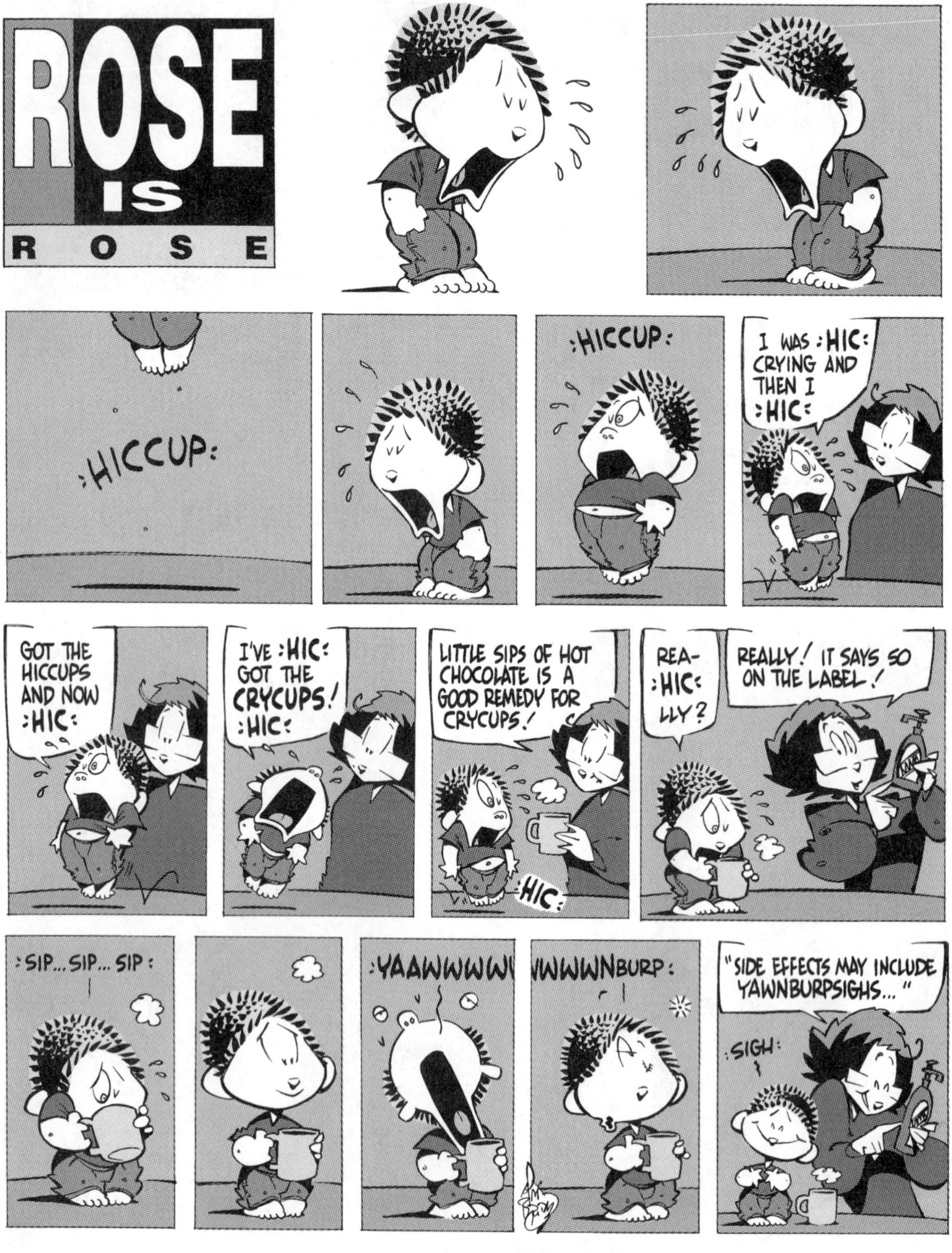
ROSE IS ROSE
:HICCUP:
:HICCUP:
I WAS :HIC: CRYING AND THEN I :HIC:
GOT THE HICCUPS AND NOW :HIC:
I'VE :HIC: GOT THE CRYCUPS! :HIC:
LITTLE SIPS OF HOT CHOCOLATE IS A GOOD REMEDY FOR CRYCUPS!
:HIC:
REA- :HIC: LLY?
REALLY! IT SAYS SO ON THE LABEL!
:SIP... SIP... SIP:
:YAAWWWWWWWWWNBURP:
"SIDE EFFECTS MAY INCLUDE YAWNBURPSIGHS..."
:SIGH:

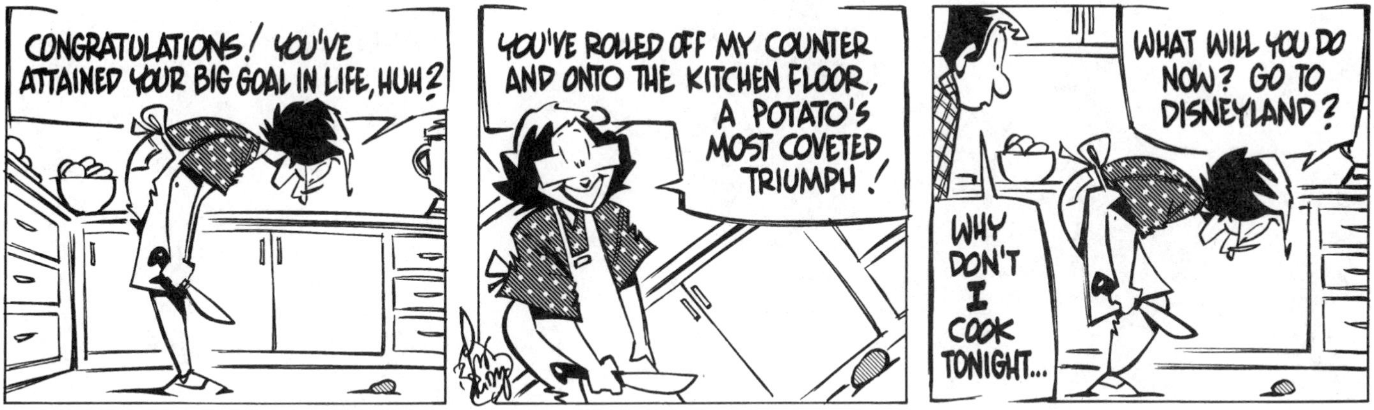
CONGRATULATIONS! YOU'VE ATTAINED YOUR BIG GOAL IN LIFE, HUH?
YOU'VE ROLLED OFF MY COUNTER AND ONTO THE KITCHEN FLOOR, A POTATO'S MOST COVETED TRIUMPH!
WHAT WILL YOU DO NOW? GO TO DISNEYLAND?
WHY DON'T I COOK TONIGHT...

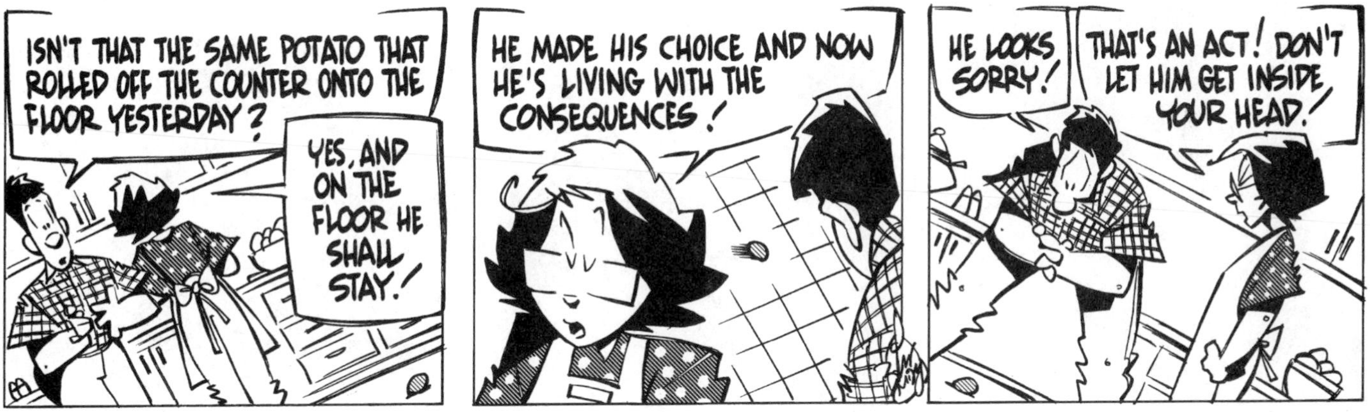
ISN'T THAT THE SAME POTATO THAT ROLLED OFF THE COUNTER ONTO THE FLOOR YESTERDAY?
YES, AND ON THE FLOOR HE SHALL STAY!
HE MADE HIS CHOICE AND NOW HE'S LIVING WITH THE CONSEQUENCES!
HE LOOKS SORRY!
THAT'S AN ACT! DON'T LET HIM GET INSIDE YOUR HEAD!

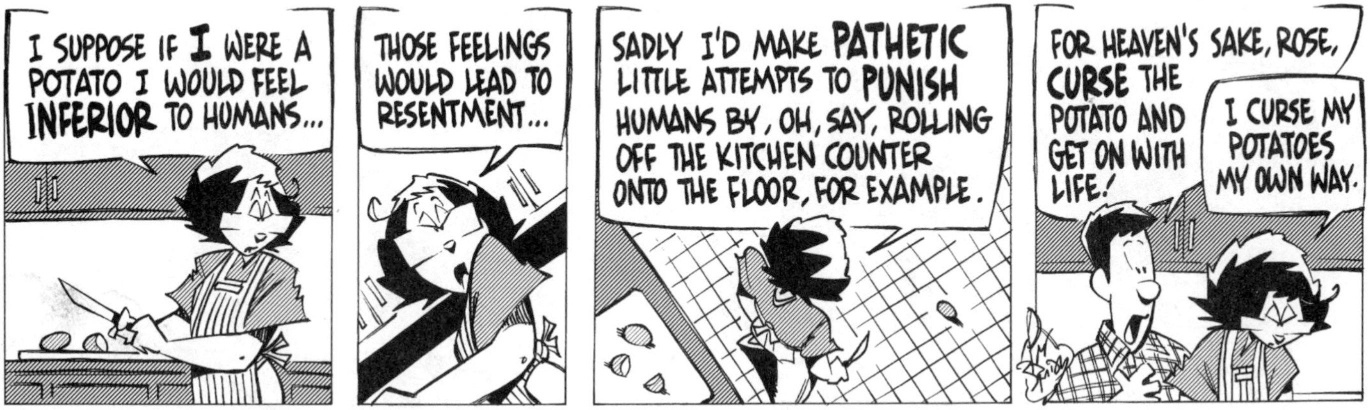
I SUPPOSE IF I WERE A POTATO I WOULD FEEL INFERIOR TO HUMANS...
THOSE FEELINGS WOULD LEAD TO RESENTMENT...
SADLY I'D MAKE PATHETIC LITTLE ATTEMPTS TO PUNISH HUMANS BY, OH, SAY, ROLLING OFF THE KITCHEN COUNTER ONTO THE FLOOR, FOR EXAMPLE.
FOR HEAVEN'S SAKE, ROSE, CURSE THE POTATO AND GET ON WITH LIFE!
I CURSE MY POTATOES MY OWN WAY.

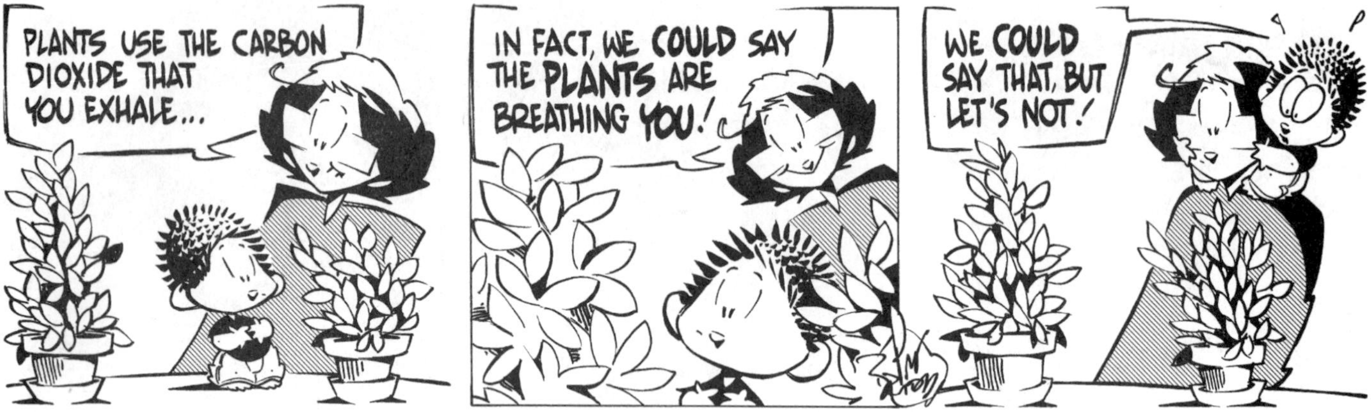
PLANTS USE THE CARBON DIOXIDE THAT YOU EXHALE...
IN FACT, WE COULD SAY THE PLANTS ARE BREATHING YOU!
WE COULD SAY THAT, BUT LET'S NOT!

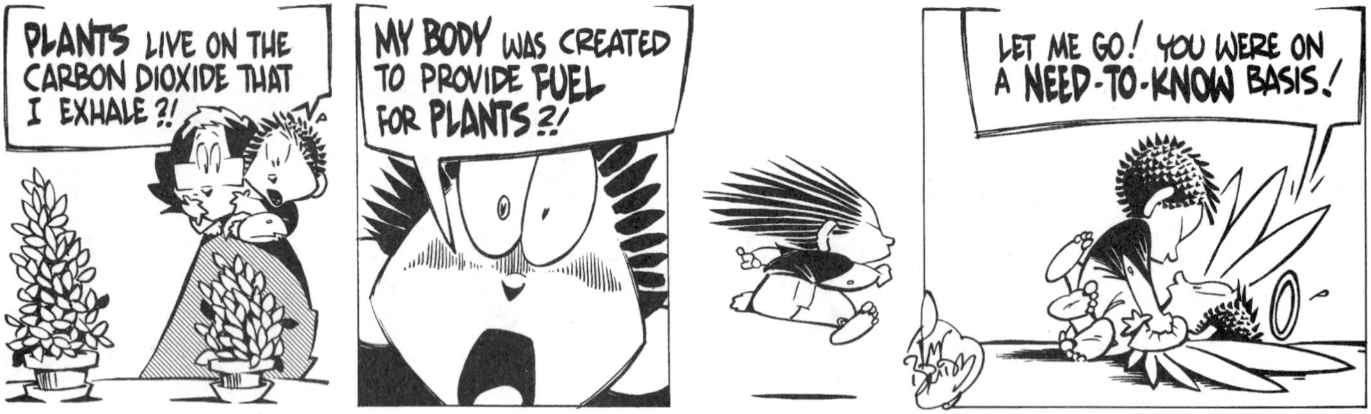
PLANTS LIVE ON THE CARBON DIOXIDE THAT I EXHALE ?!
MY BODY WAS CREATED TO PROVIDE FUEL FOR PLANTS ?!
LET ME GO! YOU WERE ON A NEED-TO-KNOW BASIS!

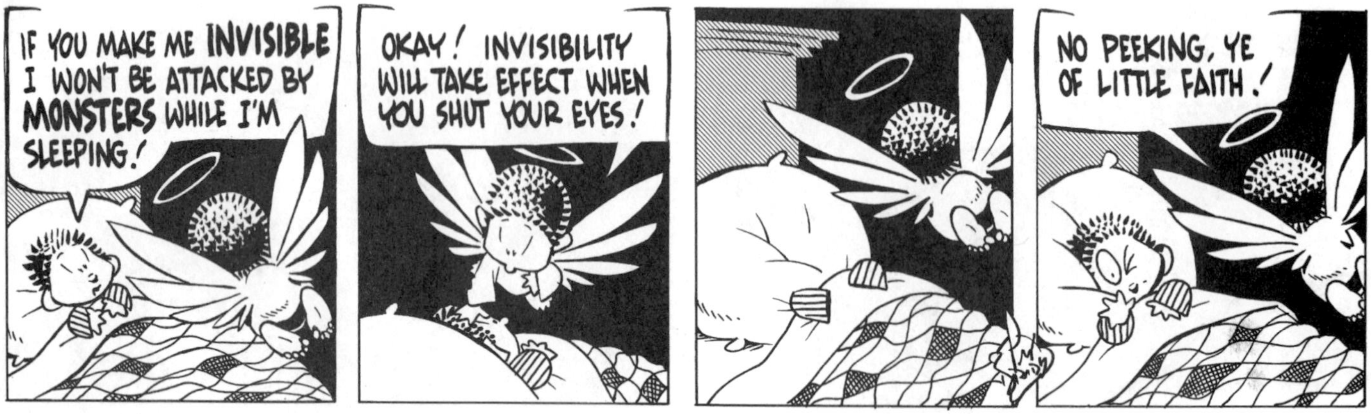
IF YOU MAKE ME INVISIBLE I WON'T BE ATTACKED BY MONSTERS WHILE I'M SLEEPING!
OKAY! INVISIBILITY WILL TAKE EFFECT WHEN YOU SHUT YOUR EYES!
NO PEEKING, YE OF LITTLE FAITH!

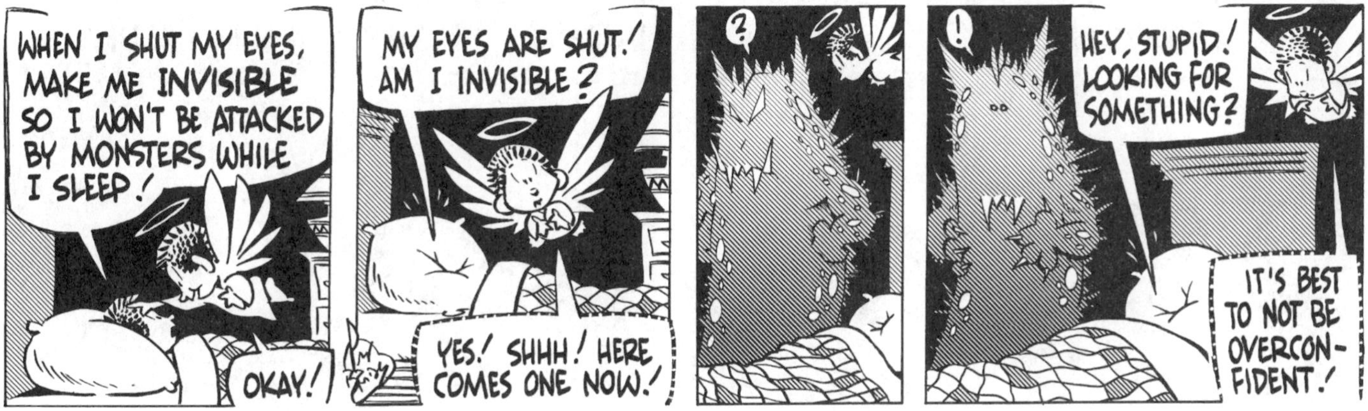
WHEN I SHUT MY EYES, MAKE ME INVISIBLE SO I WON'T BE ATTACKED BY MONSTERS WHILE I SLEEP!
OKAY!
MY EYES ARE SHUT! AM I INVISIBLE?
YES! SHHH! HERE COMES ONE NOW!
?
!
HEY, STUPID! LOOKING FOR SOMETHING?
IT'S BEST TO NOT BE OVERCON-FIDENT!

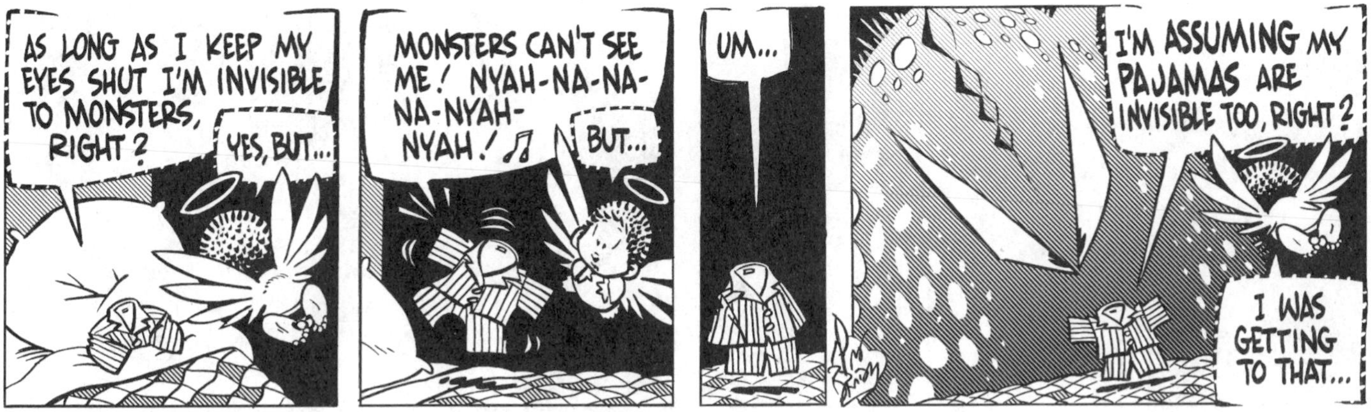
AS LONG AS I KEEP MY EYES SHUT I'M INVISIBLE TO MONSTERS, RIGHT?
YES, BUT...
MONSTERS CAN'T SEE ME! NYAH-NA-NA-NA-NYAH-NYAH!
BUT...
UM...
I'M ASSUMING MY PAJAMAS ARE INVISIBLE TOO, RIGHT?
I WAS GETTING TO THAT...

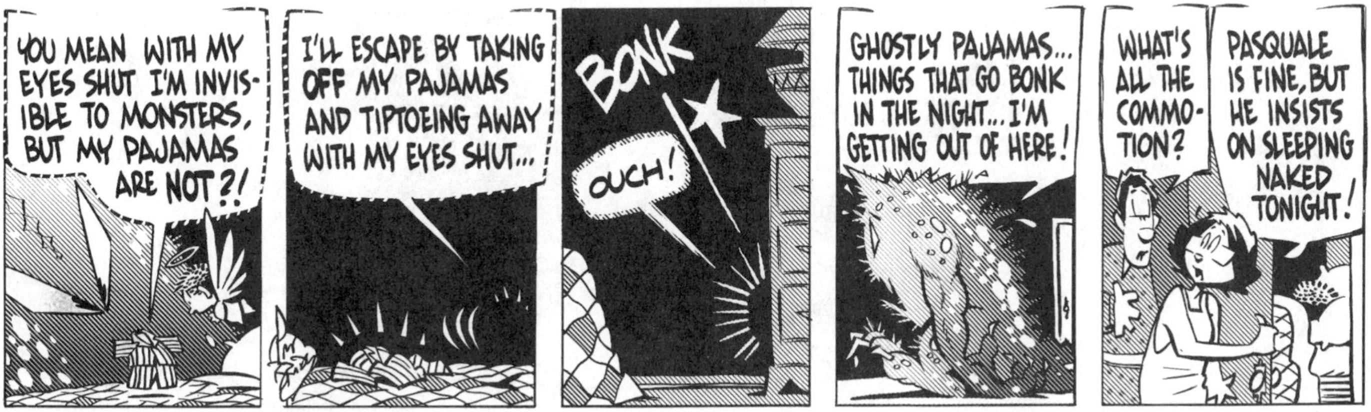
YOU MEAN WITH MY EYES SHUT I'M INVIS-IBLE TO MONSTERS, BUT MY PAJAMAS ARE NOT?!
I'LL ESCAPE BY TAKING OFF MY PAJAMAS AND TIPTOEING AWAY WITH MY EYES SHUT...
BONK
OUCH!
GHOSTLY PAJAMAS... THINGS THAT GO BONK IN THE NIGHT... I'M GETTING OUT OF HERE!
WHAT'S ALL THE COMMO-TION?
PASQUALE IS FINE, BUT HE INSISTS ON SLEEPING NAKED TONIGHT!

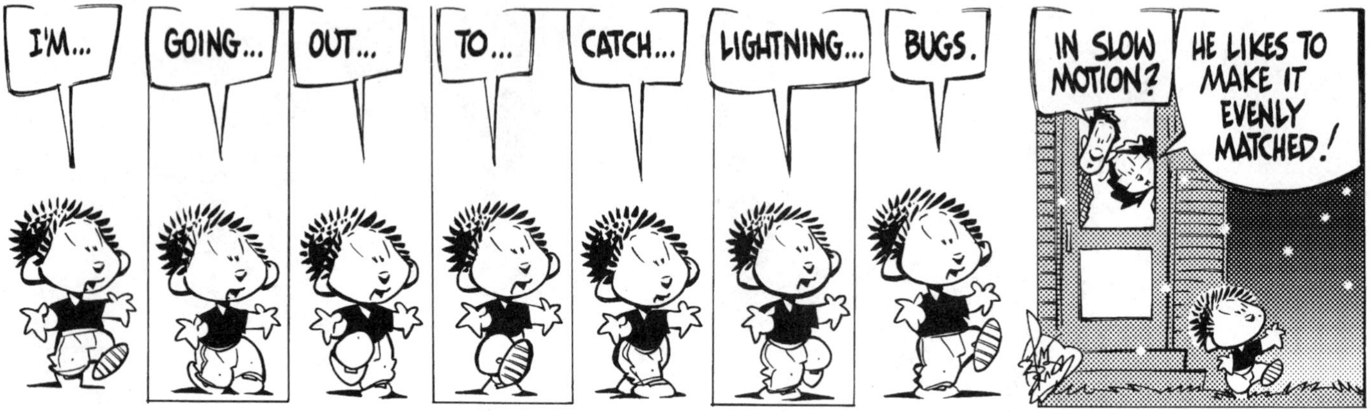
I'M...
GOING...
OUT...
TO...
CATCH...
LIGHTNING...
BUGS.
IN SLOW MOTION?
HE LIKES TO MAKE IT EVENLY MATCHED!

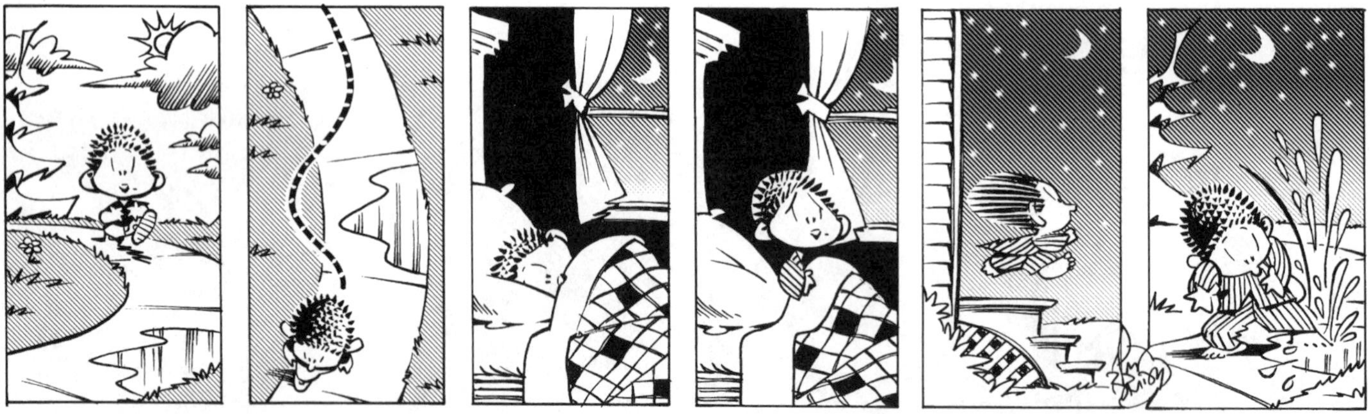

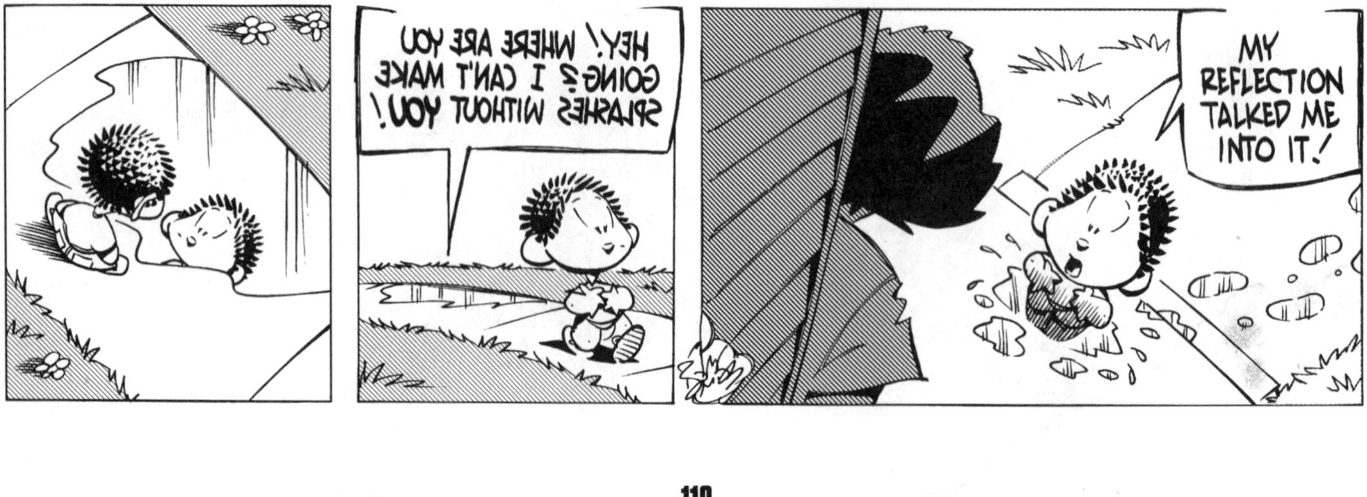
HEY! WHERE ARE YOU GOING? I CAN'T MAKE SPLASHES WITHOUT YOU!
MY REFLECTION TALKED ME INTO IT!

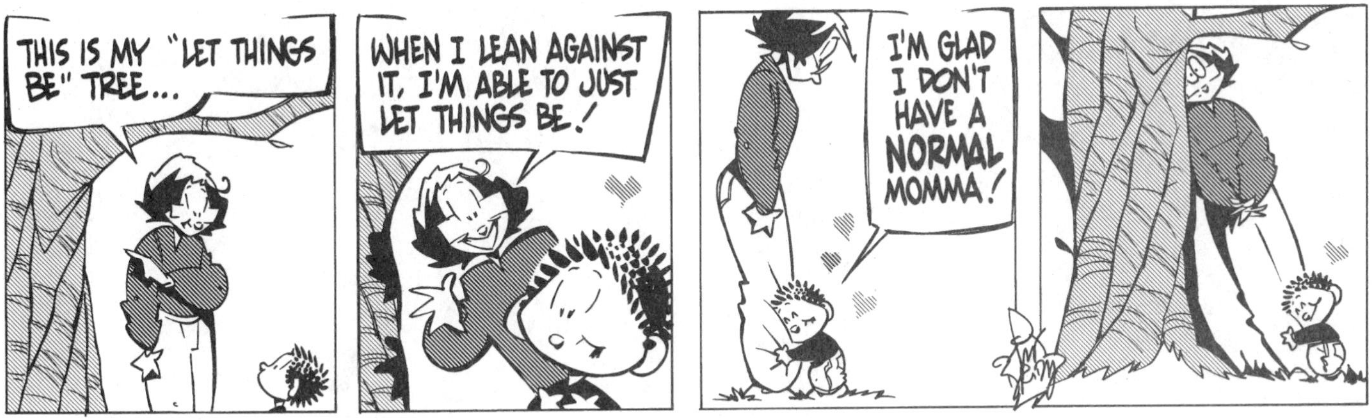
THIS IS MY "LET THINGS BE" TREE...
WHEN I LEAN AGAINST IT, I'M ABLE TO JUST LET THINGS BE!
I'M GLAD I DON'T HAVE A NORMAL MOMMA!

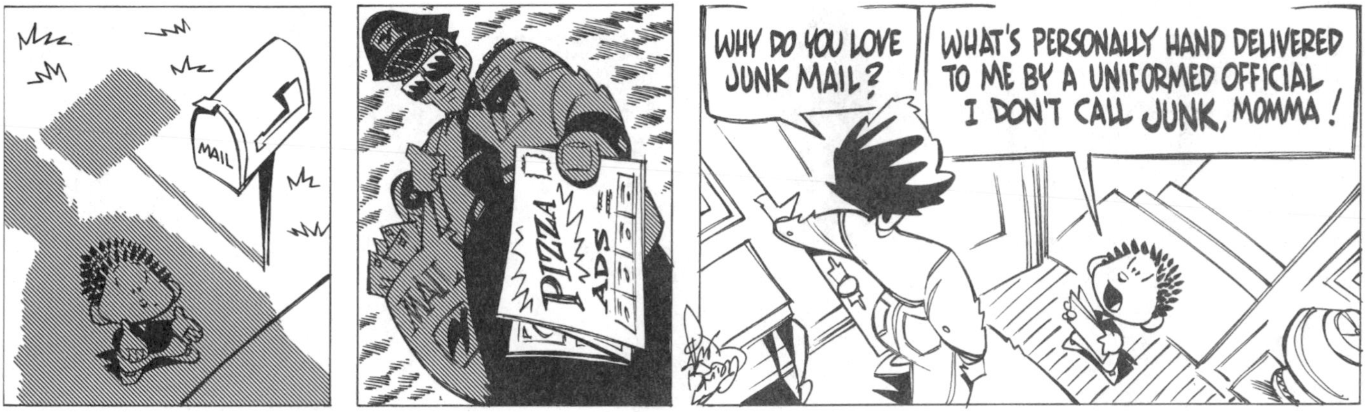
MAIL
PIZZA
ADS
WHY DO YOU LOVE JUNK MAIL?
WHAT'S PERSONALLY HAND DELIVERED TO ME BY A UNIFORMED OFFICIAL I DON'T CALL JUNK, MOMMA!

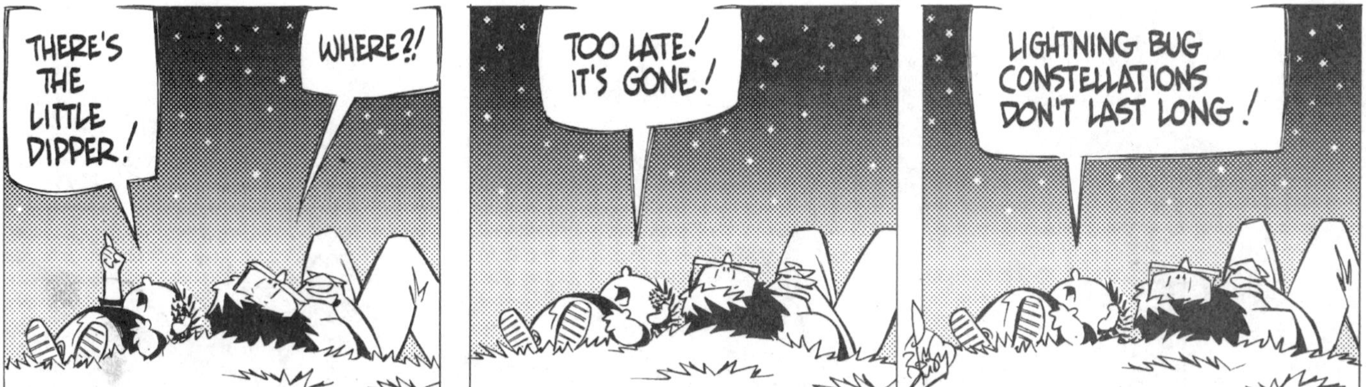
THERE'S THE LITTLE DIPPER!
WHERE?!
TOO LATE! IT'S GONE!
LIGHTNING BUG CONSTELLATIONS DON'T LAST LONG!

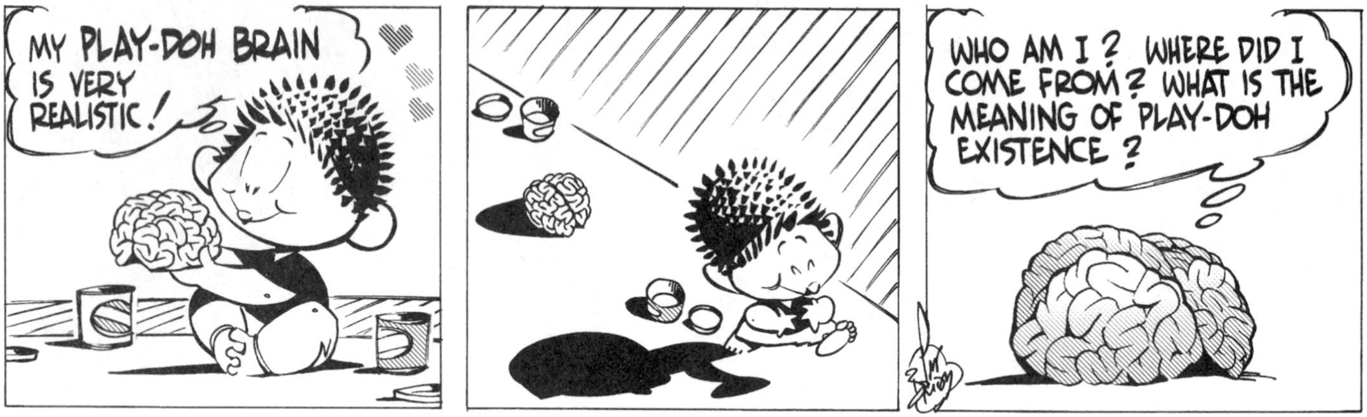
MY PLAY-DOH BRAIN IS VERY REALISTIC!
WHO AM I? WHERE DID I COME FROM? WHAT IS THE MEANING OF PLAY-DOH EXISTENCE?

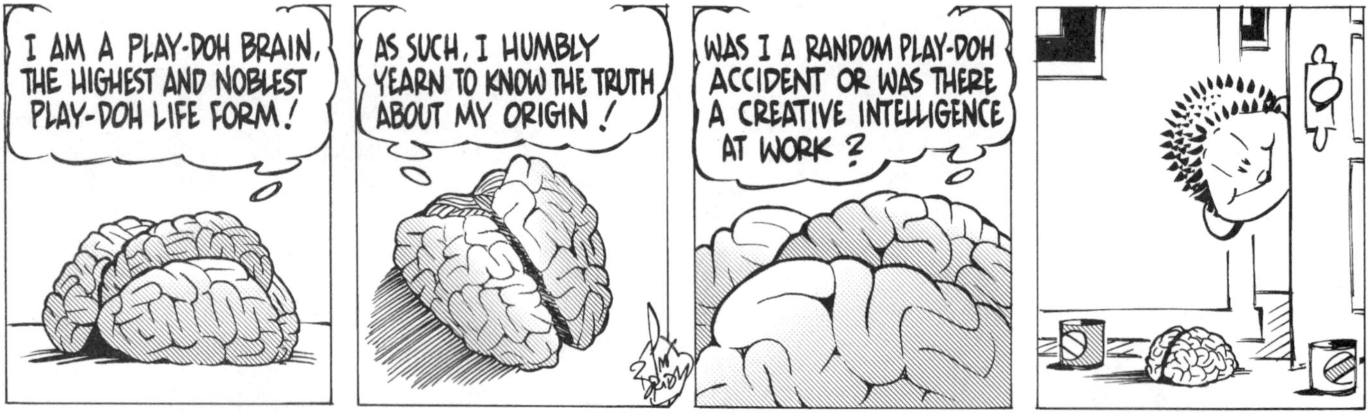
I AM A PLAY-DOH BRAIN, THE HIGHEST AND NOBLEST PLAY-DOH LIFE FORM!
AS SUCH, I HUMBLY YEARN TO KNOW THE TRUTH ABOUT MY ORIGIN!
WAS I A RANDOM PLAY-DOH ACCIDENT OR WAS THERE A CREATIVE INTELLIGENCE AT WORK?

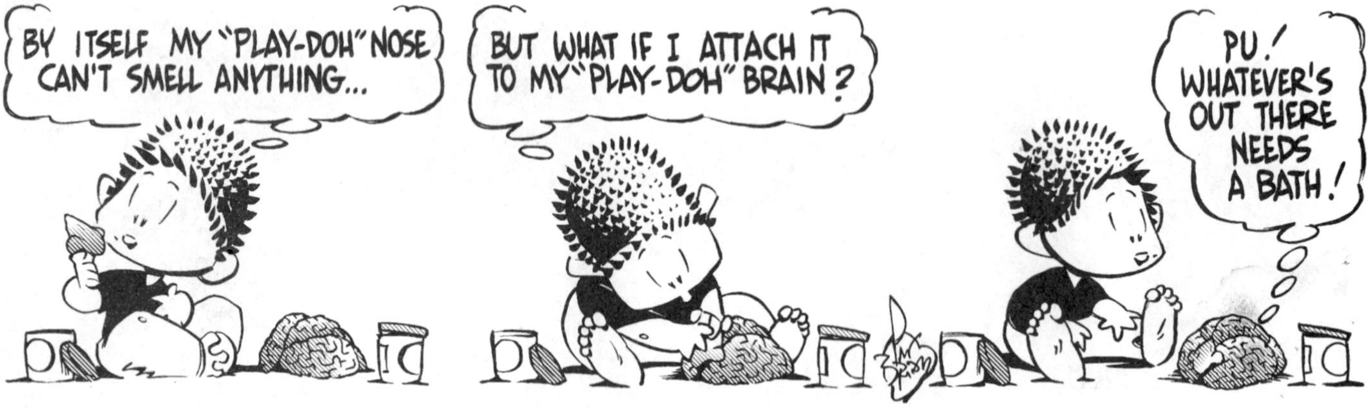
BY ITSELF MY "PLAY-DOH" NOSE CAN'T SMELL ANYTHING...
BUT WHAT IF I ATTACH IT TO MY "PLAY-DOH" BRAIN?
PU! WHATEVER'S OUT THERE NEEDS A BATH!

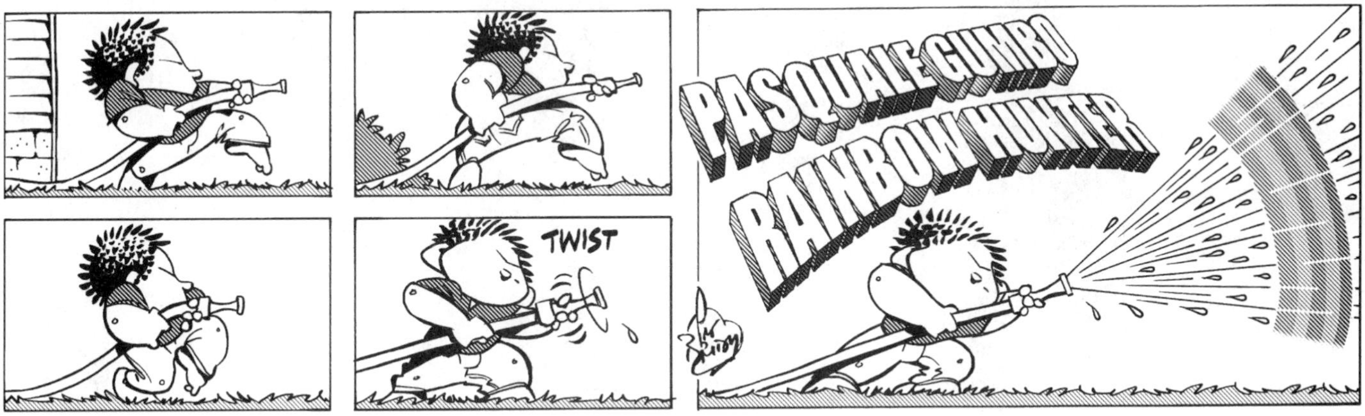
TWIST
PASQUALE GUMBO
RAINBOW HUNTER

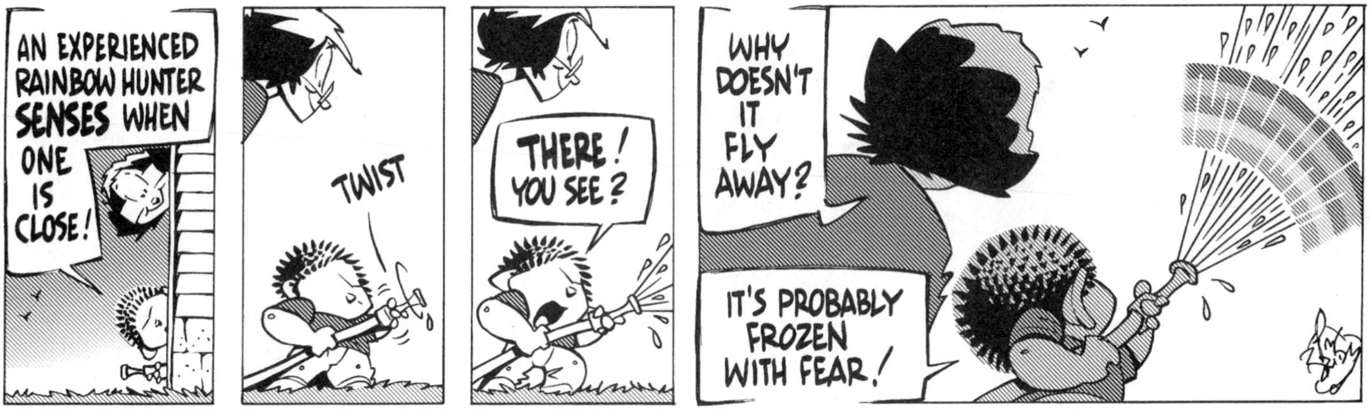
AN EXPERIENCED RAINBOW HUNTER SENSES WHEN ONE IS CLOSE!
TWIST
THERE! YOU SEE?
WHY DOESN'T IT FLY AWAY?
IT'S PROBABLY FROZEN WITH FEAR!

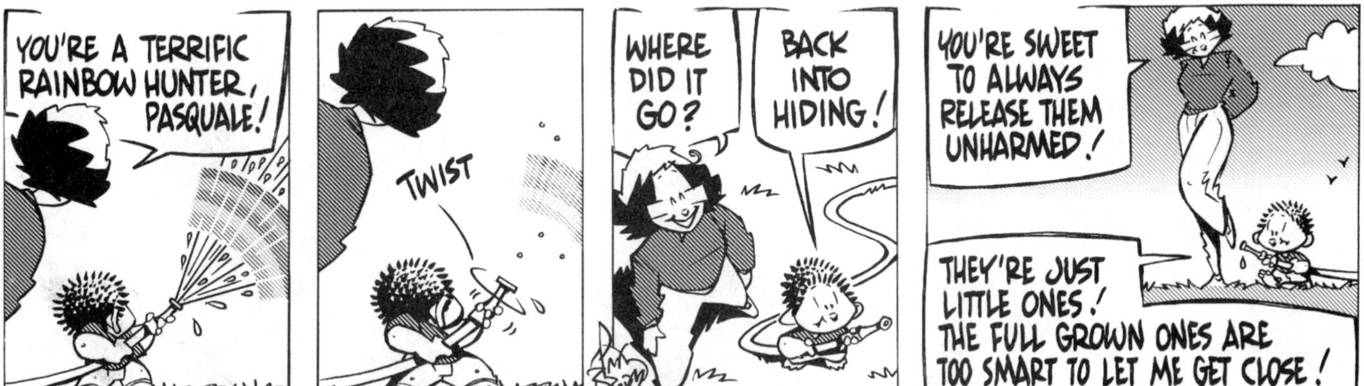
YOU'RE A TERRIFIC RAINBOW HUNTER, PASQUALE!
TWIST
WHERE DID IT GO?
BACK INTO HIDING!
YOU'RE SWEET TO ALWAYS RELEASE THEM UNHARMED!
THEY'RE JUST LITTLE ONES! THE FULL GROWN ONES ARE TOO SMART TO LET ME GET CLOSE!

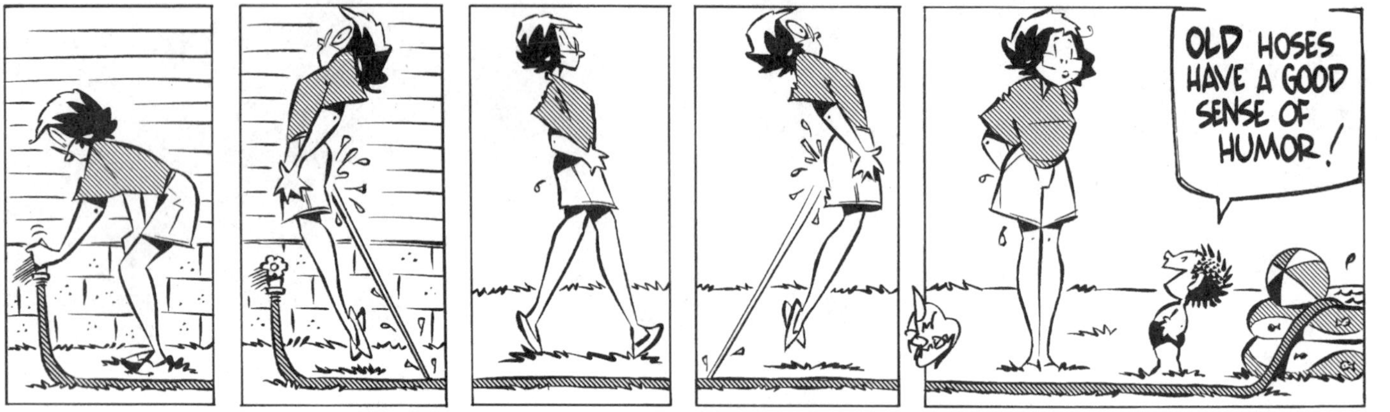
OLD HOSES HAVE A GOOD SENSE OF HUMOR!

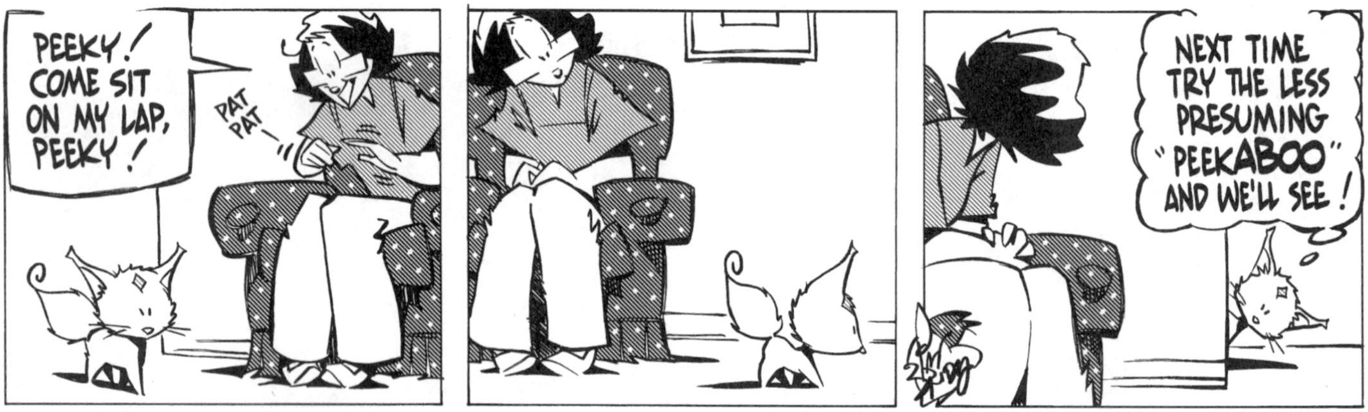
PEEKY! COME SIT ON MY LAP, PEEKY!
PAT PAT
NEXT TIME TRY THE LESS PRESUMING "PEEKABOO" AND WE'LL SEE!

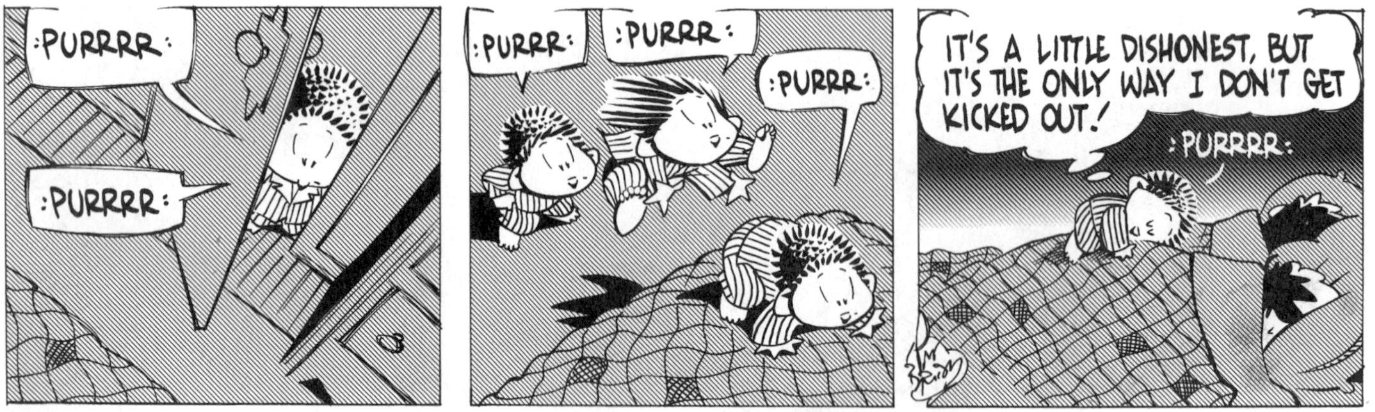
:PURRRR:
:PURRRR:
:PURRR:
:PURRR:
:PURRR:
IT'S A LITTLE DISHONEST, BUT IT'S THE ONLY WAY I DON'T GET KICKED OUT!
:PURRRR:

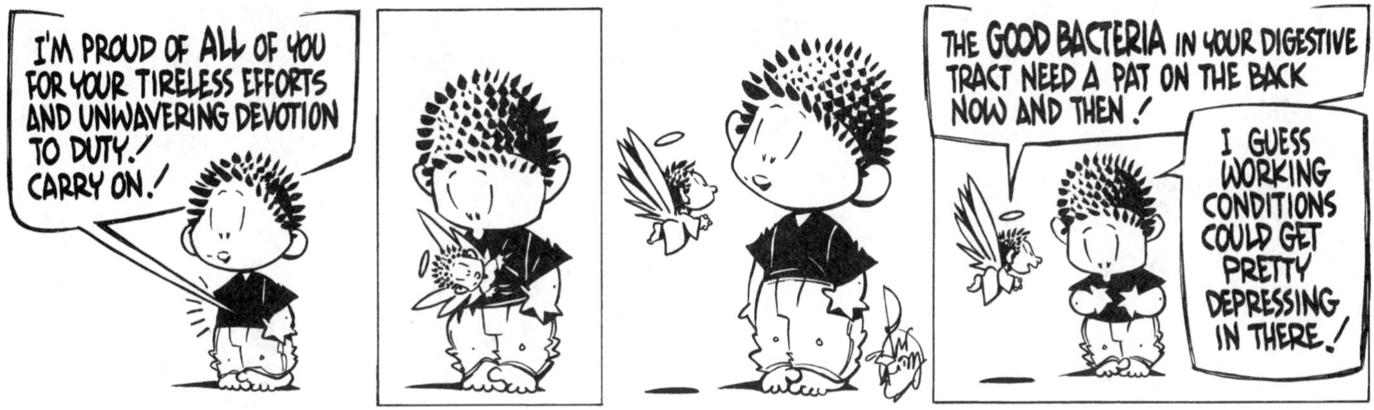
I'M PROUD OF ALL OF YOU FOR YOUR TIRELESS EFFORTS AND UNWAVERING DEVOTION TO DUTY! CARRY ON!
THE GOOD BACTERIA IN YOUR DIGESTIVE TRACT NEED A PAT ON THE BACK NOW AND THEN!
I GUESS WORKING CONDITIONS COULD GET PRETTY DEPRESSING IN THERE!

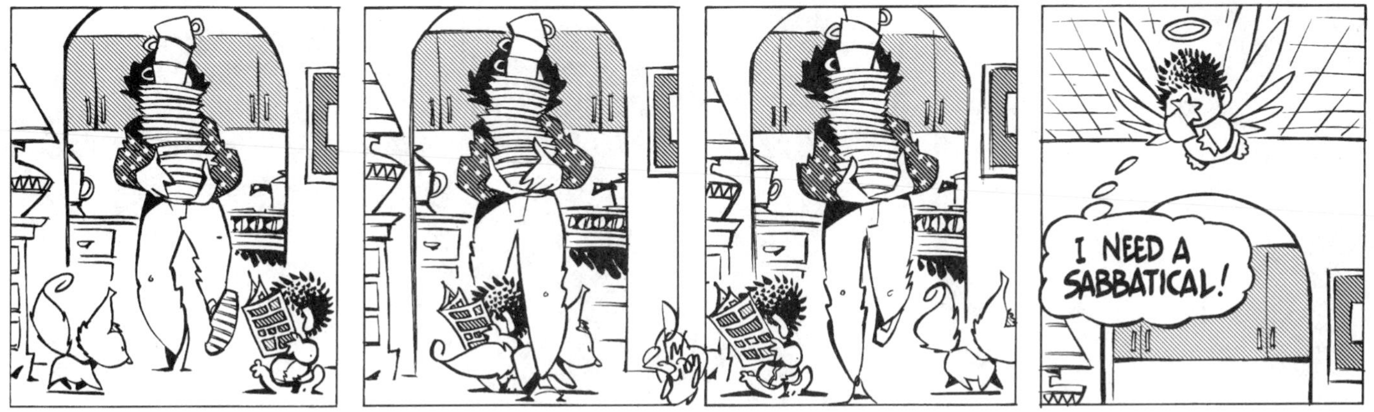
I NEED A SABBATICAL!

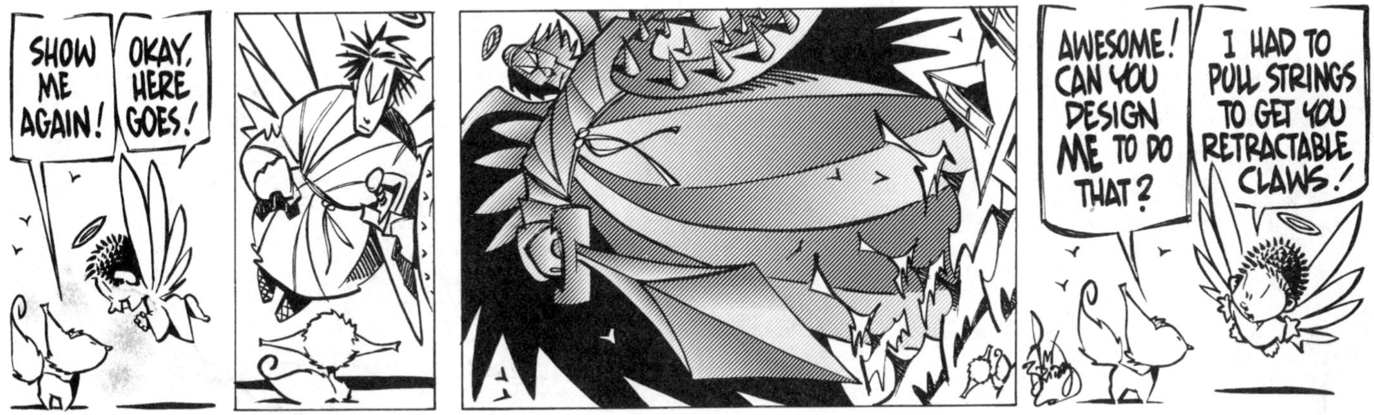
SHOW ME AGAIN!
OKAY, HERE GOES!
AWESOME! CAN YOU DESIGN ME TO DO THAT?
I HAD TO PULL STRINGS TO GET YOU RETRACTABLE CLAWS!

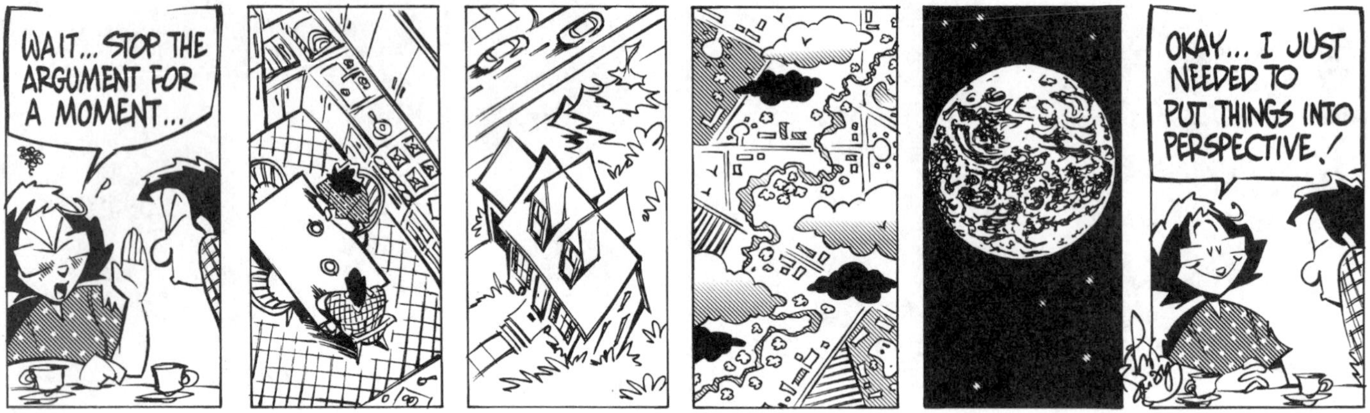
WAIT... STOP THE ARGUMENT FOR A MOMENT...
OKAY... I JUST NEEDED TO PUT THINGS INTO PERSPECTIVE!

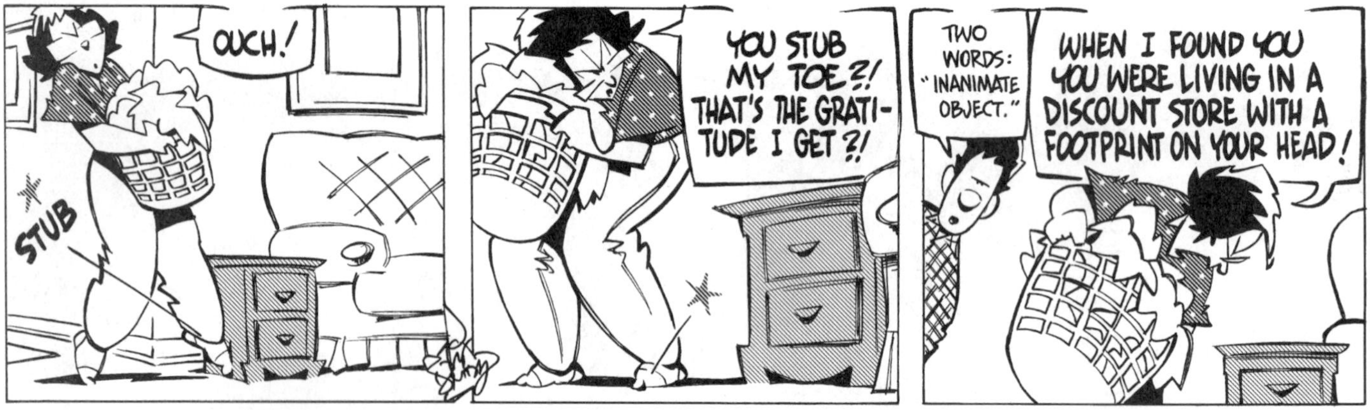
OUCH!
STUB
YOU STUB MY TOE?! THAT'S THE GRATITUDE I GET?!
TWO WORDS: "INANIMATE OBJECT."
WHEN I FOUND YOU YOU WERE LIVING IN A DISCOUNT STORE WITH A FOOTPRINT ON YOUR HEAD!

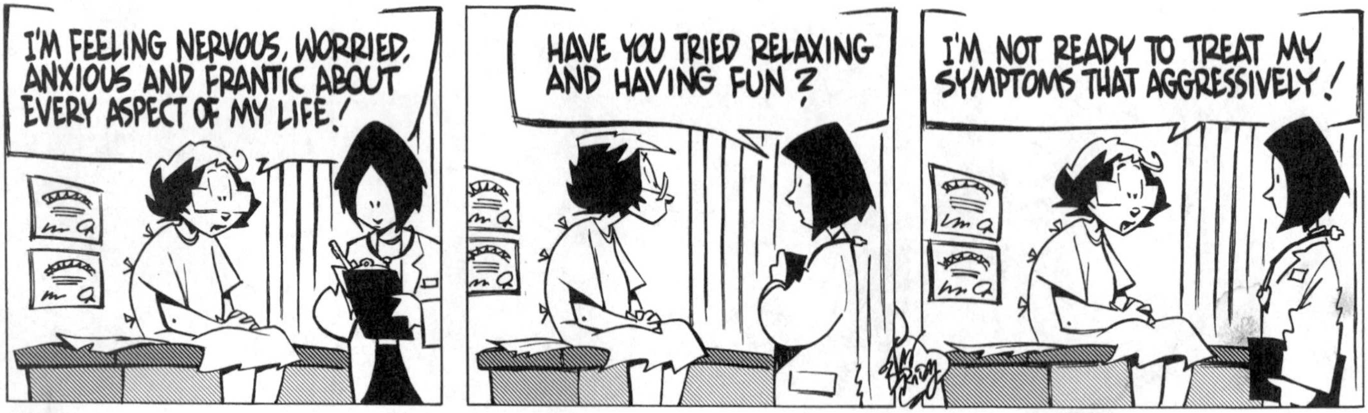
I'M FEELING NERVOUS, WORRIED, ANXIOUS AND FRANTIC ABOUT EVERY ASPECT OF MY LIFE!
HAVE YOU TRIED RELAXING AND HAVING FUN?
I'M NOT READY TO TREAT MY SYMPTOMS THAT AGGRESSIVELY!

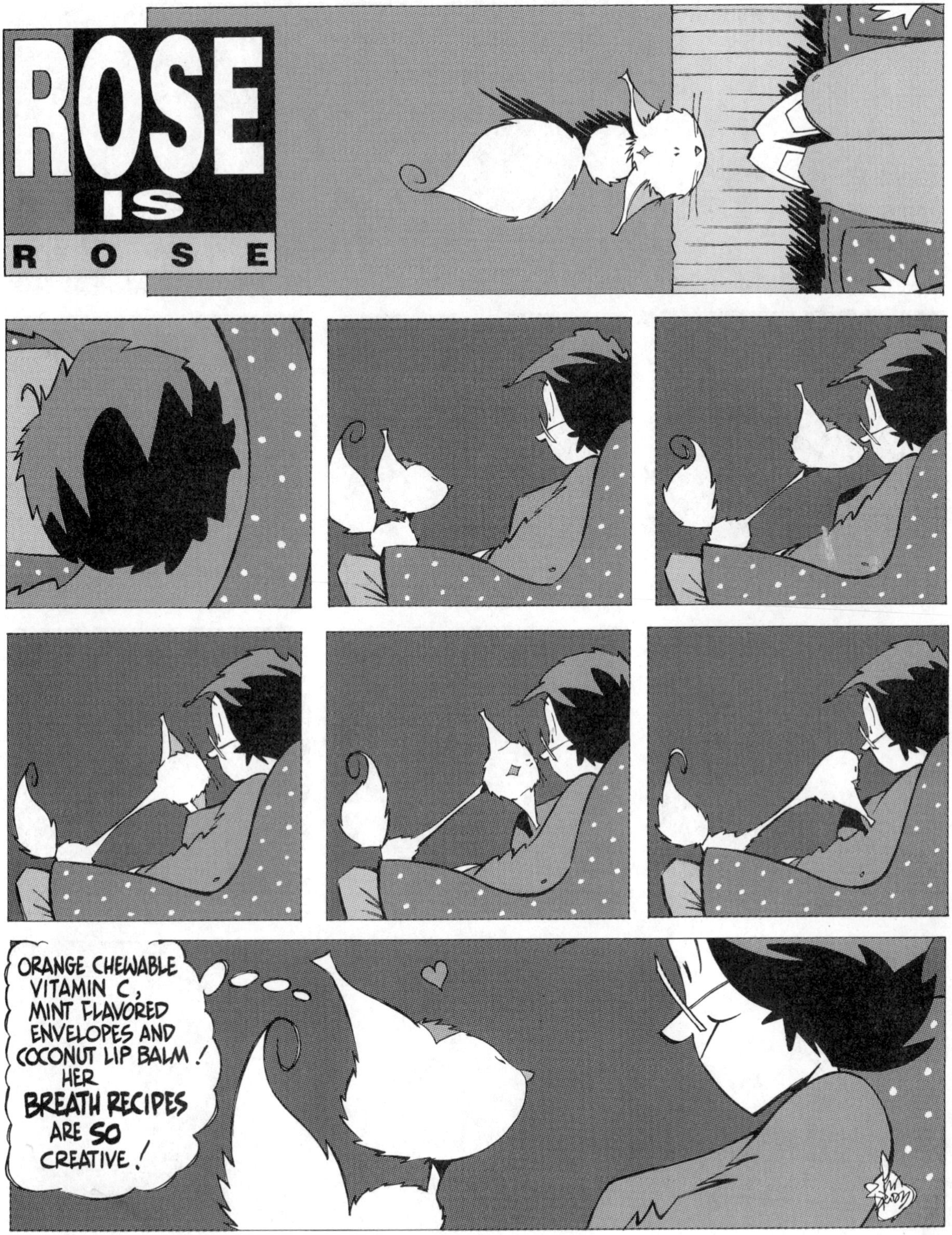
ROSE IS ROSE
ORANGE CHEWABLE VITAMIN C, MINT FLAVORED ENVELOPES AND COCONUT LIP BALM! HER BREATH RECIPES ARE SO CREATIVE!

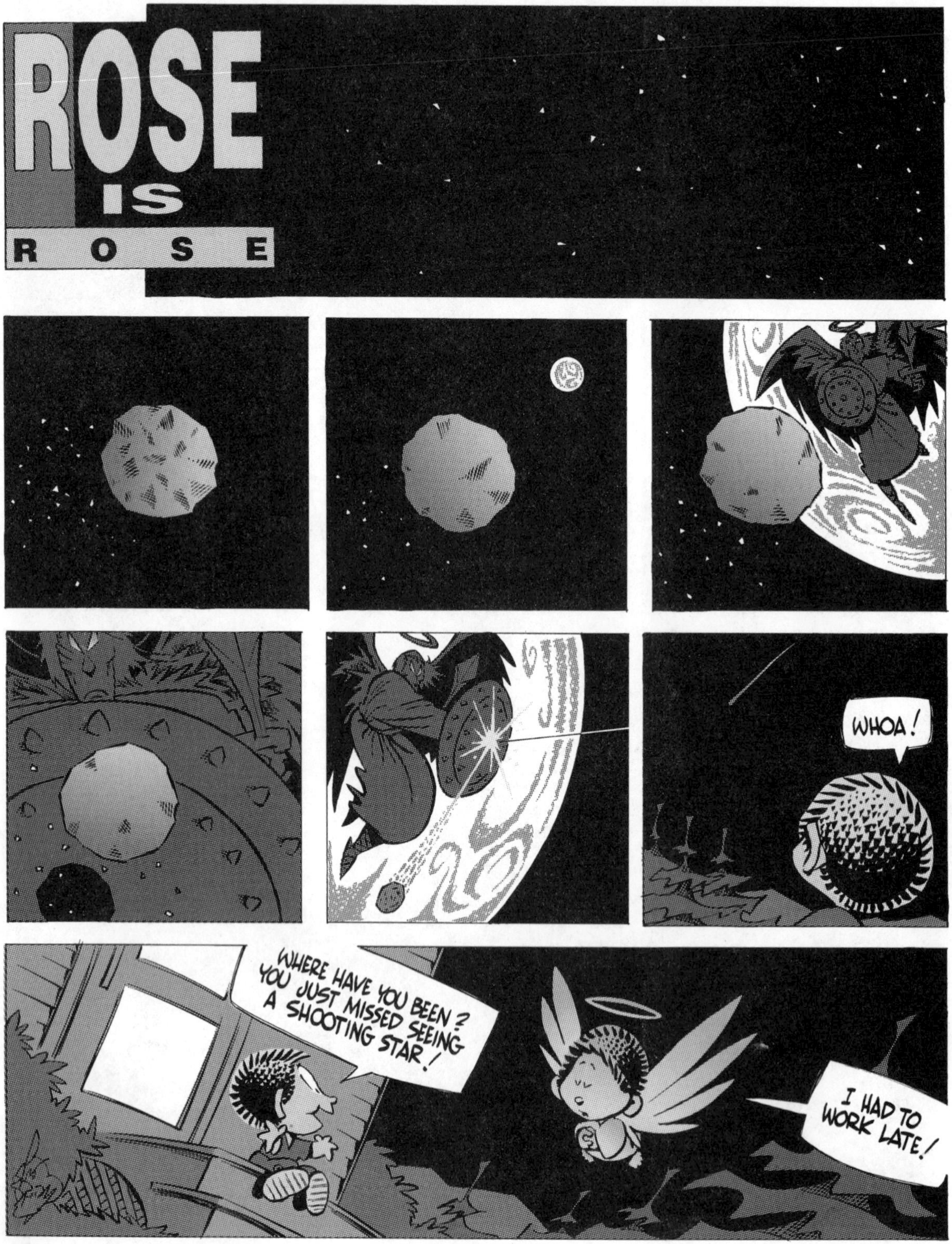
ROSE IS ROSE
WHOA!
WHERE HAVE YOU BEEN? YOU JUST MISSED SEEING A SHOOTING STAR!
I HAD TO WORK LATE!

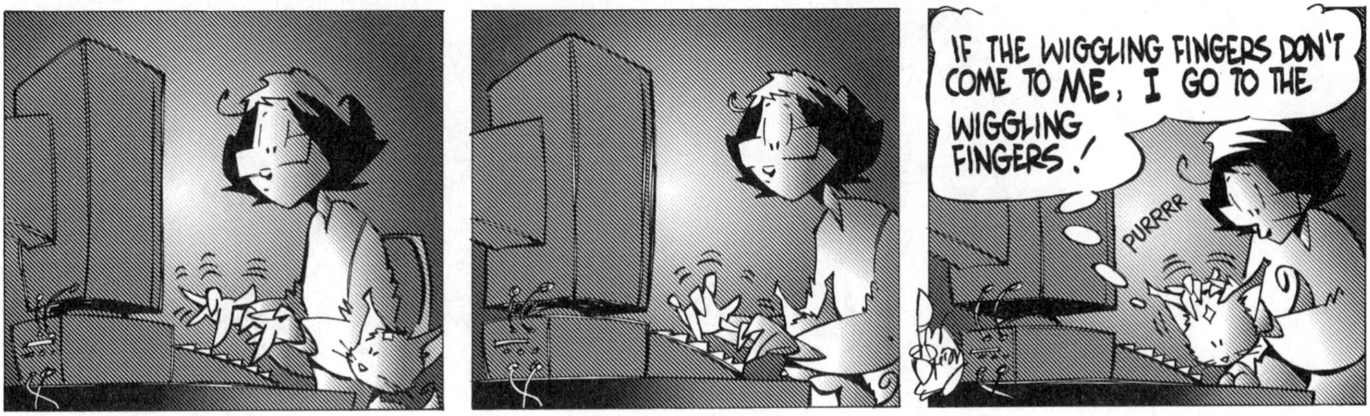
IF THE WIGGLING FINGERS DON'T COME TO ME, I GO TO THE WIGGLING FINGERS!
PURRRR

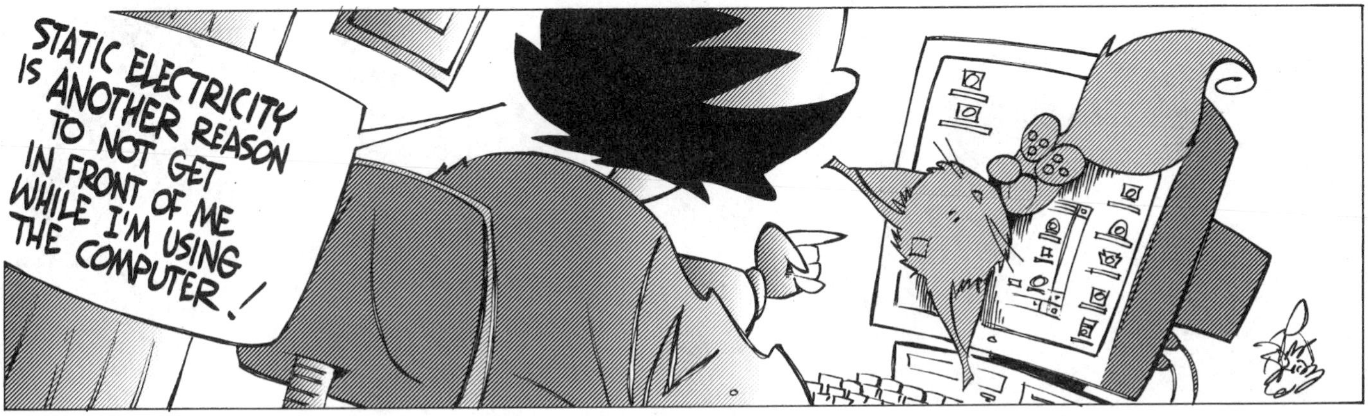
STATIC ELECTRICITY IS ANOTHER REASON TO NOT GET IN FRONT OF ME WHILE I'M USING THE COMPUTER!

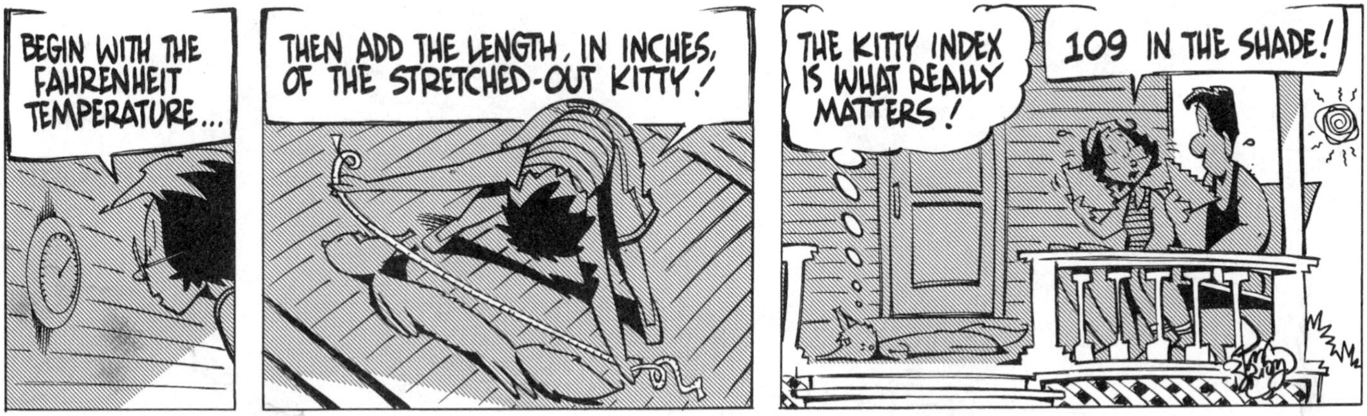
BEGIN WITH THE FAHRENHEIT TEMPERATURE...
THEN ADD THE LENGTH, IN INCHES, OF THE STRETCHED-OUT KITTY!
THE KITTY INDEX IS WHAT REALLY MATTERS!
109 IN THE SHADE!

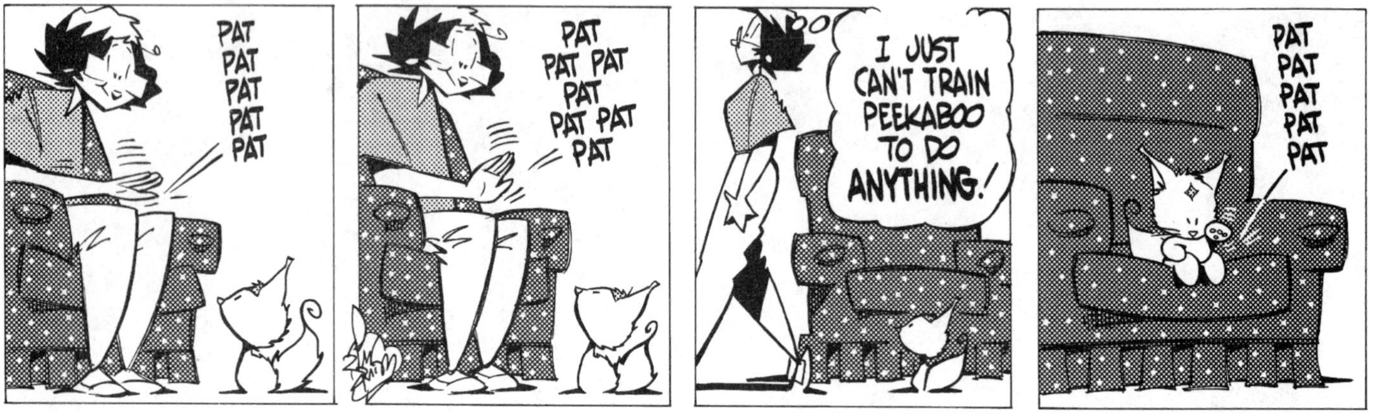
PAT
PAT
PAT
PAT
PAT
PAT
PAT PAT
PAT
PAT PAT
PAT
I JUST CAN'T TRAIN PEEKABOO TO DO ANYTHING!
PAT
PAT
PAT
PAT
PAT

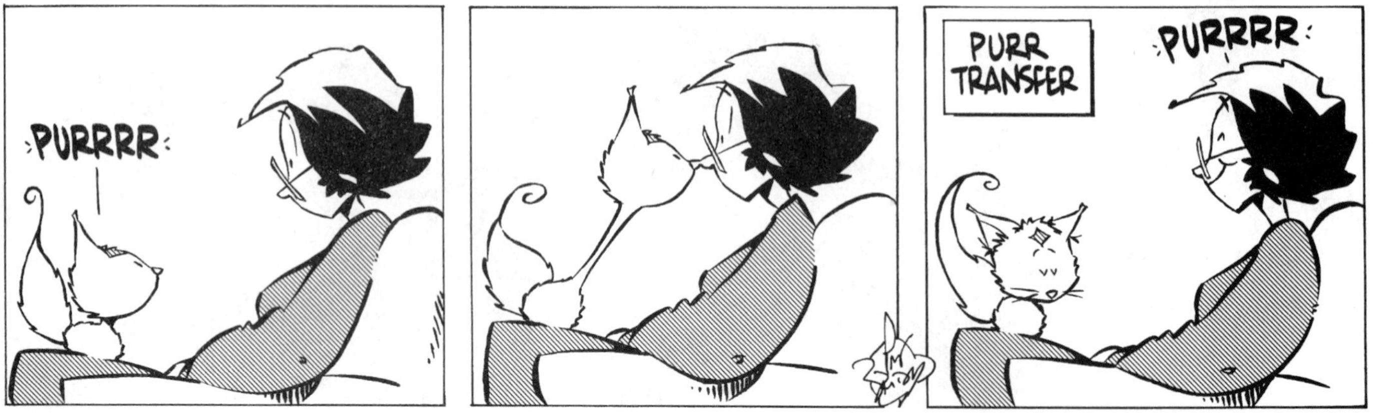
PURRRR
PURR TRANSFER
PURRRR

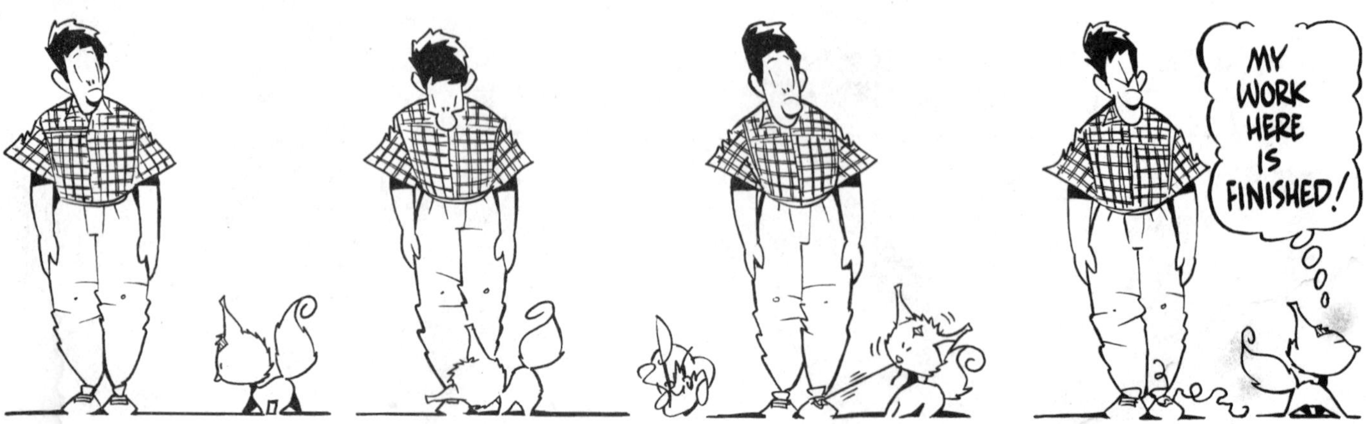
MY WORK HERE IS FINISHED!

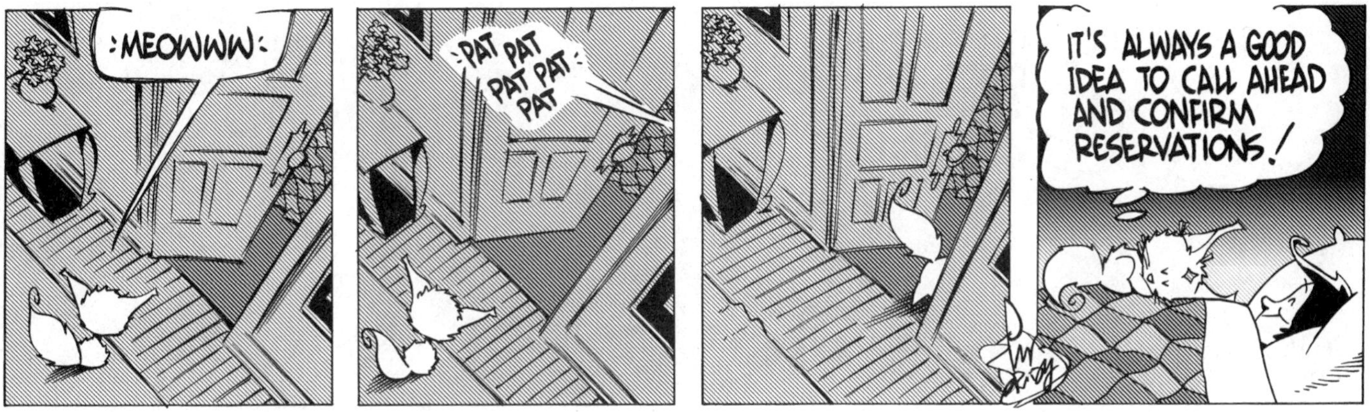
MEOWWW
PAT PAT PAT PAT PAT
IT'S ALWAYS A GOOD IDEA TO CALL AHEAD AND CONFIRM RESERVATIONS!

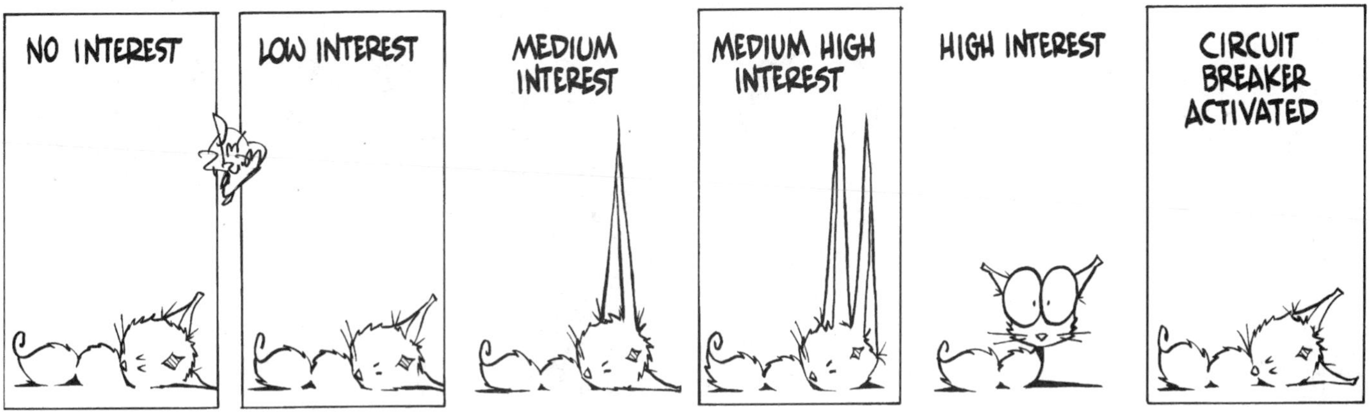
NO INTEREST
LOW INTEREST
MEDIUM INTEREST
MEDIUM HIGH INTEREST
HIGH INTEREST
CIRCUIT BREAKER ACTIVATED

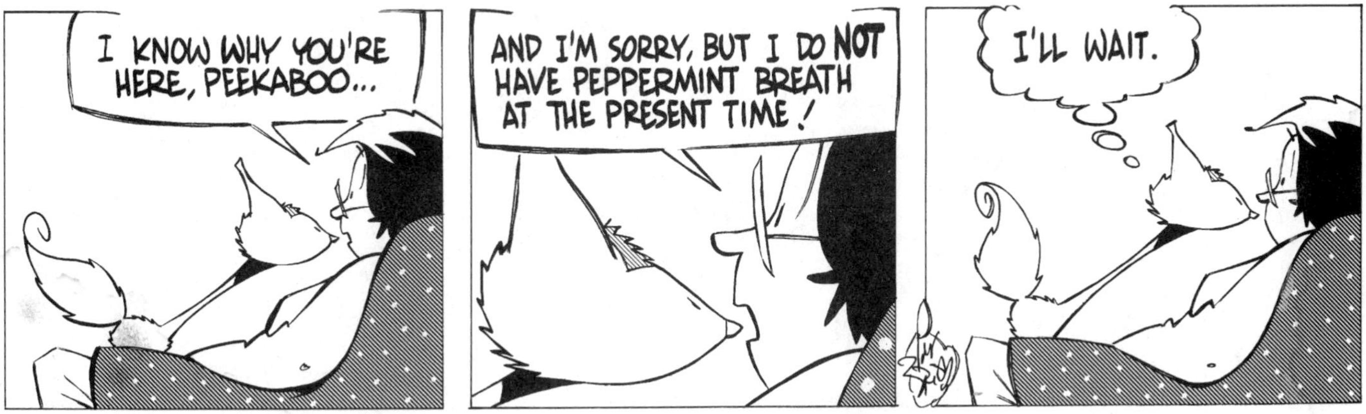
I KNOW WHY YOU'RE HERE, PEEKABOO...
AND I'M SORRY, BUT I DO NOT HAVE PEPPERMINT BREATH AT THE PRESENT TIME!
I'LL WAIT.

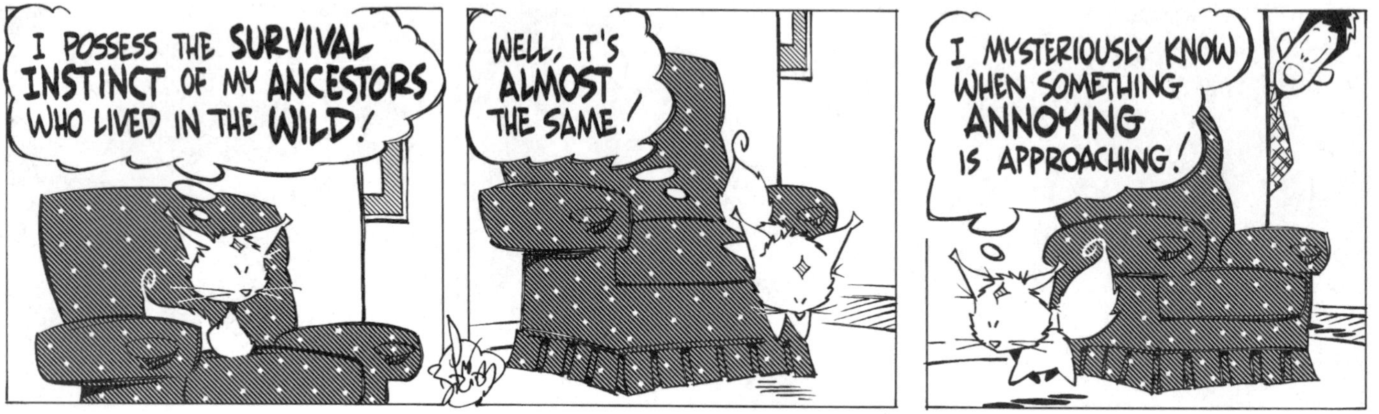
I POSSESS THE SURVIVAL INSTINCT OF MY ANCESTORS WHO LIVED IN THE WILD!
WELL, IT'S ALMOST THE SAME!
I MYSTERIOUSLY KNOW WHEN SOMETHING ANNOYING IS APPROACHING!

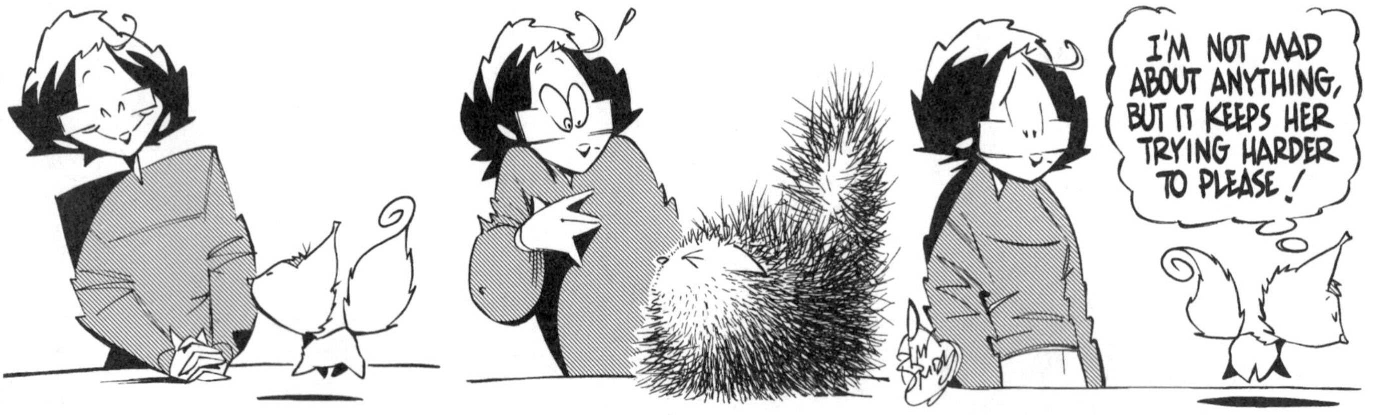
I'M NOT MAD ABOUT ANYTHING, BUT IT KEEPS HER TRYING HARDER TO PLEASE!

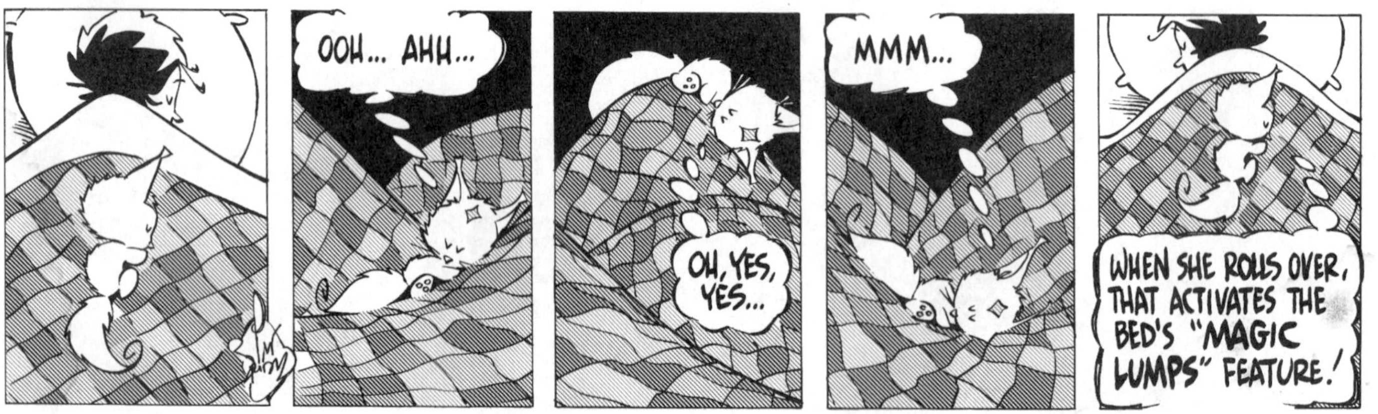
OOH... AHH...
OH, YES, YES...
MMM...
WHEN SHE ROLLS OVER, THAT ACTIVATES THE BED'S "MAGIC LUMPS" FEATURE!

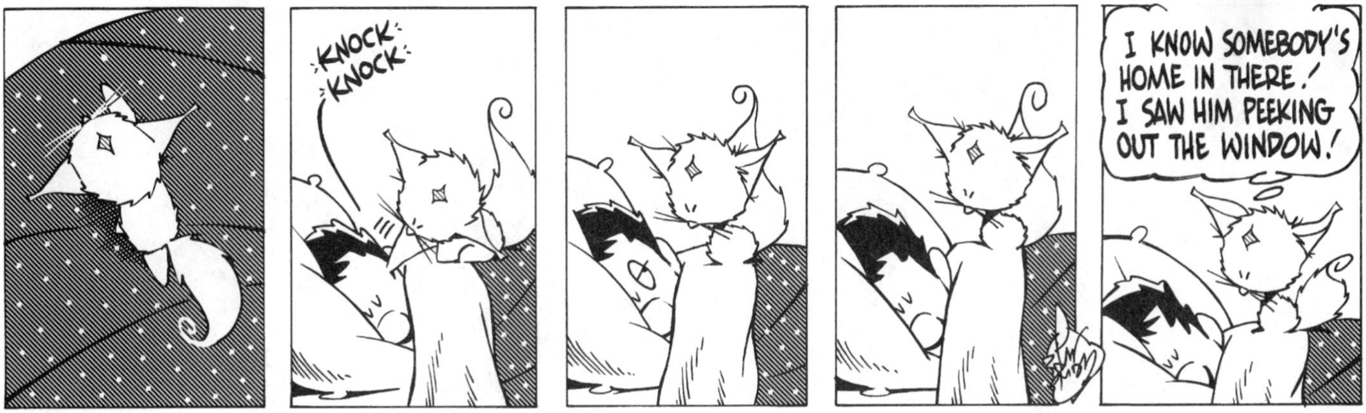
KNOCK KNOCK
I KNOW SOMEBODY'S HOME IN THERE! I SAW HIM PEEKING OUT THE WINDOW!

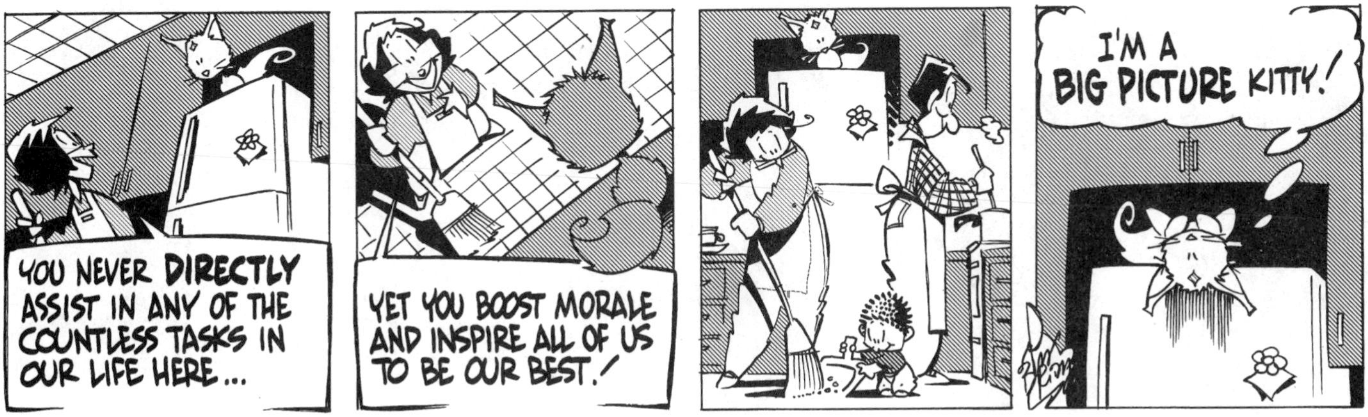
YOU NEVER DIRECTLY ASSIST IN ANY OF THE COUNTLESS TASKS IN OUR LIFE HERE...
YET YOU BOOST MORALE AND INSPIRE ALL OF US TO BE OUR BEST!
I'M A BIG PICTURE KITTY!

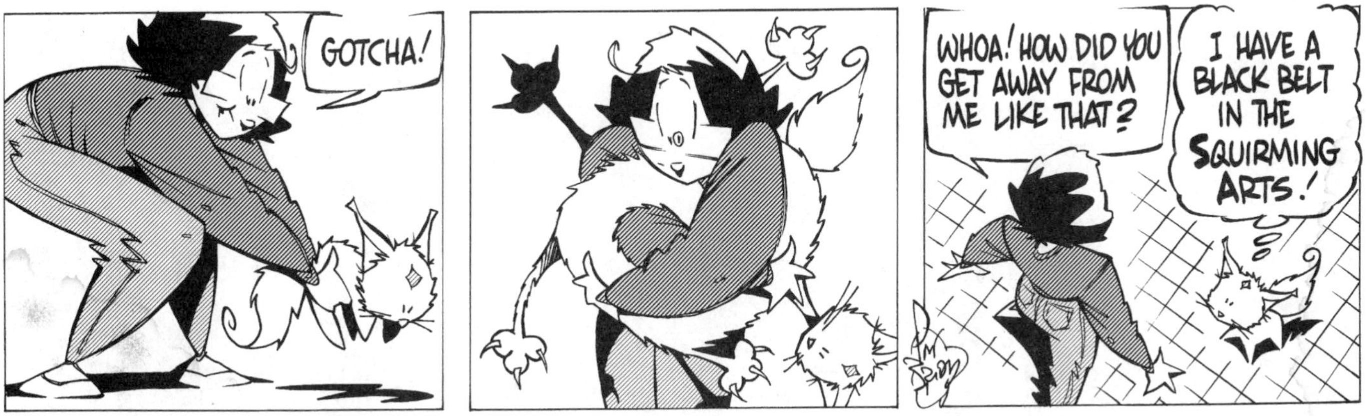
GOTCHA!
WHOA! HOW DID YOU GET AWAY FROM ME LIKE THAT?
I HAVE A BLACK BELT IN THE SQUIRMING ARTS!

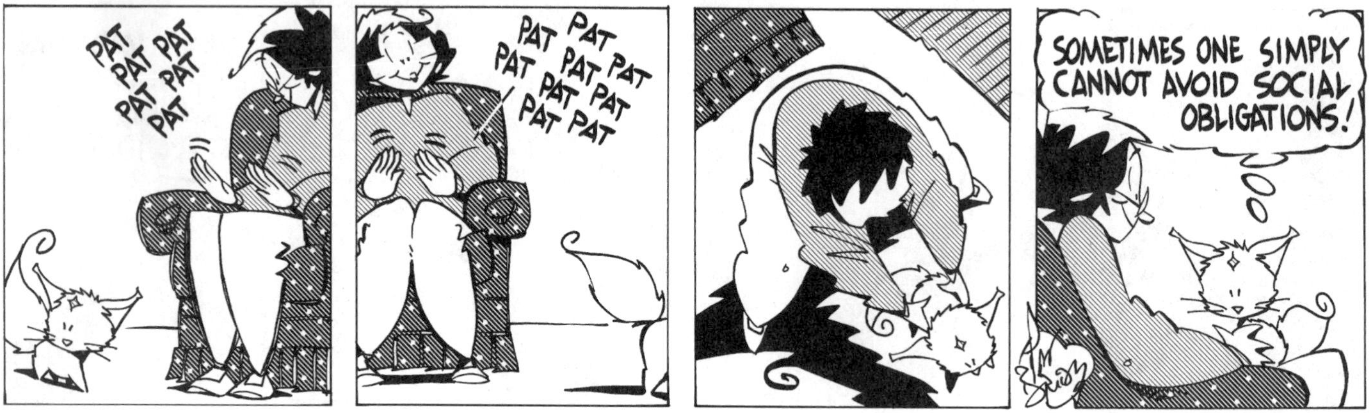
PAT PAT PAT PAT PAT PAT
PAT PAT PAT PAT PAT PAT PAT PAT PAT PAT
SOMETIMES ONE SIMPLY CANNOT AVOID SOCIAL OBLIGATIONS!

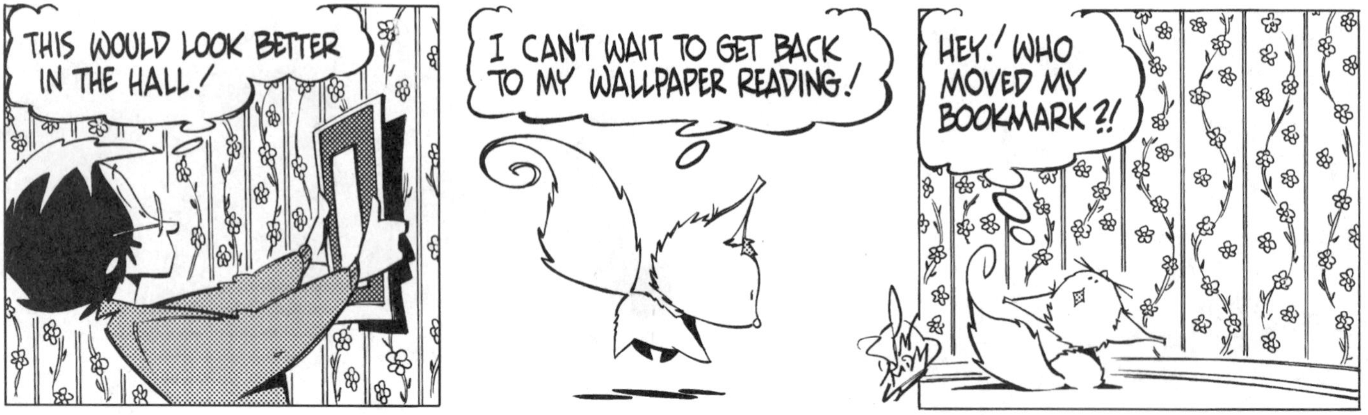
THIS WOULD LOOK BETTER IN THE HALL!
I CAN'T WAIT TO GET BACK TO MY WALLPAPER READING!
HEY! WHO MOVED MY BOOKMARK?!

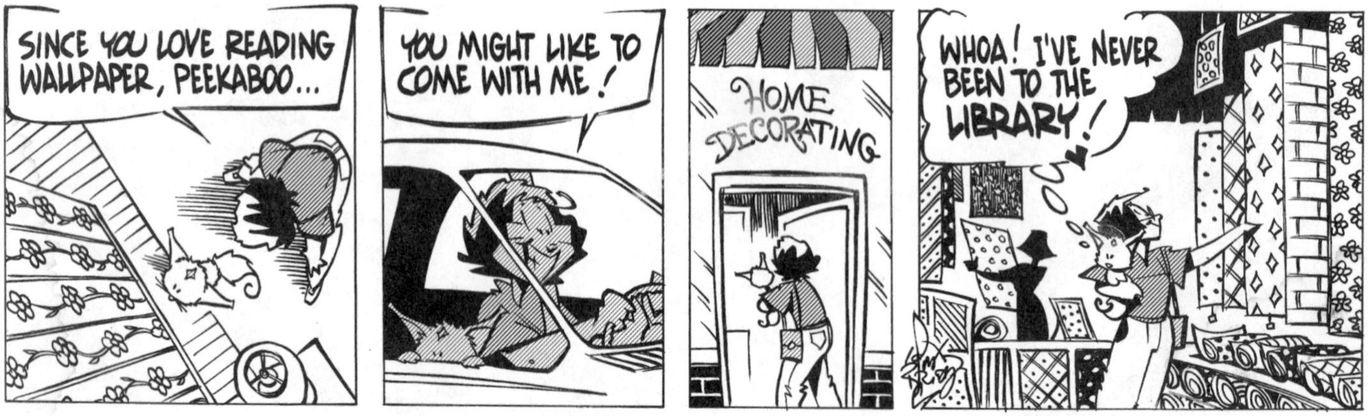
SINCE YOU LOVE READING WALLPAPER, PEEKABOO...
YOU MIGHT LIKE TO COME WITH ME!
HOME DECORATING
WHOA! I'VE NEVER BEEN TO THE LIBRARY!

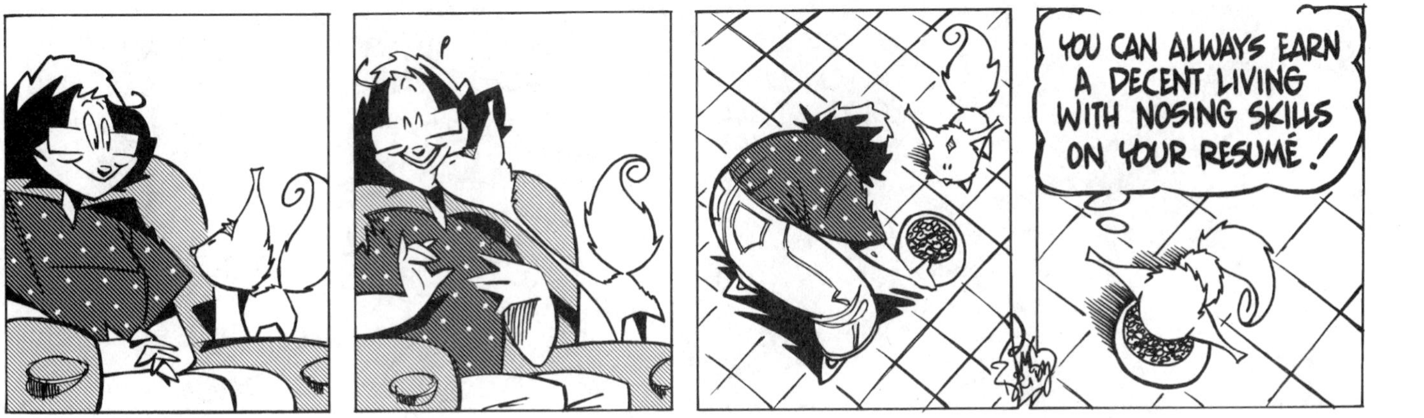
YOU CAN ALWAYS EARN A DECENT LIVING WITH NOSING SKILLS ON YOUR RESUMÉ!

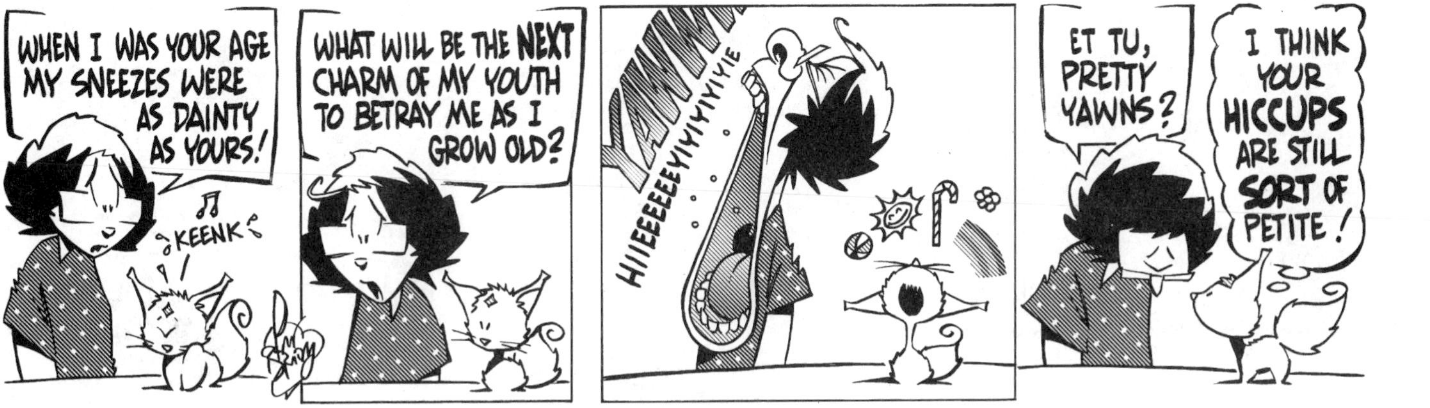
WHEN I WAS YOUR AGE MY SNEEZES WERE AS DAINTY AS YOURS!
KEENK
WHAT WILL BE THE NEXT CHARM OF MY YOUTH TO BETRAY ME AS I GROW OLD?
ET TU, PRETTY YAWNS?
I THINK YOUR HICCUPS ARE STILL SORT OF PETITE!

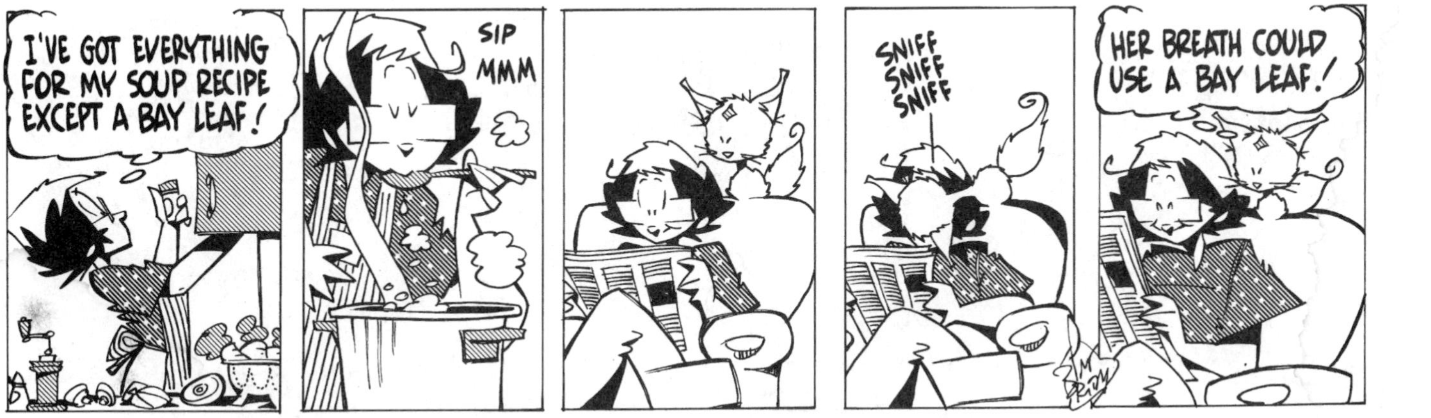
I'VE GOT EVERYTHING FOR MY SOUP RECIPE EXCEPT A BAY LEAF!
SIP
MMM
SNIFF SNIFF SNIFF
HER BREATH COULD USE A BAY LEAF!

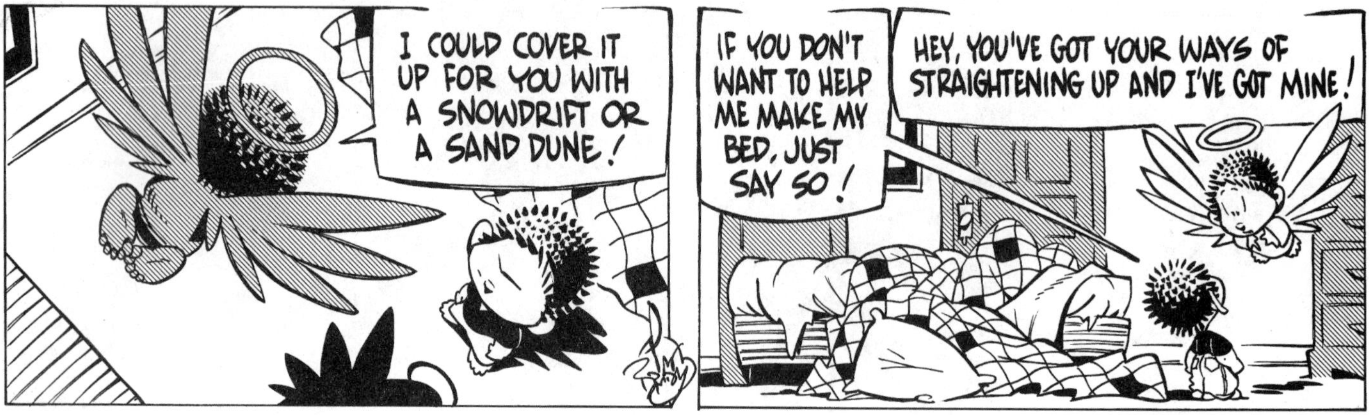
I COULD COVER IT UP FOR YOU WITH A SNOWDRIFT OR A SAND DUNE!
IF YOU DON'T WANT TO HELP ME MAKE MY BED, JUST SAY SO!
HEY, YOU'VE GOT YOUR WAYS OF STRAIGHTENING UP AND I'VE GOT MINE!

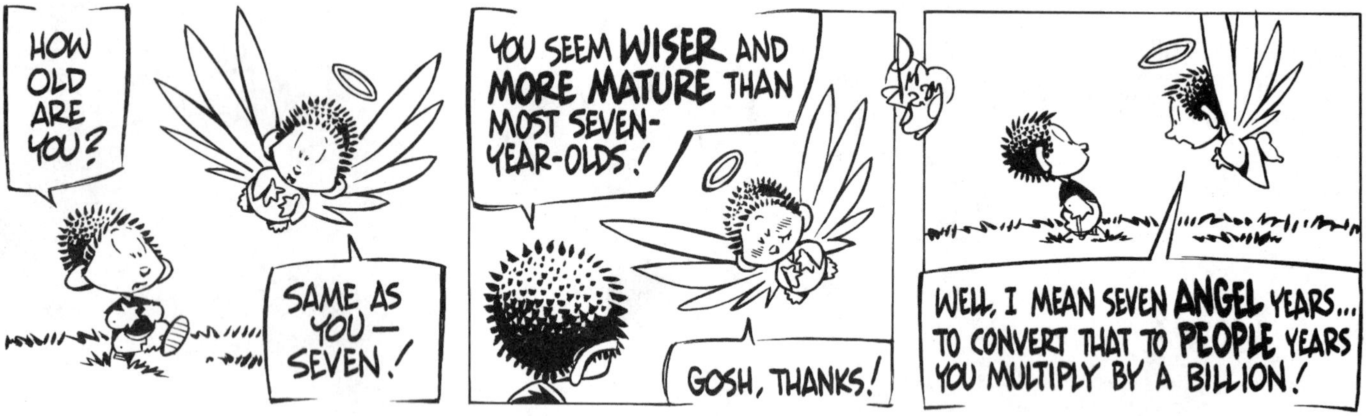
HOW OLD ARE YOU?
SAME AS YOU— SEVEN!
YOU SEEM WISER AND MORE MATURE THAN MOST SEVEN-YEAR-OLDS!
GOSH, THANKS!
WELL, I MEAN SEVEN ANGEL YEARS... TO CONVERT THAT TO PEOPLE YEARS YOU MULTIPLY BY A BILLION!

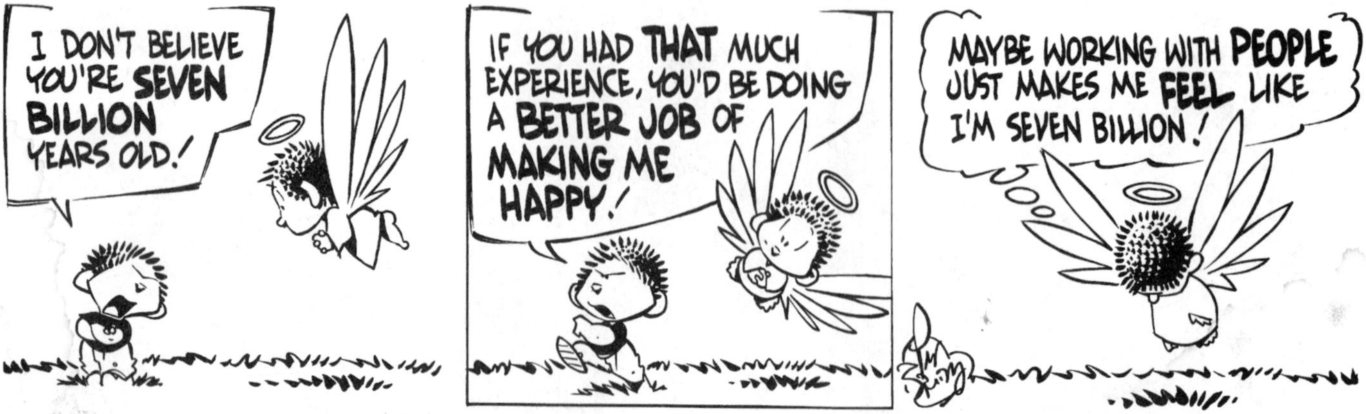
I DON'T BELIEVE YOU'RE SEVEN BILLION YEARS OLD!
IF YOU HAD THAT MUCH EXPERIENCE, YOU'D BE DOING A BETTER JOB OF MAKING ME HAPPY!
MAYBE WORKING WITH PEOPLE JUST MAKES ME FEEL LIKE I'M SEVEN BILLION!

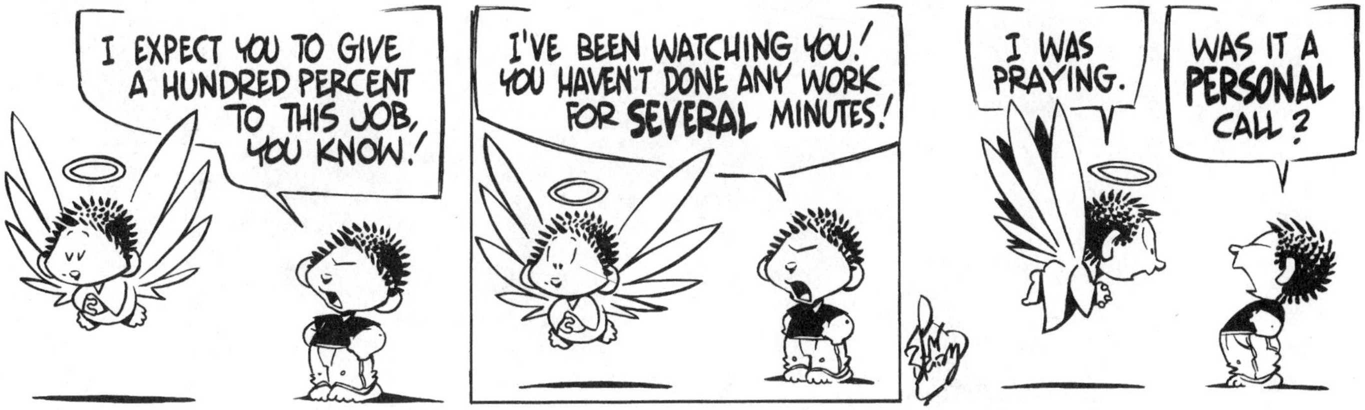
I EXPECT YOU TO GIVE A HUNDRED PERCENT TO THIS JOB, YOU KNOW!
I'VE BEEN WATCHING YOU! YOU HAVEN'T DONE ANY WORK FOR SEVERAL MINUTES!
I WAS PRAYING.
WAS IT A PERSONAL CALL?

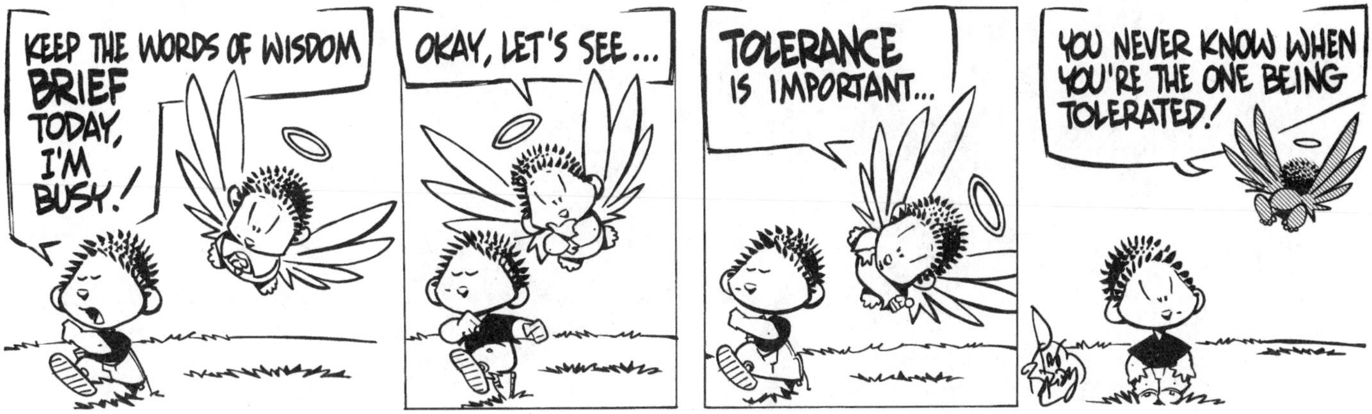
KEEP THE WORDS OF WISDOM BRIEF TODAY, I'M BUSY!
OKAY, LET'S SEE...
TOLERANCE IS IMPORTANT...
YOU NEVER KNOW WHEN YOU'RE THE ONE BEING TOLERATED!

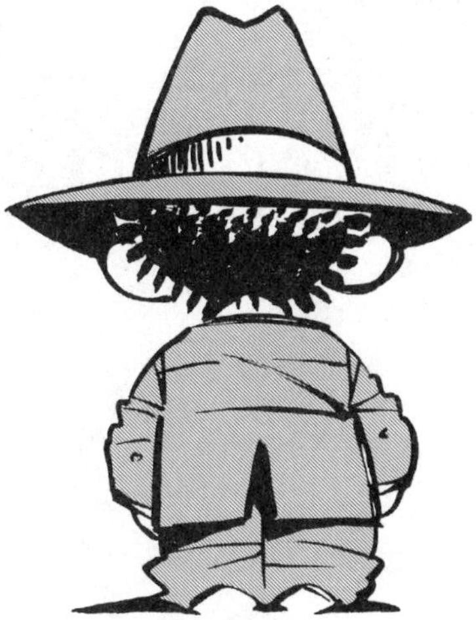

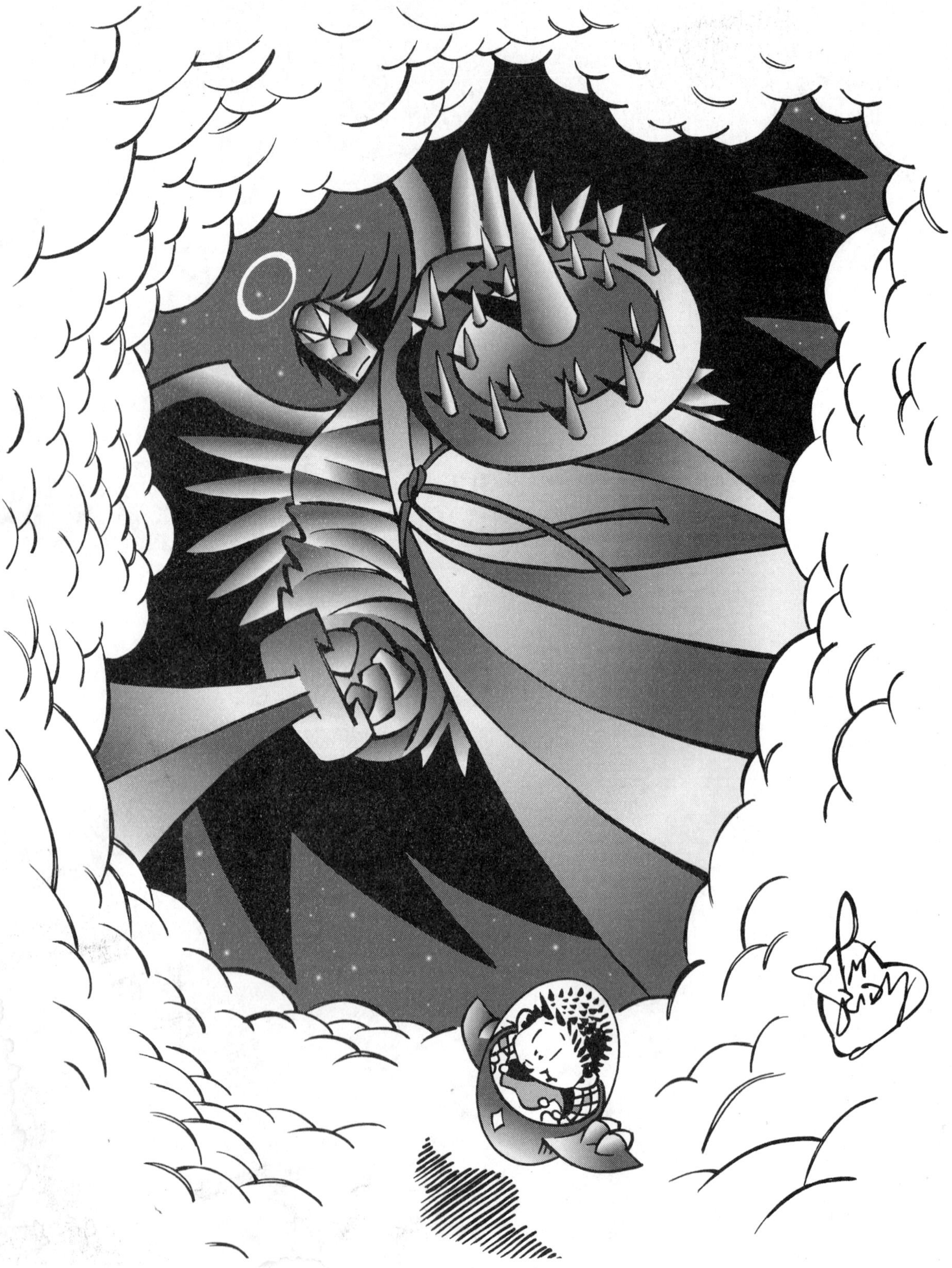